Preparing Culturally Efficacious Bilingual Counselors through Theory and Case Studies

Critical Studies of Latinxs in the Americas

Yolanda Medina and Margarita Machado-Casas
Series Editors

Vol. 31

Claudia G. Interiano-Shiverdecker,
Belinda Bustos Flores, Cristina Thornell,
Jessenia García, and Isanely Guerrero Kurz

Preparing Culturally Efficacious Bilingual Counselors through Theory and Case Studies

PETER LANG

New York · Berlin · Bruxelles · Chennai · Lausanne · Oxford

Library of Congress Cataloging-in-Publication Data

Names: Interiano-Shiverdecker, Claudia G., author. | Flores, Belinda
Bustos, author. | Thornell, Cristina, author. | García, Jessenia,
author. | Kurz, Isanely Guerrero, author.
Title: Preparing culturally efficacious bilingual counselors through theory
and case studies / Claudia G. Interiano-Shiverdecker, Belinda Bustos
Flores, Cristina Thornell, Jessenia García, Isanely Guerrero Kurz.
Description: New York : Peter Lang, 2024. | Series: Critical studies of
Latinxs in the Americas, 2372-6822 ; volume 31 | Includes
bibliographical references and index.
Identifiers: LCCN 2023036337 (print) | LCCN 2023036338 (ebook) |
ISBN 9781433196997 (paperback) | ISBN 9781636676302 (pdf) |
ISBN 9781636676319 (epub)
Subjects: LCSH: Counseling–Social aspects. | Hispanic Americans–Social
conditions. | Education, Bilingual.
Classification: LCC BF636.6 .I56 2023 (print) | LCC BF636.6 (ebook) |
DDC 158.3–dc23/eng/20230927
LC record available at https://lccn.loc.gov/2023036337
LC ebook record available at https://lccn.loc.gov/2023036338
DOI 10.3726/b21157

Bibliographic information published by the Deutsche Nationalbibliothek.
The German National Library lists this publication in the German
National Bibliography; detailed bibliographic data is available
on the Internet at http://dnb.d-nb.de.

Cover design by Peter Lang Group AG

ISSN 2372-6822 (print)
ISBN 9781433196997 (paperback)
ISBN 9781636676302 (ebook)
ISBN 9781636676319 (epub)
DOI 10.3726/b21157

© 2024 Peter Lang Group AG, Lausanne
Published by Peter Lang Publishing Inc., New York, USA
info@peterlang.com - www.peterlang.com

This publication has been peer reviewed.

CONTENTS

PREFACE

Until I am free to write bilingually and to switch codes without having always to translate, while I still have to speak English or Spanish when I would rather speak Spanglish, and as long as I have to accommodate the English speakers rather than having them accommodate me, my tongue will be illegitimate. I will no longer be made to feel ashamed of existing. I will have my voice: Indian, Spanish, white.
— **Gloria Anzaldúa**

In her book, *Borderlands/La Frontera: The New Mestiza*, Gloria Anzaldúa (1987) wrote about her experiences with her native language, Spanish, in the chapter titled *"How to Tame a Wild Tongue."* Gloria Anzaldúa was an American scholar of Chicana cultural theory, feminist theory, and queer theory. Throughout her work, she used a mix of English and Spanish words without translation to challenge the influence of English as the dominant language in the text and legitimize the power of her Spanish language. We (Claudia, Belinda, Cristina, Jessenia, and Isanely) seek to bring Anzaldúa's powerful message to the field of counseling. As five Spanish-speaking Latina scholars, with professional experience as bilingual counselors, we recognized the multitude of challenges encountered when providing services in Spanish without any formal training. Despite our passion and pride in serving our community, we all agreed that the adequate preparation of bicultural-bilingual counselors remains limited. As you read this text, know that this book was created by bilingual counselors, and for bilingual counselors, to raise our collective voice.

Throughout our first conversations we realized a significant problem in the field: the overall assumption that for bilingual counselors to be culturally and linguistically efficacious, they simply must be bilingual. We counter this false assumption by offering that the professional community would never agree that a counselor simply must speak English or another first language to be an effective counselor. This also becomes an ethical issue if bilingual counselors are prepared entirely using traditional Euro-American counseling theories and techniques. Several publications address the fact that "Euro-American" therapy models grounded in Western European philosophical assumptions (Sue & Sue, 2015, p. 36) do not match other cultural backgrounds (e.g., Alvarado et al., 2019; Arredondo et al., 2014; Fuertes, 2004; Guilman, 2015; Hernandez-Wolfe, 2013; Ibrahim & Heuer, 2016; McCaffery & Moody, 2015). Bilingual counselors must also know clinical terms and concepts in both English and Spanish. Throughout this book, we present appropriate translations for clinical terminology and intentionally did not italicize our words in Spanish. Bilingual counselors can benefit from books that like Anzaldúa use a mix of English and Spanish words.

Therefore, our book is unique because it provides adequate knowledge and resources to prepare culturally efficacious bilingual counselors (Fuertes, 2004; McCaffery & Moody, 2015). Our focus is upon the Latine population to ensure access to materials in Spanish and to attend to Latine mental health issues (Arredondo et al., 2014). We have engaged in this critical work to provide the profession a resource in which theory and practices intersect.

Overview of the Book

In Chapter 1, *Preparing Culturally Efficacious Bilingual Counselors Through Theory and Case Studies*, we provide the theoretical and research grounding for preparing culturally efficacious bilingual counselors. Specifically, we use a social justice lens and weave in self-efficacy research. We also provide a snapshot of the topics discussed in subsequent chapters of the book.

Chapter 2, *Developing Linguistic-Communicative Competence in Bilingual Counseling Settings*, discusses the importance of considering the client's language preference and modality during the counseling session. Given the role of language in expressing emotion, it further explores bilingual counselors' communicative competence, which includes bilingual proficiency, understanding clinical terms in Spanish, and code-switching to establish rapport and trust with the client. We further stipulate that attending to the client's communication style and language preferences can advance the therapeutic outcomes. We also offer several Spanish resources and forms that can be used in the bilingual clinical setting. The case study presented highlights the importance of considering language as a socio-cultural factor within the counseling setting.

In Chapter 3, *Cultural Choques and Acculturation: Sociocultural Considerations for Serving the Counseling Needs of the Latine Populations*, we extend our discussion on hegemonic discourse that results in cultural choques (clash/tensions) for Latine bicultural clients. Within the United States, the rhetoric in which the Latine population is given monolithic expectations to fully embrace the majority groups' monolingual ideals and cultural practices positions the Latine population as a minoritized group. As a result, these cultural choques impact individuals' psychological well-being and identity. To understand these choques, we explore several cultural considerations and provide a case study illustrating the cultural choques that clients may experience. We also extend the conversation regarding traditional counseling theories and how these can be employed using a sociocultural lens to meet the needs of bilingual populations. We further consider other theories, such as Acculturation, Borderland Theory, and LatCrit, that can serve to underpin counselors' approaches when working with bilingual clients.

Bilingual Supervision for Developing and Guiding Culturally Efficacious Counselors is discussed in Chapter 4 considering the specialized skills needed by bilingual counselors. In this chapter, we present various topics/concerns applicable to bilingual supervision. The goal of this chapter is to support bilingual counselors training to develop communicative competence, cultural competence, and an understanding of the sociopolitical issues that may be impacting the psychological well-being of the Latine client. Additionally, we present resources that can help supervisors and educators provide guidance and feedback that augment bilingual counselors' development. The case study presented here incorporates the nuances present within the bilingual client-counselor-supervisor relationship.

Chapter 5, *Bilingual Casos: Becoming Culturally Efficacious by Applying Theory to Practice*, provides six different case studies situated in our social justice framework. For each case, we offer abbreviated research to ground the clinical skills employed. Each of the cases is followed by resources and reflective questions. These sample cases can be used to prepare bilingual counselors.

Our book provides a final reflection on bilingual counselor training and supervision that will assist the field in moving towards bilingual/bicultural responsive practices.

Closing Thoughts

Our vision for this text was to provide theoretical grounding and practical approaches that are responsive to serving the distinct Latine/bilingual population. We hope that our book assists others in moving away from a monocultural/linguistic perspective situated in Western thought. We conclude by reiterating that one cannot assume that if a counselor is bilingual, they possess the requisite knowledge and skills to provide care to bilingual clients. In preparing culturally efficacious bilingual counselors, there is ethically necessary foundational training, and it should not just be an afterthought. We trust that this introductory text will provide the substantive foundation from which bilingual counselors can continue their growth, recognize the power of their language, and prepare efficiently to provide a space that allows clients to express themselves in their native tongue.

References

Alvarado, M., Lerma, E., & Vela, J. C. (2019). Experiences of Spanish speaking counseling students: Implications for the profession. *The Journal of Counselor Preparation and Supervision, 12*(4). https://digitalcommons.sacredheart.edu/jcps/vol12/iss4/1

Anzaldúa, G. (1987). *Borderlands/La Frontera: The new mestiza.* Aunt Lute Books.

Arredondo, P., Gallardo-Cooper, M., Delgado-Romero, E. A., & Zapata, A. L. (2014). *Culturally responsive counseling with Latinas/os.* American Counseling Association.

Fuertes, J. N. (2004). Supervision in bilingual counseling: Service delivery, training, and research considerations. *Journal of Multicultural Counseling and Development, 32*(2), 84–94. https://doi.org/10.1002/j.2161-1912.2004.tb00363.x

Guilman, S. R. (2015). Beyond interpretation: The need for English-Spanish bilingual psychotherapists in counseling centers. *James Madison Undergraduate Research Journal, 2*(1), 26–30. http://commons.lib.jmu.edu/cgi/viewcontent.cgi?article=1010&context=jmurj

Hernandez-Wolfe, P. (2013). *A borderlands view on Latinos, Latin Americans, and decolonization: Rethinking mental health.* Jason Aronson.

Ibrahim, F. A., & Heuer, J. R. (2016). *International and cultural psychology. Cultural and social justice counseling: Client-specific interventions.* Springer International Publishing.

McCaffrey, A., & Moody, S. J. (2015). Providing equitable services: Implementing bilingual counseling certification in counselor education programs. *VISTAS Online*, Article 33, 1–11. https://www.counseling.org/docs/default-source/vistas/article_33625c21f16116603ab cacff0000bee5e7.pdf?sfvrsn=6

Sue, D., & Sue, D. (2015). *Counseling the culturally diverse: Theory and practice* (7th ed.). Wiley.

FOREWORD

Language is the "how" of the counseling process. A shared language allows a client to encode their feelings and experiences and the counselor to decode these messages. What is more, it is a tool for the counselor to express empathy and facilitate client healing.

Aside from being a means of communication, language is also an instrument to access and convey culture. Though language does not define identity, it enables access to elders, literature, film, and music—means of transmitting and constructing knowledge and values. As such, the ability to speak the client's native language is critical for understanding the client's values and lived experience.

What then when a monolingual English-speaking counselor tries to provide services to a Spanish-speaking or a bilingual Spanish- and English-speaking client? Typically, the client is compelled to adapt to the counselor's language: the client is forced to assimilate to English. In this case, we must ask what is lost, and what aspects of the client's culture and experience are left out of the counseling process.

The importance of language to the counseling process is likely lost on monolingual English-speaking counselors. The privilege of speaking only the dominant language of the United States leaves most monolingual counselors ignorant of how social structures, businesses, and media cater to their needs. Alas, they will never know the feeling of having to instantaneously decipher if written words are in English or Spanish, of having to translate for Spanish-speaking relatives, or the pain of being chastised for speaking Spanish. English monolingual counselors will also miss the cultural validation of conversing in Spanish with a colleague, the more nuanced ways to express emotions across two languages, and the seamless transitions of going from listening to Punk Rock to immediately belting out a Ranchera.

"Preparing Culturally Efficacious Bilingual Counselors Through Theory and Case Studies" is a groundbreaking text: The first to fully consider bilingualism in counseling—giving attention to a topic that has too long gone neglected in the counseling literature. This text moves beyond basic vocabulary to consider intersectionality and social justice frames in bilingual counseling—topics missed in most counseling texts. What is more, the application of theory, attention to cultural values, discussion of supervision, and various case studies provide resources necessary for counselors across experience levels.

With the Latine community now firmly the second largest ethnic group in the United States, the need for more bilingual counselors will only continue to grow. To effectively and ethically serve this growing population, one that has historically underutilized counseling, action must be taken. This text has inspired me, as a counselor educator, to consider how we might better recruit and train bilingual professionals. I hope that this text similarly inspires other counselors and counselor educators to recruit and train more bilingual counselors.

Carlos P. Hipolito-Delgado | Professor
University of Colorado Denver
School of Education and Human Development |Counseling
carlos.hipolito@ucdenver.edu
he/him/el

AUTHOR BIOGRAPHIES

Claudia G. Interiano-Shiverdecker, Ph.D., is a Fulbright Scholar and an Assistant Professor at the University of Texas at San Antonio (UTSA). She received her master's degree in Clinical Mental Health Counseling from the University of Wisconsin-Stout and a Ph.D. in Counselor Education and Supervision from the University of North Carolina at Charlotte. She is a Licensed Professional Counselor in Texas specializing in providing bilingual counseling services to Spanish-speaking populations. Previously, she worked for four years as a licensed psychologist in Honduras with Spanish-speaking adolescents. Her research primarily focuses on (a) social justice and multicultural considerations for marginalized communities, particularly the Latine community; (b) counseling competencies to work with trauma and specific populations vulnerable to trauma; (c) advocating for underrepresented populations in higher education; and (d) bilingual counseling and supervision. Dr. Interiano-Shiverdecker serves as part of the committee in charge of the Bilingual Counseling Certificate in the Department of Counseling at UTSA.

Belinda Bustos Flores, Ph.D., is currently an Associate Dean of Strategic Partnerships, Preparation, and Growth, Bicultural-Bilingual Studies in the College of Education and Human Development at the University of Texas at San Antonio. Prior to becoming a faculty member, Flores was a bilingual education teacher and bilingual counselor. Flores's research focuses on teacher development and preparing culturally efficacious teachers. Flores was the recipient of the 2015 AERA *Hispanic Research Issues SIG Elementary, Secondary, and Postsecondary Award*. In 2019, Flores was the recipient of the *AERA Bilingual Education Research SIG Lifetime Achievement Award*.

Cristina "Cristy" Thornell (née Martínez-Smith), Ph.D., is a Licensed Professional Counselor in Texas and has extensive experience working in community agencies and higher education. As a former full-time faculty, she has taught master-level counseling students and supervised bilingual counselors-in-training who offered services in the community. As a bilingual counselor, she has provided services in both English and Spanish, to people living in diverse community settings, to adults during their recovery process living in transitional programs, and to people living in homeless shelters. She has also facilitated court-mandated group therapy for teens and parents, as well as working with clients holding different immigration statuses. Now she is in the process of building her practice where her focus is to provide mental health services to the Spanish-speaking community.

Jessenia García, Ph.D., is an Assistant Professor of counseling at St. Edward's University and a Licensed Professional Counselor in the state of Texas. She received both her master's degree in counseling and doctoral degree in counselor education and supervision from The University of Texas at San Antonio. Her research interests include bilingual counseling and supervision, first-generation Latine college students, bicultural stress and identity development, and other Latine issues in counseling. She currently operates her private practice where she focuses on adult BIPOC and Latine issues in mental health. She was named a graduate fellow for the Texas Association of Chicanos in Higher Education in 2019 and a faculty fellow for the Association for Hispanics in Higher Education in 2022.

Isanely "Isa" Kurz, Ph.D., (she/her/ella) is a Licensed Professional Counselor in Texas. She enjoys teaching adjunct on diversity and social justice competencies within counseling courses. She has had experience counseling individuals, couples, and families from rural communities experiencing trauma while also utilizing equine-assisted therapy. She has also worked extensively with neurodiverse individuals and their families across multiple settings. Isa is currently pursuing certifications in Eye Movement Desensitization and Reprocessing (EMDR) and Perinatal Mental Health. Her research interests consist of diversity, equity, and inclusivity issues in counseling, including using centering Latine and QIPOC ways of knowing. When she is not teaching or counseling, she loves spending time with her family, eating cheesy pizza, and listening to scary stories and true crime podcasts.

ACKNOWLEDGMENTS

Yo, Claudia Gabriela Interiano-Shiverdecker, quiero agradecerles a mis padres, Juan José Interiano González y Maria Isabel Estrada de Interiano, mi esposo Darren Shiverdecker, mis hermanos Juan José Interiano Estrada e Ilan Francisco Interiano Starkman, mi tía Elena de Acosta, y al resto de mi familia por su apoyo incondicional y por todas sus palabras de aliento. Este logro no hubiera sido posible sin ustedes. Muchas gracias por creer en mí. Cuando comencé mi carrera como consejera bilingüe nunca pensé que yo podría ser parte de un equipo que está creando recursos para desarrollar la formación de consejeros bilingües. Por ende, quiero agradecerles a Derek Robertson, Elias Zambrano, Heather Trepal, y Thelma Duffey, profesores del Departamento de Consejería de la Universidad de Texas en San Antonio por invitarme a ser parte del Departamento de Consejería que ofrece unos de los pocos certificados bilingües para la formación de consejeros bilingües en la nación. Fue así como conocí a mis coautores y tuve la oportunidad de ser parte de este proyecto. Belinda, muchísimas gracias por creer en mí y convencerme de que este libro no solo era posible sino necesario. Me has inspirado de muchas formas a creer en mi voz cómo Latina. Jessenia, Cristina, Isa ha sido un honor crear este libro juntas. Durante estos años nos hemos desarrollado profesionalmente y personalmente y me lleno de felicidad al vernos prosperar. Quiero también agradecer a mis estudiantes, particularmente a Sofia Santillan, quienes me han ofrecido sugerencias para este libro basado en sus experiencias como consejeros bilingües. Este libro definitivamente fue hecho para todos los clientes, consejeros, supervisores y educadores bilingües y esperamos que ayude a mejorar el acceso y calidad de nuestra salud mental.

I, Belinda Bustos Flores, want to acknowledge my familia, especially my querido esposo, Mario Enrique Flores, and my hija de oro, Janelle Beth Flores, as well as my parents, Arturo Silvano Bustos and Frances Salazar Bustos, for their constant support and love. The inspiration for this book was when I taught a course for bilingual counselors; together with doctoral students, now faculty at various universities, we worked on developing a much-needed resource. We then invited Dr. Claudia Interiano-Shiverdecker to the team, who has successfully led this project to fruition. I want to thank my fellow authors, my colegas, who have greatly contributed to the success of the book for bilingual counselors. I am also thankful to my former students Austin Bonecutter, Maria Avila, and Maricela Saavedra, who assisted in the editing process. Lastly, I like to dedicate our book to our gente who deserve equitable bilingual counseling services. ¡Sí se puede y sí se hizo!

Yo, Cristina Thornell, tomo esta oportunidad para darle gracias a la vida por lo que tengo y por lo que no. Gracias a mi familia y a mis colegas por ser como son y por aceptarme como soy. De nosotras para ustedes escribimos este libro para todos nosotros que creemos en la magia de nuestra voz y el poder de nuestras emociones. Gracias a Belinda por empezar este proyectó y nunca darse por vencida. Claudia, gracias por ser la capitana de este barco. Por último, gracias a Isa y a Jessenia por su cooperación y amistad. Sin todas ustedes este libro no sería lo que es.

I, Cristina Thornell, take this opportunity to give thanks to life for what I have and for what I do not. Thank you to my family and my colleagues for being who they are and for accepting me as I am. From us to you we wrote this book for all of us who believe in the magic of our voice and the power of our emotions. Thanks to Belinda for starting this project and never giving up. Claudia, thank you for being the captain of this ship. Lastly, thanks to Isa and Jessenia for their cooperation and friendship. Without all of you, this book would not be what it is.

I, Jessenia García, express my deepest gratitude to my family and husband who fan my flames and give me the courage to continue fighting the good fight. Youssef, Gabriela, Josue, Beckita, and Josh thank you for your continuous love and support. You are so loved and appreciated! I have also been incredibly lucky to have wonderful mentors. Thank you to Dr. Angelica Tello and Dr. Heather Trepal for having faith in me in those developmental years as a doctoral student. You poured so much into me and helped instill a love and confidence in myself to do this work! Lastly, thank you to mis colegas, chingona sisters, las meras meras Claudia, Isanely, Cristina, and Belinda for being such a wonderful team. This book is work from the heart and is filled with so much love for the community of counselors and clients for whom we hope this book reaches.

I, Isanely Kurz, would like to express my love and appreciation for my boys, my husband Zack, and my son Zachary Ryan Jr. Mi vida, I hope that you are inspired by my actions to embrace my destiny and as you grow up to follow your path, may you take the strength of nuestra gente to guide you always. Gracias a mis padres Isanely y Tony, y a mis hermanos Tony y Diego que me han apoyado toda mi vida. Thank you to my best friend and Zachary's madrina, Nancy, who has been my sounding board and fellow chingona at a time when our paths needed to cross. I am grateful to my fellow authors, Belinda, Claudia, Jessenia, and Cristina who have attested to the value of this book as a resource to help our communities in need. Lastly, I would like to acknowledge all the bilingual counselors, educators, and supervisors who are out there doing the hard work every day. La lucha sigue my friends, I see you, I hear you, I am you.

· 1 ·

PREPARING CULTURALLY EFFICACIOUS BILINGUAL COUNSELORS THROUGH THEORY AND CASE STUDIES

Our book focuses on the preparation of bilingual counselors for the ever-growing Latine community. As of July 2021, the Latine community was the largest ethnic group in the United States, with over 61.4 million people, or 18.5% of the nation's total population (U.S. Census Bureau, n.d.). The Latine community is far from a homogenous group, as there are many generational, immigration, and heritage language differences (Krogstad & Lopez, 2017). Throughout this book, we use the gender-inclusive term "Latine" in reference to individuals living in the United States with ancestry from Spanish-speaking (e.g., Mexico, Puerto Rico, Cuba, Dominican Republic) and non-Spanish-speaking (e.g., Brazil), South and Central American countries. However, preferences for this pan-ethnic self-identification vary from person to person; some prefer the gendered terms "Latina" and "Latino," while others prefer the term "Hispanic," more specific ethnic terms such as "Chicana," "Mexican American," or country-based identifications such as "Honduran." We also acknowledge that although the term "Latine" engenders greater acceptance due to its gender neutrality, many may perceive the use of this term as an example of language imperialism (the transfer of a dominant language to other people) or extranjerismo (an expression taken from another language to fulfill a semantic void). We, therefore, encourage the reader to consider the cultural and clinical implications of using this term.

Throughout this book, we also employ the notion of cultural efficacious-ness and situate our work within a social justice framework. The Academy for Teacher Excellence, founded in 2003, introduced the concept of *cultural efficaciousness* (Flores et al., 2007; Guerra, 2016). Cultural and linguistic effi-caciousness draws from Bandura (1993), who suggests that individuals attain self-efficacy through verbal or social persuasion, physiological emotional arousal, and mastery experiences. In expanding Bandura's work, Flores and colleagues (Flores et al., 2007; Flores et al., 2018; Gist et al., 2015) proposed that in contrast to cultural competency, cultural efficaciousness includes an outcome expectation in which the individual possesses both the competence and the ability to enact change.

While their work has focused on preparing culturally efficacious teachers, the notion of cultural efficaciousness is appropriate for bilingual counselors as they should possess strong personal and professional identities, positive cultural and linguistic competence, critical reflective counseling skills, and a belief that they can make a difference in their clients' lives. This book, therefore, seeks to prepare culturally efficacious bilingual counselors through readings and clini-cal case studies that will address issues related to bilingualism (how to counsel in two languages) while also considering important aspects of biculturalism (cultural identity integration for the client and the counselor). We believe that this framework will not only facilitate important skills and terminology but also promote counselor self-efficacy and identity development among bilingual counselors.

Social Justice Framework

The social justice framework that encapsulates the contents of this book carries a vision of a society in which the distribution of resources is equita-ble and all members are physically safe and secure (Bell, 1997). This book is intentionally situated within this perspective to provide bilingual counselors with the tools to increase access and quality of care to the communities they serve. Social justice advocacy refers to actions taken to facilitate the removal of external barriers to opportunity and well-being (Toporek & Liu, 2001). Social justice counseling, therefore, includes social and political action that seeks to (a) produce conditions that allow for equal access and opportunity; (b) reduce or eliminate disparities in education, resources, employment, and services; (c) encourage mental health professionals to consider micro, meso, and macro levels in the assessment, diagnosis, and treatment of clients and client systems; and (d) broaden the role of the helping profession (e.g., advocate, consultant, psychoeducator, change agent, community worker; Goodman et al., 2004; Ibrahim & Heuer, 2016; Sue et al., 2019).

To begin, a culturally efficacious bilingual counselor must understand (a) their cultural conditioning and how this conditioning affects their personal beliefs, values, and attitudes; (b) the worldviews and life experiences of diverse groups; and (c) the skills required to use culturally appropriate intervention strategies when working with different groups in society (Arredondo et al., 1996). A new model for conceptualizing counselors' cultural competency emerged when the Association for Multicultural Counseling and Development (AMCD) published the Multicultural and Social Justice Counseling Competencies (MSJCC), proposing social justice as the fifth force in counseling (Ratts et al., 2016). For each situation, counselors were asked to consider four quadrants (based on marginalized and privileged dimensions for both client and counselors), and, for each quadrant, four levels (counselor self-awareness, client worldview, counseling relationship, counseling and advocacy interventions) and four competencies (attitudes and beliefs, knowledge, skills, and action; Ratts et al., 2016). By doing so, this model illustrates, in the context of intersectionality, how both clients and counselors may experience marginalization concerning identity and privilege in another. Furthermore, social justice advocacy interventions recommend counselors take action on multiple levels including interpersonal, institutional, community, public policy, and international/global (Ratts et al., 2016).

Thus, if bilingual counselors are concerned with bettering the life circumstances of individuals, families, and communities in our society, then social justice counseling and advocacy is the overarching umbrella guiding their work. The main thesis of this book is that to best serve the Latine population we must recognize that counseling does not take place in a vacuum isolated from larger sociopolitical influences (Sue et al., 2019). Latine research shows that services are frequently antagonistic or inappropriate to the life experiences of this population, lack sensitivity and understanding, and can leave clients feeling oppressed and discriminated against (Bridges et al., 2012). A social justice framework requires culturally efficacious bilingual counselors to recognize that in addition to developing cultural awareness of self and others and using culturally appropriate intervention strategies, they must also learn to identify systemic obstacles to well-being and help community members harness their strengths and resources to confront those obstacles. To accomplish this goal, culturally efficacious counselors work collaboratively with their clients to gain access to the resources needed to improve well-being, while also working to pass legislation and social policy that serve oppressed communities (e.g., affirmative action, civil rights voting protections).

Social Justice Framework Concepts

Several key concepts exemplify the tenets of the social justice framework. Counselors seeking to operate from this framework must be concerned with the positionality of privilege and oppression, power, and advocacy.

Positionality of Privilege and Oppression

Privilege, o privilegio, refers to unearned access to benefits and advantages for members of dominant groups as a result of ongoing exploitation and oppression of non-dominant group members (Sue et al., 2019). Privileged status often resides outside the awareness of the person possessing it (McIntosh, 1992; Robinson & Howard-Hamilton, 2000). On the other hand, oppression, u opresión, is the systemic and institutional abuse of power by one group at the expense of others and the use of force to maintain this dynamic (Allport, 1982). An oppressive system stems from the ideology of the superiority of some groups and inferiority of others and operates, intentionally and unintentionally, on individual, institutional, and cultural levels. In other words, oppressive systems seek to keep some individuals at an advantage, while keeping others at a disadvantage based on social group membership (Allport, 1982). Examples of these include patriarchy, misogyny, sexism, heterosexism, racism, ableism, ageism, and colonialism.

Many discussions of privilege and oppression focus primarily on gender, race, or both (Sue et al., 2019). However, these conversations require an understanding of intersections, intricacies, and influences that are part and parcel of an individual's life and experiences. Categories of privilege and oppression include other socially constructed categories of sexual orientation, socioeconomic status, age, degree of ableness, politics of appearance, language, education, colorism, and religious affiliation. This constellation of social categories, known as *positionalities*, classify, categorize, and construct the social value that is assigned to individuals according to various components (Robinson, 1999). Positionalities, therefore, "possess rank, have value, and are constructed hierarchically, particularly those that are visible and discernible" (Robinson, 1999, p. 73). Intersectionality, o interseccionalidad, is a framework that considers the various backgrounds and personal experiences that shape the lives and outcomes of marginalized populations, defined by their positionality in different categories (i.e., gender, age, race, language). Intersectionality suggests that people have unique experiences based on the combination of their identities and that it is impossible to understand discrimination and oppression by considering one singular identity, especially given that institutions use identity to discriminate against some and privilege others.

At this point, it is common to think of oppression and privilege in the context of personal experience, or maybe about a specific client population. Yet culturally efficacious bilingual counselors consider how privilege, oppression, and positionality apply to the counselor, the client, and their relationship. Exploration of different positionalities of privilege and oppression, therefore, facilitates multicultural counseling competency in all counselors, including bilingual counselors. The consequences of not addressing privilege and oppression may obstruct the therapeutic process, damage the client's perspective and actions, and/or result in a misunderstanding or misinterpretation of the client. Bilingual counselors must understand that although they may work with clients with whom they share certain positionalities (e.g., Latine identity, physical features, gender), client-counselor differences in positionality may create different and even contrasting perspectives, values, and behaviors. For example, a Latine, female, straight counselor working with a Latine, female, bisexual client may share similar oppressive experiences as part of the Latine community; however, the counselor's positionality as a straight woman provides privilege in terms of sexual orientation (e.g., ability to openly speak about their partner with colleagues, family, and friends without any personal or professional repercussions) that the client may not experience.

Power

Failure to address power imbalances, o desbalances de poder, constructed by the hierarchy of positionalities in the counseling relationship may lead to avoidance, distancing, and detachment from clients in the professional practice (Vodde, 2001). Power is the ability or official authority to decide what is best for others and who will have access to resources. It also refers to the capacity to exercise control over others and to direct or influence the behavior of others, oneself, and/or the course of events. Counselors who examine their privileged statuses are less likely to succumb to racial stereotypes, more likely to view problems from a systemic perspective, more likely to gain culturally specific knowledge from their clients, and less likely to impose ethnocentric values onto their clients (Sue et al., 2019). Counselors must address these issues to avoid power imbalances and thus unethical practices. The counseling relationship can be affected by different levels of cultural power between individuals and how they respond to clients of various cultural backgrounds, as well as how their interactions with clients facilitate their awareness of privilege and oppression. For example, with clients who experience privilege in several areas, counselors may struggle to openly discuss instances in which clients' behaviors or attitudes were discriminatory to them or others. If so, the bilingual counselor might consider consulting with colleagues and supervisors to evaluate if broaching these discriminatory remarks is needed in the counseling relationship. If it is not appropriate, the counselor may need support to process their emotions when clients, including other Latine clients, are discriminatory against them. On the other hand, if counselors ignore power imbalances favoring the counselor, the client may not feel comfortable or safe to discuss vulnerable topics. If we hold a space of power for the client, whether it is skin color (being a White-skinned Latine) or sexual orientation (identifying as straight), it may be helpful to ask the client if this impacts their relationship. A question like, "¿Como te sientes con el hecho de que yo soy de tez blanca (o no parte de la comunidad LGBTQ)? ¿Afecta nuestra relación de alguna manera?"

Advocacy

Since the development of Multicultural Counseling Competencies (MCC) (Sue et al., 1992), the needs of culturally diverse clients became pertinent to counselor training, practice, and research. In 2002, the American Counseling Association (ACA) published the Advocacy Competencies (Lewis et al., 2002) to guide counselors pursuing advocacy work as an ethical aspect of service delivery. Social justice advocacy, o la defensa de la justicia social, involves acting with or on behalf of oppressed individuals on different levels by understanding individuals in the context of their social environment, recognizing the negative influence of oppression on mental health and well-being, and advocating for justice and equality (Ratts et al., 2016). Counselors recognize their privilege and use social advocacy skills to help bring about individual and systemic changes. Proponents of social justice advocacy in counseling suggest counselors need to discern when they act within the boundaries of individual or family counseling and when to branch out in the community to raise awareness, educate, and advocate for issues pertaining to marginalized clients. Adopting a social justice framework in this book, we guide counselors to use their knowledge, skills, and awareness to best serve the Latine population both in an office setting and through community outreach, thus changing individuals' lives and shaping their communities.

Social Justice Framework and Bilingual Counseling

The Council for Accreditation of Counseling and Related Educational Programs (CACREP, 2016), charged with creating professional academic standards for counseling graduate programs, has made judicious efforts to mandate curriculum changes that promote multicultural competencies. The 2016 CACREP Standards require counselor education programs to incorporate "advocacy processes needed to address institutional and social barriers that impede access, equity, and success for clients" (Standard F.1.e), and to address "multicultural and pluralistic characteristics within and among diverse groups nationally and internationally" (Standard F.2.a). Preparing culturally efficacious bilingual counselors through a social justice framework thus requires curricula specifically designed to promote knowledge, skills, and awareness to best work with Spanish-speaking communities.

We observe two current factors that impede counselor education program efforts to address this issue. First, there is an underrepresentation of Latine mental health professionals, including counselors and social workers, (U.S. Department of Health and Human Services, 2017) to meet the needs of the bilingual populace. Undoubtedly, there is a need for ethnic/racial and linguistic representation in the counseling profession, as studies have shown that a linguistic and cultural match impacts the quality of services available to multilingual populations (Meyer & Zane, 2013; Valentine et al., 2017). Given the over-representation of White counselors and the under-representation of ethnic/racial minoritized bilingual counselors, counseling programs must engage in the recruitment, preparation, and retention of bilingual counselors committed to social justice issues.

Second, researchers (Biever et al., 2011; Verdinelli & Biever, 2009) noted that bilingual counselors trained in English felt less confident providing services in Spanish, experiencing an increase of negative self-talk when counseling in Spanish. To prepare culturally efficacious bilingual counselors, there is a need for appropriate linguistic and cultural materials adapted or reimagined to meet bilingual counselors' needs (Trepal et al., 2014). Most bilingual counselors providing services in Spanish do not receive any additional clinical training or supervision to provide services in Spanish or work with the Latine community. The lack of attention to training bilingual counselors is based on the implicit, yet faulty, assumption that students with conversational proficiency in Spanish can easily translate professional concepts obtained in English to their work with Spanish-speaking clients. Similar to educator preparation (Flores et al., 2018), we cannot assume that having a linguistic and/or cultural match will ensure social justice or the competency of counselors. This belief also ignores cultural nuances in language and may leave bilingual counselors at risk of providing services with insufficient skills. In addition, the resources and materials available for training are limited (Guilman, 2015).

Rationale for the Book

For these reasons, the authors designed this book framed within the concepts of social justice to train culturally efficacious bilingual counselors through theory and case studies. Bilingual counselor education can advance the social justice mission of the counseling profession and address the needs of the growing Latine population. We believe that bilingual counselors can develop a greater sense of professional identity and efficacy when they can consult with others about bilingual counseling issues, thus ultimately improving their performance.

Our social justice framework draws from the notion that language, culture, and multicultural competencies are critical components to consider within the bilingual counseling context. Language is the conduit to the healing process, allowing clients to express their most intimate thoughts (Oliva, 2017). However, language does not function in isolation but rather reflects the cultural understandings and worldview of an individual. Traditional counseling therapeutic approaches developed, practiced, and evaluated based on a Euro-American/ Western society are rooted in and reflect Euro-American worldviews (Sue et al., 2019). These worldviews identify a particular philosophy of life (i.e., individualism, autonomy, internal locus of control, and personal responsibility) as normal in counseling and supervisory relationships (Sue et al., 2019). Therapeutic approaches developed using a Euro-American perspective may not match cultural norms embraced by Latine communities.

Several researchers also suggested that to assist bilingual clients, counselors must understand the context in which their clients engage in their daily lives and move away from colonizing practices (Arredondo et al., 2014; Goodman & Gorski, 2015; Ibrahim & Heuer, 2016; McCaffrey & Moody, 2015).

Bilingual counselors seeking to best serve the Latine community must also be concerned with the welfare of society, seeking to enhance the quality of life for all persons and address the obstacles that oppress, denigrate, and harm those in our society. Issues of power, marginalization, and inequities must be treated from a decolonial perspective, not a colonial lens that looks at clients simply as victims or individuals struggling to fit into society (Hernandez-Wolfe, 2013). As McCaffrey and Moody (2015) observed:

> While stressors are central to any individual adapting to a new culture, the collectivist nature of many Latino cultures presents an additional challenge. In comparison to the individualistic and achievement-oriented disposition of the United States, the Latino lifestyle, mentality, and motivation are identified by the importance of family and sense of community. (p. 3)

Key Elements of Bilingual Counseling

As an answer to this professional concern, this book describes key elements of bilingual counseling to offer supplemental training for students and licensed professionals to effectively meet the growing needs of the Latine community. In the chapters that follow, we introduce components of bilingual counseling training and describe the implementation of these features into case studies designed to train competent bilingual counselors. We provide a short introduction of these elements below and their connection to bilingual counseling training.

Language Competency

Language competence refers to the "ability to communicate effectively via grammatical, conversational, sociolinguistic, and strategic accuracy and flexibility" (Schwartz et al., 2010, p. 211). Communication is a principal tool in counseling. Neglecting language competence may amplify any existing obstacles to access and quality of services. Individuals with limited English proficiency report more barriers to healthcare access (Artiga et al., 2015), and worse quality of healthcare (Nguyen & Reardon, 2013). They often turn away from counseling services because they feel uncomfortable speaking in another language or struggle to convey thoughts or feelings in English (Castaño et al., 2007), which has the effect of distancing themselves from emotions (Javier,

2007). Non-English-speaking clients must often rely on translators, interpreters, or language brokers to obtain services despite documented concerns about these practices such as omissions, role exchange, and ethical concerns with using children or family members as translators (Paone & Malott, 2008). Language also carries over important cultural values.

Bilingual counselors allow clients whose English is limited or who prefer Spanish to express themselves on a deeper level while validating their cultural identity. Bilingual clients will have a range of bilingual proficiency in which they may be more Spanish or English-dominant or may function equally in both languages. Bilingual clients may code-switch (alternate Spanish and English) when speaking about personal issues. They may recall childhood memories in their heritage language or the language spoken at home. Further, clients may be struggling with acculturative stress in which they grapple with their cultural/ethnic attitudes, beliefs, behaviors, identities, or values (Miranda & Matheny, 2000; Schwartz et al., 2010). Thus, the bilingual counselor must adapt to clients' language modalities and preferences.

Cultural Competency

The growing prevalence of Spanish-speaking and bilingual households in the United States requires mental health care services to be delivered by culturally trained professionals. Latine populations continue to face the challenge of identifying competent practitioners capable of providing culturally appropriate linguistic services (Flores, 2013; Rios-Ellis, 2005; Fripp & Carlson, 2017). Latines' lack of access to services may make them less likely to receive care for treatment of diagnoses such as depression, anxiety, and substance use. Inequitable access to mental health services can lead to missed educational and career opportunities, thus deepening the socioeconomic divide and putting these communities at greater risk for suicide and trauma. Furthermore, this population is vulnerable to possible misdiagnosis by less competent practitioners who may exhibit bias and lack knowledge of cultural systems and relationships (Softas-Nall et al., 2015).

The MSJCC maintains that counselors must possess knowledge of clients' worldviews, assumptions, attitudes, values, biases, social identities, social group statuses, and experiences with power, privilege, and oppression (Ratts et al., 2016). Awareness and understanding of the intersectionality of sociopolitical realities and cultural elements are vital in ensuring a culturally informed standard of care for Spanish-speaking clients. Training in bilingual counseling must therefore equip students with tools to expand their knowledge of culture and subcultures, as well as societal and institutional contexts that impact healthcare disparities and unequal access to resources (Delgado-Romero et al., 2018). Other multicultural considerations include cross-cultural awareness and considerations of cultural paradigms such as acculturation, oppression, discrimination, collectivism, religiosity, and the overall rhetoric surrounding Latine communities (McCaffrey & Moody, 2015).

Supervision and Practice

Supervised clinical practice is a requirement for adequate training and ethical practice in counseling programs. Existing professional mandates assert that supervisors must attend to multicultural issues, including language and cultural competence. While the ACA's (2014) *Code of Ethics* mentions the importance of counselors attending to the language preferences of clients, bilingual counselors typically receive supervision in English regardless of the language used in the session. In these instances, bilingual counselors translate their work with Spanish-speaking clients into English, creating a potential ethical issue as the supervisor entrusts the supervisee with the adequate translation of the session.

Proficiency standards for bilingual supervision represent a limited area in the counseling literature (Arredondo et al., 2014; Trepal et al., 2019). Bilingual supervision must protect client welfare, promote trainee skill development, create an effective supervisory alliance, and simultaneously attend to the impact of culture and language in counseling and supervision (Fuertes, 2004; González et al., 2015). Additional components of bilingual supervision include (a) differences in background, acculturation, or sociocultural realities between supervisor, counselor, and client (González et al., 2015); (b) language switching in session and supervision; and (c) conveying complex emotional concepts in another language that may not always directly translate (McCaffrey & Moody, 2015). To adequately prepare bilingual counselors through a social justice lens, it is important to consider Bandura's (1993) notion of self-efficacy and Flores et al.'s (2007, 2018) notion of cultural efficaciousness. We must ensure that bilingual counselors not only feel confident but are also able to demonstrate competence. We believe that programs must provide bilingual counselors with various experiences in which they acquire bilingual counselor self-efficacy and competence. For example, vicarious experiences can be achieved through intentional efforts of offering internship placements where counselors can work with bilingual clients and receive critical feedback on counseling sessions.

This can also occur during debriefing activities within practicum or internship classes. Further, it is important for bilingual counselors to critically reflect on their role within the counseling session in terms of attention to language and cultural issues.

Clinical Cases and Implications for Bilingual Counselors

An essential component of this book is the inclusion of clinical case studies in both English and Spanish to exemplify common elements and/or clinical considerations in bilingual counseling. Case studies were written in contexts that reflect linguistic, cultural, ethical, and socio-political considerations when working with the Latine community. Therefore, the case studies selected highlight contemporary issues and relevant themes that are prevalent in the lives of the Latine community (e.g., code-switching, trauma and immigration, family dynamics). These case studies are designed to extend the breadth and depth of classroom discussion and case conceptualizations. They also provide bilingual counselors with hands-on, useful, concrete, and workable applications that will offer opportunities for skill and theory development.

The bilingual description of the clinical case studies is two-fold. First, we believe this structure supports our efforts to develop linguistic competency among culturally efficacious counselors. Bilingual counselors providing services in Spanish should receive clinical training and supervision in Spanish to learn how to effectively translate and/or discuss core elements of the counseling process. Clinical cases in Spanish allow bilingual counselors to develop conceptualization and treatment skills, while also learning and/or enhancing counseling terminology in Spanish. Second, we recognize that bilingual counselors may vary in language proficiency, and may even differ between written, verbal, and reading capabilities. Therefore, we provide the English translation as a guide.

Conclusion

In the subsequent chapters, we will delineate the topics presented within this introductory chapter. Each of the chapters will present a deeper exploration and discussion of these critical topics for preparing culturally efficacious bilingual counselors. A clinical case study follows each topic, with accompanying reflective questions and implications for clinical practice to facilitate the application of concepts and terms discussed in each chapter.

Points to Remember

- Social justice counselors seek to take actions that facilitate the removal of external barriers to opportunity and well-being.
- Culturally efficacious bilingual counselors must recognize that in addition to developing cultural awareness of self and others, as well as using culturally appropriate intervention strategies, they must also engage in social justice counseling and advocacy.
- Training of bilingual counselors must include developing language and cultural competence.
- In addition to the curriculum, standards, and materials used to prepare bilingual counselors, the counselor supervisor plays a key role in the development of culturally efficacious bilingual counselors.
- Practice through case studies can facilitate self-efficacy and competency to develop culturally efficacious bilingual counselors.

References

Allport, G. W. (1982). *The nature of prejudice.* Addison-Wesley Publishing Company.

American Counseling Association. (2014). *2014 ACA code of ethics.* https://www.counseling.org/Resources/aca-code-of-ethics.pdf

Arredondo, P., Gallardo-Cooper, M., Delgado-Romero, E. A., & Zapata, A. L. (2014). *Culturally responsive counseling with Latinas/os.* American Counseling Association.

Arredondo, P., Toporek, R., Brown, S. P., Jones, J., Locke, D. C., Sanchez, J., & Stadler, H. (1996). Operationalization of the multicultural competencies. *Journal of Multicultural Counseling and Development, 24*(1), 42–78. https://doi.org/10.1002/j.2161-1912.1996.tb00288.x

Artiga, S., Young, K., Conrachione, E., & Garfield, R. (2015). The role of language in health care access and utilization for insured Hispanic adults. *Disparities Policy.* https://www.kff.org/report-section/the-role-of-language-in-health-care-access-and-utilization-for-insured-hispanic-adults-issue-brief/

Bandura, A. (1993). Perceived self-efficacy, cognitive development and functioning. *Educational Psychologist, 28*(2), 117–148. https://doi.org/10.1207/s15326985ep2802_3

Bell, L. A. (1997). Theoretical foundation for social justice education. In M. Adams, L. A. Bell & P. Griffin (Eds.), *Teaching for diversity and social justice: A sourcebook* (pp. 3–15). Routledge.

Biever, J. L., Gómez, J. P., González, C. G., & Patrizio, N. (2011). Psychological services to Spanish-speaking populations: A model curriculum for training competent professionals. *Training and Education in Professional Psychology, 5,* 81–87. https://doi.org/10.1037/a0023535

Bridges, A. J., Andrews, A. R., & Deen, T. L. (2012). Mental health needs and service utilization by Hispanic immigrants residing in mid-southern United States. *Journal of Transcultural Nursing, 23*(4), 359–368. https://doi.org/10.1177/1043659612451259.

Castaño, M. T., Biever, J. L., González, C. G., & Anderson, K. B. (2007). Challenges of providing mental health services in Spanish. *Professional Psychology: Research and Practice, 38*(6), 667–673. https://doi.org/10.1037/0735-7028.38.6.667

Council for Accreditation of Counseling and Related Educational Programs. (2016). *CACREP 2016 standards.* http://www.cacrep.org/wp-content/uploads/2017/08/2016-Standards-with-citations.pdf

Delgado-Romero, E. A., De Los Santos, J., Raman, V. S., Merrifield, J. N., Vazquez, M. S., Monroig, M. M., Bautista, E. C., & Durán, M. Y. (2018). Caught in the middle: Spanish-speaking bilingual mental health counselors as language brokers. *Journal of Mental Health Counseling, 40*(4), 341–352. https://doi.org/10.17744/mehc.40.4.06

Flores, B. B., Claeys, L. C., & Gist, C. (2018). *Culturally efficacious teacher preparation and pedagogies for social justice.* A Rowman Littlefield Subsidary.

Flores, B. B., Clark, E. R., Claeys, L., & Villarreal, A. (2007). Academy for teacher excellence: Recruiting, preparing, and retaining Latino teachers through learning communities. *Teacher Education Quarterly, 34*(4), 53–69. https://www.jstor.org/stable/23479111

Flores, Y. (2013). *Chicana and Chicano mental health: Alma, corazón y mente.* University of Arizona.

Fripp, J. A., & Carlson, R. G. (2017). Exploring the influence of attitude and stigma on participation of African American and Latino populations in mental health services. *Journal of Multicultural Counseling and Development, 45*(2), 80–94. https://doi.org/10.1002/jmcd.12066

Fuertes, J. N. (2004). Supervision in bilingual counseling: Service delivery, training, and research considerations. *Journal of Multicultural Counseling and Development, 32*(2), 84–94. https://doi.org/10.1002/j.2161-1912.2004.tb00363.x

Gist, C., Flores, B. B., & Claeys, L. (2015). A competing theory of change: Critical teacher development. In C. Sleeter, L. V. Neal, & K. Kumashiro (Eds.), *Diversifying the teacher workforce: Preparing and retaining highly effective teachers* (pp. 19–31). Routledge Publishers.

Gonzalez, L. M., Ivers, N. N., Noyola, M. C., Murillo-Herrera, A., & Davis, K. M. (2015). Supervision in Spanish: Reflections from supervisor-trainee dyads. *The Clinical Supervisor, 34*(2), 184–203. https://doi.org/10.1080/07325223.2015.1058208

Goodman, L. A., Liang, B., Helms, J. E., Latta, R. E., Sparks, E., & Weintraub, S. (2004). Training counseling psychologists as social justice agents: Feminist and multicultural perspectives. *Counseling Psychologist, 32*(6), 793–837. https://doi.org/10.1177/0011000004268802

Goodman, R. D., & Gorski, P. C. (Eds.). (2015). *Decolonizing "multicultural" counseling through social justice.* Springer-Verlag.

Guerra, N. S. (2016). *Addressing challenges Latinos/as encounter with the LIBRE Problem-Solving Model. Critical studies of Latinos/as in the Americas series.* Peter Lang Publishing.

Guilman, S. R. (2015). Beyond interpretation: The need for English-Spanish bilingual psychotherapists in counseling centers. *James Madison Undergraduate Research Journal, 2*(1), 26–30. http://commons.lib.jmu.edu/cgi/viewcontent.cgi?article=1010&context=jmurj

Hernandez-Wolfe, P. (2013). *A borderlands view on Latinos, Latin Americans, and decoloniza-tion: Rethinking mental health*. Jason Aronson.

Ibrahim, F. A., & Heuer, J. R. (2016). *Cultural and social justice counseling: Client-specific inter-ventions*. Springer International Publishing.

Javier, R. A. (2007). *The bilingual mind: Thinking, feeling, and speaking in two languages*. Springer.

Krogstad, J. M., & Lopez, M. H. (2017). *Use of Spanish declines among Latinos in major U.S. met-ros*. PEW Reports. http://www.pewresearch.org/fact-tank/2017/10/31/use-of-spanish-decli nes-among-latinos-in-major-u-s-metros/

Lewis, J. A., Arnold, M. S., House, R., & Toporek, R. L. (2002). *ACA advocacy competencies*. http://www.counseling.org/Publications/

McCaffrey, A., & Moody, S. J. (2015). Providing equitable services: Implementing bilingual counseling certification in counselor education programs. *VISTAS Online.* https://www. counseling.org/docs/default-source/vistas/article_33625c21f16116603abcacff0000bee5e7. pdf?sfvrsn=8

McIntosh, P. (1992). White and male privilege: A personal accounting of coming to see corre-spondences through work in women's studies. In M. L. Anderson & P. H. Collins (Eds.), *Race, class, and gender: An anthology* (pp. 70–81). Wadsworth.

Meyer, O. L., & Zane, N. (2013). The influence of race and ethnicity in clients' experiences of mental health treatment. *Journal of Community Psychology, 41*(7), 884–901. https://doi. org/10.1002/jcop.21580

Miranda, A. O., & Matheny, K. B. (2000). Socio-psychological predictors of acculturative stress among Latino adults. *Journal of Mental Health Counseling, 22*(4), 306–317. http://coshima. davidrjfikis.com/EPRS8550/articles/regression_baily.pdf

Nguyen, D., & Reardon, L. J. (2013). The role of race and English proficiency on the health of older immigrants. *Social Work in Health Care, 52*(6), 599–617. https://doi.org/10.1080/00981 389.2013.772554

Oliva, M. E. (2017). A healing journey of the bilingual self: In search of the language of the heart. *Journal of Ethnic & Cultural Diversity in Social Work.* https://doi.org/10.1080/15313 204.2017.1384946.

Paone, T. R., & Malott, K. M. (2008). Using interpreters in mental health counseling: A liter-ature review and recommendations. *Journal of Multicultural Counseling and Development, 36*(3), 130–142. https://doi.org/10.1002/j.2161-1912.2008.tb00077.x

Ratts, M. J., Singh, A. A., Nassar-McMillan, S., Butler, S. K., & McCullough, J. R. (2016). Multicultural and social justice counseling competencies: Guidelines for the counseling profession. *Journal of Multicultural Counseling and Development, 44*(1), 28–48. https://doi. org/10.1002/jmcd.12035

Rios-Ellis, B. (2005). *Critical disparities in Latino mental health: Transforming research into action*. National Council of La Raza.

Robinson, T. L. (1999). The intersections of dominant discourses across race, gender, and other identities. *Journal of Counseling and Development, 77*(1), 73–79. https://doi. org/10.1002/j.1556-6676.1999.tb02423.x

Robinson, T. L., & Howard Hamilton, M. F. (2000). *The convergence of race, ethnicity and gen-der: Multiple identities in counseling*. Merrill.

Schwartz, A., Rodríguez, M. M. D., Santiago-Rivera, A. L., Arredondo, P., & Field, L. D. (2010). Cultural and linguistic competence: Welcome challenges from successful diversification. *Professional Psychology: Research and Practice, 41*(3), 210–220. https://doi.org/10.1037/a0019447

Softas-Nall, L., Cardona, B., & Barritt. J. (2015). Challenges and diversity issues working with multilingual and bilingual couples and families: Implications for counseling. *The Family Journal, 23*(4), 13–17. https://doi.org/10.1177/1066480714548402

Sue, D. W., Arredondo, P., & McDavis, R. J. (1992) Multicultural competencies/ standards: A pressing need. *Journal of Counseling & Development, 70*(4), 477–486. https://doi.org/10.1002/j.1556-6676.1992.tb01642.x

Sue, D. W., Sue, D., Neville, H. A., & Smith, L. (2019). *Counseling the culturally diverse: Theory and practice* (8th ed.). Wiley.

Toporek, R. L., & Liu, W. M. (2001). Advocacy in counseling: Addressing race, class, and gender oppression. In D. B. Pope-Davis & H. L. K. Coleman (Eds.), *The intersection of race, class, and gender in multicultural counseling* (pp. 285–413). Sage.

Trepal, H., Ivers, N., & Lopez, A. (2014). Students' experiences with bilingual counselors. *The Journal of Counselor Preparation and Supervision, 6*(2). https://doi.org/10.7729/62.1096

Trepal, H., Tello, A., Haiyasoso, M., Castellon, N., Garcia, J., & Martinez-Smith, C. (2019). Supervision strategies used to support Spanish-speaking bilingual counselors. *Teaching and Supervision in Counseling, 1*(1), 19–31. https://doi.org/10.7290/tsc010103.

U.S. Census Bureau (n.d.). *Quickfacts.* https://www.census.gov/quickfacts/fact/table/US/RHI725219

U.S. Department of Health and Human Services, Health Resources and Services Administration, National Center for Health Workforce Analysis. (2017). *Sex, race, and ethnic diversity of U.S. health occupations (2011–2015).* https://bhw.hrsa.gov/sites/default/files/bhw/nchwa/diversityushealthoccupations.pdf

Valentine, S. E., Borba, C. P., Dixon, L., Vaewsorn, A. S., Guajardo, J. G., Resick, P. A., Wiltsey Stirman, S., & Marques, L. (2017). Cognitive processing therapy for Spanish-speaking Latinos: A formative study of a model-driven cultural adaptation of the manual to enhance implementation in a usual care setting. *Journal of Clinical Psychology, 73*(3), 239–256. https://doi.org/10.1002/jclp.22337.

Verdinelli, S., & Biever, J. L. (2009). Experiences of Spanish/English bilingual supervisees. *Psychotherapy: Theory, Research, Practice, Training, 46*, 158–170. https://doi.org/10.37/a0016024

Vodde, R. (2001). De-centering privilege in social work education: Whose job is it anyway? *Race, Gender, & Class, 7*(4), 139–160. https://www.jstor.org/stable/41955731

· 2 ·

DEVELOPING LINGUISTIC-COMMUNICATIVE COMPETENCE IN BILINGUAL COUNSELING SETTINGS

In Chapter 1, we briefly discussed the importance of bilingual counselors' capacity to adapt to the clients' language modality and preferences. In this chapter, we discuss language considerations when working with the Latine community and provide resources, activities, and a case study to develop linguistic-communicative competence in bilingual counseling settings. Linguistic-communicative competence moves beyond only acquiring linguistic competence—the ability to use grammar, syntax, and vocabulary of the language (Chomsky, 1965). Linguistic-communicative competence includes (a) linguistic competence, (b) sociolinguistic competence (c) discourse competence, and (d) strategic competence (Canale & Swain, 1980). Sociolinguistic competence refers to the ability to use and respond to language appropriately given the setting, topic, and relationships among the people communicating (Canale & Swain, 1980). It helps the speaker answer questions such as "What words or phrases fit this setting and this topic?" Discourse competence refers to the ability to interpret the larger context and construct longer stretches of language so that the parts make up a coherent whole (Canale & Swain, 1980). This allows speakers to connect words, phrases, and sentences in conversations. Strategic competence is knowing how to recognize and repair communication breakdowns, how to work around gaps in one's language, and how to learn more about using the language in specific contexts. This form of competence allows the speaker to recognize when they have misunderstood someone or someone has misunderstood them. Moreover, it allows them to repair miscommunication and express ideas correctly (Canale & Swain, 1980).

Developing linguistic-communicative competence is essential for bilingual counselors for a myriad of reasons. First, language is a counselor's main tool because both counselors and clients express beliefs, feelings, and thinking mostly by speaking. Within a counseling session, language is key in establishing rapport with clients and guiding clients in the resolution of their presenting issues (Artiga et al., 2015; Santiago-Rivera et al., 2009). Neglecting language competence may amplify any existing obstacles to access and quality of services.

Therefore, bilingual counselors must take additional steps to best use this tool. They must effectively translate counseling terms in Spanish, codeswitch between Spanish and English, and understand the intricate relationship between culture and language. In 2004, Fuertes noted that bilingual counseling must cover counseling standards (e.g., theory, case conceptualization, assessment, setting goals, treatment planning, and evaluation), while also addressing the role of language to the aforementioned standards. According to McCaffrey and Moody (2015), characteristics of linguistic competence for counselors include a demonstration of advanced language fluency and a skilled ability to conduct interviews.

Second, bilingual Latine are a heterogeneous group from diverse cultural and linguistic contexts. The latest U.S. Census (2019) showed that by 2018, over 40.5 million individuals over 5 years of age spoke Spanish at home, making it the second most spoken language in the United States. However, according to the PEW Research Center Report (2018), Latine ages 18–35 are 41% English dominant, 40% bilingual, and 19% Spanish dominant, while Latine ages 36 and over are 24% English dominant, 32% bilingual, and 44% Spanish dominant. This group also includes immigrants, refugees, and first, second, third, and beyond generations of Latine living in the United States. The Latine population originates from over 20 countries that make up Latin America and the Caribbean (PEW Research Center, 2019). Thus, even though the majority (62%) of Latine living in the United States are of Mexican descent (PEW Research Center, 2019), bilingual counselors must recognize each country's unique cultural/racial make-up, the client's immigration history to the United States, the client's life experience in the United States (González et al. 2015), and language nuances particular to different countries and regions

(Interiano-Shiverdecker et al., 2021). Counselors must acknowledge these within-group differences to maintain multicultural sensitivity and avoid engaging in hegemonic practices that lead to the eradication of cultural practices. Therefore, linguistic competence requires counselors to not only acquire the proper terminology in Spanish, articulate and interpret clients' thoughts and feelings, and translate/express general clinical terms in Spanish (Alvarado et al., 2019; Trepal et al., 2014), but to also consider language as a multicultural factor and understand language incongruences between Spanish-speaking groups.

Social Justice Theoretical Framework

If we consider language from a social justice framework, the role of the bilingual counselor is to provide opportunities and the vocabulary for bilingual clients to freely express their innermost feelings and thoughts. Within a social justice framework, bilingual counselors provide linguistic justice by making Spanish-speaking services not only desirable but available and achievable. However, we must not take a simplistic approach to conceptualizing linguistic justice within the counseling session. Dialect, upbringing, income, and access to education influence language development (Sonnenschein et al., 2017). These factors contribute to language competency, anxiety, clinical skill level, and code-switching practices. We must consider our clients' language preferences as well as our own language competence, language anxiety, and code-switching practices. In this chapter, we discuss how these concepts impact our work with Spanish-speaking clients and then provide resources that facilitate our ability to counsel efficiently in both languages.

Language Considerations in Bilingual Counseling Clinical Settings

Language as an Expression of Autonomy

Our sense of self, our identity, and our culture intimately tie to language. As such, it is an expression of our autonomy, o autonomía, as individuals. Santiago-Rivera and Altarriba (2002) considered language a transmitter of culture and traditional beliefs. U.S.-born Latine and those who have immigrated from different countries may prefer to speak their heritage or native language, and they may have strong ties to their culture of origin. From a social justice stance, we must provide our clients autonomy by honoring their language preferences for expressing themselves. As Brown (1994) surmised, "language is a part of a culture, and a culture is a part of a language; the two are intricately interwoven so that one cannot separate the two without losing the significance of either language or culture" (p. 165). While the United States does not have an official language, many consider speaking English as a positive social value. Individuals who speak other languages (e.g., Spanish) have at times received hostile and discriminatory responses (Borden, 2014). For example, many Spanish-speaking individuals report getting yelled at for speaking Spanish and receiving derogatory statements such as "Go back to your country". If a person feels forced to learn a new language, they may perceive it as a threat to their cultural origins and sense of self, thereby resulting in a cultural choque (see Chapter 3). At the same time, a person may choose to speak English to avoid discrimination and alienation. Language preference can be an indicator of a person's level of acculturation (Gallardo et al., 2014; see also Chapter 3). It is important to recognize that individuals may self-determine their degree of acculturation in terms of cultural, linguistic, and political views. Rafieyan and colleagues (2013) introduced the notion of acculturation attitudes to indicate the level of commitment a person must adopt to a new culture. Rafieyan et al.'s (2013) study demonstrated a positive correlation between acculturation attitudes and an individual's linguistic knowledge. The findings suggested that the higher the level of commitment to immersion into a new culture, the easier it is to learn a new language. However, we must also consider that despite individual commitment, hegemonic forces within society often circumvent these efforts. Individuals may feel marginalized; thereby as an act of linguistic resistance and to maintain their identity, they may refuse to acquire or speak the majority language (Norton, 2012). The next chapter will discuss this topic to a greater extent as well as the impact of generational status on the acculturation process and heritage language loss. Nevertheless, the bilingual counselor must understand that the client's use of their heritage language may be a form of resistance to avoid the issues discussed or a form of resistance to oppressive hegemonic discourses evident in society.

Intersectionality of Culture, Language, and Identity

Mary Eaton (1994) defined the concept of intersectionality, as "oppression [that] arises out of the combination of various oppressions which, together, produce something unique and distinct from any one form of discrimination standing alone" (p. 229). Scholars caution against the use of intersectionality in research as merely a watered-down and simplistic "multiple identities" notion that tends to ignore the systems of power, inequity, and oppression which create and perpetuate these identities in the first place (Moradi & Grzanka, 2017). An intersectional approach considers the historical, social, and political context and recognizes the unique experience of the individual based on the intersection of all relevant grounds (Freedman, 2018). As such, analyses that focus on gender, race, or language independently are insufficient because these social positions exist simultaneously. According to Flores and Clark (2017), an individual's heritage or native language connects not only to their cultural practices but also to the individual's ethnic/bicultural identity.

Anzaldúa's (1987, 2002) conceptual lens of "borderland spaces" contributes greatly to understanding the intersectionality of culture, language, and identity, in which Latine continually encounter, wrestle with, and cross borders of "language," "culture," and "identity." Borderlands present blurry overlapping areas of "shared influence" between "regions" lacking "clear edges" (Clandinin & Rosiek, 2007, p. 38), and encompass ambiguity, duality, and intersectionality. Learning a new language involves experiencing such borderland spaces in which language learners "juggle" languages and cultures (Anzaldúa, 1987, p. 101). Through this "juggling" in cultural and linguistic practices, they experience "border-crossings," "in-betweenness" (Ramos & Sayer, 2017; Rudolph, 2016), and a struggle of borders both internally and externally (Anzaldúa, 1987). These borderland experiences include negotiating and reimagining borders and play a significant role in how language learners construct identities. Hence, it is impossible to separate language from culture. As Anzaldúa (1987) pronounces, "Ethnic identity is twin skin to linguistic identity—I am my language" (p. 81).

Although bilingual Latine engage in two distinct linguistic and cultural groups as well as hybrid communities, many experience difficulties navigating their borderland experiences of culture, language, and identity. For many, language is an expression of their cultural ways of being, a reflection of their identity, and a window into their essence. For example, some clients may prefer to use their heritage language for emotional expression or when processing traumatic events (Santiago-Rivera et al., 2009). Others may communicate using dichos laden with cultural meanings (Castaño et al., 2007) that perfectly express their experience. Yet, most dichos lose their essence when translated into English. Therefore, the inability to understand the client's borderland experience and its connection to language, culture, and identity expression can significantly decrease utilization and quality of services and disrupt rapport building between client and counselor.

Code-Switching Practices

In addition to having the competency to engage in either language, the bilingual counselor should also be able to code-switch during the counseling session. Code-switching, o alternancia de código, is alternating between two languages or linguistics in a verbal or written text (Bialystok et al., 2009). For the Latine community, this is commonly known as speaking Spanglish, and it is a naturally occurring phenomenon. Many may reject the notion of code-switching, feeling that it waters down each language. However, scholars agree that code-switching can not only serve as a coping mechanism to navigate languages, but as a strength of bilingual speakers (Reyes, 2004; Tigert et al., 2019). Young children raised bilingually demonstrate this metalinguistic capacity to code-switch when speaking to their bilingual peers and other adults. They also recognize the need to code-switch when speaking to another individual without the same proficiency (Reyes, 2004). Bilingual children use code-switching to explain a task, build rapport, express their emotions, and perform affective check-ins with peers (Reyes, 2004; Tigert et al., 2019). As adults, bilinguals continue to have this metalinguistic capacity and code-switch as needed with other bilinguals (Adelsope et al., 2010).

As a bilingual counselor, the capacity to code-switch and demonstrate metalinguistic awareness is key in establishing rapport and trust with the client. Within the counseling session, code-switching often occurs when emotions are high (Santiago-Rivera et al., 2009; Trepal et al., 2019). The intersectionality of emotion and memory may result in clients expressing these in their native/heritage language or second language (Altarriba, 2014). Frequently, the expression of these emotions is linked to when a specific event occurred. Such life events and accompanying emotions are "encoded in memory in the language in which the experience occurred" (Santiago-Rivera et al., 2009, p. 437). If a traumatic event occurred in childhood, then clients might discuss the event in their heritage or native language. Bilingual counselors must pay attention to how clients code-switch and assess whether clients do so to express emotion strongly or to avoid emotion. Both counselors and clients should freely code-switch because not all emotion words are translatable (Altariba, 2014). As bilingual counselors, it is important to create a safe space that allows clients to freely choose their language modality to best convey their thoughts and emotions.

Code-switching also serves to validate the bilingual client's experience. The use of both Spanish and English centers around the realities of language and life for bilingual Latine living in the United States who have felt marginalized. This fact is especially true because the conversation around language in the United States is often heavily politicized, and anti-immigration and racist sentiments support the idea that only English should be spoken in the United States. Thus, by weaving both Spanish and English into the counseling session, when clients prefer to do so, bilingual counselors are directly rejecting this idea and asserting the legitimacy of code-switching, a practice in which many bilingual individuals engage in within their day-to-day lives. By code-switching or using the native language, the bilingual counselor signifies to the client, "I hear you; I am listening. Here, you do not need to choose." You may have noticed by now the use of code-switching in this book by presenting terms in both languages. We also intentionally did not italicize words in Spanish. We want to present both languages as equal. Our use of code-switching does not intend to alienate a monolingual, English-speaking reader, but rather to encourage all counselors to think differently about language.

Bilingual Counselors' Experiences with Linguistic-Communicative Competence

Given the language preference modality of bilingual clients, bilingual counselors must possess a full repertoire in both languages to engage professionally. The American Counseling Association's (ACA, 2014) *Code of Ethics* clearly states that counselors should accommodate clients' language preferences to maintain cultural sensitivity, ensure comprehension, and account for client diversity in areas such as assessment and informed consent. While the ACA's *Code of Ethics* encourages attending to clients' preferred language, bilingual counselors, regardless of Spanish fluency, receive their clinical training and supervision in English. Implicit yet faulty assumptions exist that students with conversational proficiency in Spanish can easily translate professional concepts obtained in English. This assumption ignores cultural differences among Latine populations. As we have previously discussed, Latine vary regarding their bilingual proficiency and their relationship to each language. Within the United States, bilingual individuals represent a wide spectrum from individuals raised in a bilingual home, speaking their heritage language to others educated in a bilingual/dual language setting, educated in a foreign country, to individuals who recently immigrated to the United States (PEW Research Center, 2019). Therefore, bilingual clients and counselors may demonstrate a different range of proficiency across language domains (reading, writing, speaking, and listening) in both English and Spanish. We found these differences even among the authors of this book. Some of us born in the United States had only spoken Spanish at home, while others born in Spanish-speaking countries had received formal training in Spanish, even to the graduate level. Yet we all found that providing services in Spanish differed from providing services in English. At times, it felt harder, challenging our sense of self-competence.

Thus, bilingual counselors must be provided with opportunities to develop their bilingual competency through coursework and practice in Spanish. Kissil et al. (2013) observed that counselors' language fluency is positively correlated with their perceptions of self-efficacy and cultural competency. In other words, increasing the levels of counselors' language proficiency augmented their self-efficacy and belief in their clinical skills. The bilingual competency that some US-born Latine possess is due to efforts within the home and not those of the school (Suarez, 2002). If bilingual counselors have participated in bilingual education, the focus may have been the acquisition of English and not necessarily maintenance of the native language. While dual language programs are increasing across the country, many of these programs do not go beyond the elementary level (Center for Applied Linguistics, 2017; Palmer et al., 2015). Hence, these rich linguistic experiences may not allow bilingual counselors to develop their full repertoire of bilingual competency. Moreover, linguistic hegemonic forces such as English-only preference within the United States do not support a bilingual society, and thus many bilingual counselors may experience language loss (Borden, 2014), which can result in feelings of alienation or marginalization.

Many bilingual counselors have expressed feeling unprepared, anxious, incompetent, and insecure when counseling in Spanish (Alvarado et al., 2019; Trepal et al., 2014, 2019). Some bilingual counselors may even experience *language shock*, (Miranda & Umhoefer, 1998) defined as the inability to communicate in a second language when the individual struggles to find the proper words to express their emotions or thoughts. For example, Haley and colleagues (2015) conducted a study with master's-level counseling students in an English-speaking program serving a sizable Hispanic population near the Mexican border. Specifically, they explored whether non-native

English-speaking counseling students experienced language anxiety, and if anxiety affected their perceptions of their counseling self-efficacy compared to their native English-speaking counterparts. Haley et al. (2015) evaluated the counseling students' perceptions in the following three areas: (a) counseling process; (b) cultural competence; and (c) awareness of value. Haley et al. (2015) found that bilingual counselors-in-training (CITs) language anxiety increased their stress level, which affected their cognitive processes as well as their ability to focus, make decisions, and solve problems. It also impacted their willingness to perform. Moreover, stress is a significant factor that negatively impacts how bilingual CITs perceive their self-efficacy and their overall clinical performance. On the other hand, more clinical preparation led bilingual CITs to report less language anxiety. Thus, bilingual CITs' positive self-efficacy correlated with a sense of success, capacity to work with clients, and, consequently, future professional decision-making (Haley et al., 2015).

Developing Bilingual Counselors' Linguistic-Communicative Competence

Following recommendations from the ACA (2014) *Code of Ethics* and scholars' consensus on evaluating counselors' Spanish language proficiency (Delgado-Romero et al., 2018; Interiano-Shiverdecker et al., 2021; McCaffrey & Moody, 2015), linguistic-communicative competence is a necessary component for bilingual counselors. We conceptualize linguistic-communicative competence for bilingual counselors in five areas: (a) overall language proficiency, (b) bilingual proficiency in clinical terminology, (c) bilingual proficiency in therapeutic concepts and interventions, (d) bilingual diagnostic proficiency, and (e) bilingual proficiency in emotional vocabulary. We provide examples of these aspects in Table 2.1

Spanish language proficiency provides students with communication skills to connect with all Latine clients, thus increasing access to mental health services and reducing the need for interpreters in counseling. It is for this reason that we review several components of the counseling process and provide accurate translations and considerations when working with Spanish-speaking Latine.

Table 2.1: *Aspects of Linguistic-Communicative Competence*

Aspectos de la Competencia Lingüística	Ejemplo
Dominio del idioma español para llevar a cabo conversaciones (es decir, estructura de oraciones, conjugaciones)	This is a red car – Este es un carro rojo
Terminología clínica en español	Informed consent – Consentimiento informado
Terminología de conceptos e intervenciones terapéuticas en español	Cognitive behavioral therapy – Terapia cognitiva conductual
Terminología de diagnósticos y criterios en español	Post Traumatic Stress Disorder – Trastorno de estrés postraumático
	Hyperarousal – Hiperactivación
Vocabulario Emocional	Frustrated-Angry – Frustrado, Enojado

Greetings

The counseling process begins when the client and counselor meet. We wanted to offer a comprehensive guide and therefore provide suggestions and considerations when meeting a client for the first time in Figure 2.2.

Considerations: It is important to know that greetings in Latine cultures may differ both in language and in behavior. Both you and your client may choose different words than the ones presented in the template based on regional preferences and the relationship towards the person you are greeting. In formal settings, you may refer to someone using their professional or personal titles. For example, you may prefer to use "Señor" (Mr.) for men and "Señora" (Mrs.) for women followed by their surname. Although counselors might use formal greetings at the beginning of a relationship and may quickly move onto a first-name basis even in professional settings, you or your client(s) may choose to continue using formal greetings as a sign of respect. Also, it is important that the client feels comfortable using first names and that you follow your client's preferences. For example, other forms of saying hello are illustrated in Figure 2.3.

Attending to clients' preferences ensures communication and reduces misunderstandings. In respecting an individual's identity, it is also important to consider how counselors and clients refer to themselves in terms of how we address them (formal vs. informal), pronunciation (Spanish vs. English), and written preference for correspondence or records. For example, is there a preference for first or last name? Is there a preference for the written name to use a

Figure 2.2: Un Cordial Saludo

Counselor: ¡Hola! Mi nombre es _____.
Client: Mucho gusto. Mi nombre es _____.
Counselor: ¡Mucho gusto! Por favor pase por acá y tome asiento.

Figure 2.3: Otros Saludos Formales e Informales

Buenas
Buenos días/ Buenas tardes/Buenas noches
¿Come te va? (informal) ¿Cómo le va? (formal) ¿cómo les va? (plural)
¿Cómo estás? (informal) ¿Cómo está? (formal) ¿cómo están? (plural)

required accent (e.g., López, González)? Depending on a client's identity, ethnic pride, affinity, and acculturation status (See Chapter 3), preference will vary.

We provide the following considerations for nonverbal communication and greetings:

- **Saludos Cordiales y Contacto visual.** Appropriate greetings in professional contexts include a firm handshake with eye contact and a smile. While handshakes and eye contact are advisable, do not be offended or surprised if handshakes are brief or clients do not reciprocate eye contact. Comfort with eye contact is regional and in some Latine groups, it is disrespectful to hold someone's gaze. Working with someone who is of the opposite gender or different in age—whether younger or older—may impact overall greeting behavior. Clients may prefer vastly different greetings for other reasons as well such as age, gender, and neurodiversity.
- **Saludos informales y culturales.** Once people become acquainted, greetings become friendlier and more informal. Clients may state "¿Qué onda?", "¿Qué tal?", "¿Qué hay?" or "¿Qué hubo?" rather than "Hola". Nonverbal greetings may also change and involve a hug accompanied by a kiss on the cheek (between men and women/women and women) or a pat on the shoulder, forearm, or elbow (between men) to indicate warmth.
- **Discusión del Estado Emocional.** It is also important to note that although "¿Cómo le va?" or "¿Cómo esta?" are common greeting phrases,

in Euro-American culture this greeting will be followed by a short state-
ment such as "Estoy bien," regardless of the emotional state in which
they are in. Latine clients may provide more honest and descriptive
answers. This is something to consider when receiving clients in open
areas such as waiting rooms or halls.

Información Personal o Encuesta Psicosocial

The intake or biopsychosocial interview occurs when clients first arrive at
the counseling session. Clients can complete this document before their first
session or during their first minutes of arrival. Clients can also complete the
forms electronically or as a hard copy. They obtain demographic information,
medical and social history, and current symptomatology. Figure 2.4 provides
an example of an intake/biopsychosocial form in Spanish. Important considerations for these forms include the following:

- Not all clients are technologically savvy, and some may struggle to complete online electronic forms.
- Clients may prefer to complete the intake form on their own or with
the counselor to ask additional questions. It is also helpful to use open-
ended questions rather than closed-ended questions to obtain information during this process. These suggestions may help build rapport and
attend to values of personalismo with Latine clients.
- Be aware that illiteracy may impede a client's ability to complete the
form. Many clients may hesitate to share this information, leading to
no-shows or early termination. You may want to consider filling out the
intake form with clients during your first session.
- Lack of access to and knowledge of mental health care in other countries may restrict clients from knowing or understanding medical and
mental health family history. You may want to consider asking, "¿Ha
habido alguien en su familia que ha presentado síntomas similares a los
suyos?" instead of asking "¿Ha habido alguien en su familia que ha presentado síntomas de depresión?"
- Lastly, while the use of Latine may be common among academic circles,
not all your clients may identify themselves in this manner; thus, your
client needs to self-identify and use their preferred cultural/ethnic/racial
labels as well as gender labels.

Figure 2.4: Información Personal o Encuesta Psicosocial

Información de Cliente		
Nombre de Cliente:		
Fecha de Nacimiento:		
¿Cómo se enteró de nosotros?		
Información de Contacto		
Dirección:		
Ciudad:	Estado:	Código Postal:
Teléfono de Domicilio:	Teléfono Celular:	Correo Electrónico:
¿Podemos dejar un mensaje en el número de contacto anteriormente anotado? ☐ Sí ☐ No		
¿Cómo le gustaría ser contactado/a para recordarle de su cita? ___ Correo Electrónico ___ ___Texto a número: _____ ___Llamada a número: _____		
Contacto de Emergencia:		Teléfono:
Relación al cliente:		¿Accede a que contactemos a esta persona en caso de emergencia? ☐ Sí ☐ Noz
Edad / Raza / Etnicidad		
Edad:	Sexo:	
Raza/Etnicidad:		
Lenguaje de Preferencia: ☐ Inglés ☐ Español ☐ Ambos ☐ Otro:		
Hogar/Empleo (PARA ADULTOS)		
Estado Civil: ☐ Casado/a ☐ Soltero (Nunca Casado) ☐ Separado/Divorciado ☐ Vive con pareja ☐ Viudo/a ☐ Otro		
Ocupación:		
Estado Laboral: ☐ Empleado ☐ Desempleado ☐ Estudiante ☐ Estudiante y Empleado ☐ Jubilado		
Status Militar: ☐ No Servicio Militar ☐ Servicio Activo ☐ Jubilado ☐ Guardia Nacional ☐ Reserva ☐ Otro		

(Continued)

Figure 2.4: (*Continued*)

Nivel Educativo completado:			
Aproximado Ingreso Anual Familiar:	☐ Menos de $12,000 ☐ $25,000–$49,999 ☐ $50,000–$100,000	☐ $12,001–$24,999 ☐ Mas de $100,000	
Información Médica			
Diagnósticos o preocupaciones médicas:			
Nombre de Doctor:		Fecha de última visita:	
Nombre de Seguro Médico:			
Consejería			
¿El cliente ha recibido anteriormente servicios de consejería? ☐ Sí ☐ No			
Anteriormente servicios de consejería en este centro ☐ Este centro: Cuándo/Quién			
Anteriormente servicios de consejería en otro centro ☐ Otro: Cuándo/Quién/Dónde			
Información adicional que le gustaría ofrecer en este momento:			

Consentimiento Informado

A key part of the therapeutic process for clinical mental health counselors is ensuring the informed consent of their clients. Throughout the process of informed consent, the counselor is responsible for clearly explaining to the client the limits of confidentiality throughout the treatment process. During this process, the counselor also explains the risks and benefits of treatment, payment policies, and client rights and responsibilities. The ACA *Code of Ethics* (2014) clearly states that the informed consent form should be explained to the client in a language they can fully understand (A.2.c.). Bilingual counselors must first assess the client's preferred language to carry out the informed consent. Although many Latine speak Spanish and may prefer to speak Spanish during the counseling process, it is best to not assume that they prefer or will understand informed consent if provided in Spanish. The same applies to Latine clients that can speak English.

Providing the client with a hard copy of the informed consent in the preferred language can also facilitate the client's overall understanding. For bilingual clients, counselors may provide copies in both English and Spanish. Code-switching, as previously discussed in this chapter, can also occur during

Figure 2.5: Consentimiento Informado para Consejería

Consentimiento Informado para Consejería

Introducción—Por favor tome tiempo para leer y entender este formulario. Este documento es para proporcionarle información general acerca de mis servicios de consejería. En caso de tener alguna pregunta sobre firmar este documento o si desea una copia del mismo, por favor solicítela y se la proporcionaremos. Este documento representa el consentimiento informado y un acuerdo entre nosotros. Al firmarlo, usted reconoce que ha recibido la información necesaria para tomar una decisión informada y voluntaria de participar en el proceso de consejería. Por favor tenga en mente que usted puede terminar este acuerdo en cualquier momento.

- Las sesiones son de 50–55 minutos de duración programada a menos que otro sea indicado.
- Precio total por sesión es de $ _____
- El pago se realizará en el momento que el servicio es prestado en forma de dinero en efectivo, cheque personal o tarjeta de crédito.

Cancelaciones – Una vez que se programa una cita, se requieren 24 horas de previo aviso para la cancelación de una cita. Para que podamos mantener las tarifas razonables y aceptar determinados seguros, usted tiene que pagar por las sesiones perdidas. Las compañías de seguros no pagan por las sesiones perdidas.

Naturaleza de la Consejería – La consejería puede tener riesgos y beneficios. Algunas veces la consejería incluye el hablar sobre aspectos desagradables de su vida. Como consecuencia, usted puede sentirse incómodo. Por otra parte, la consejería puede ayudar con sus relaciones con otros y proporcionar un mejor entendimiento de usted mismo, sus valores y sus metas. Por favor entienda que no hay forma de garantizar lo que usted va a sentir durante la consejería. En su primera sesión hablaremos sobre la consejería y la forma en que trabajaremos juntos para lidiar con sus preocupaciones. Por favor hágame saber si tiene alguna pregunta. Usted tiene derecho a preguntar o rehusarse a cualquier parte de su consejería. También tiene derecho a solicitar un nuevo consejero. Tiene derecho a recibir una explicación sobre cualquier papelería que usted llene.

Emergencia – En algunas ocasiones, usted puede necesitar asistencia inmediata cuando yo no esté disponible o no pueda regresar su llamada. Estas emergencias pueden ser pensamientos de lastimarse a usted mismo o a otros, o pensamientos en hacer actos peligrosos. Si usted se encuentra en cualquier situación de emergencia, por favor de contactar al 911 o vaya a la sala de emergencias más cercana.

Confidencialidad – La ley protege su privacidad entre cliente y consejero. La única forma en que yo puedo liberar su información es si usted firma una autorización por escrito.

Límites de Confidencialidad – Existen algunas situaciones en las cuales yo tenga que tomar acción para protegerlo a usted u otros de daños. Es mi obligación por ley divulgar información a las instituciones competentes en las siguientes situaciones específicas:

(Continued)

Figure 2.5: *(Continued)*

- En caso de que yo tenga alguna razón para creer que un menor o un adulto vulnerable no está siendo cuidado o es abusado, la ley exige que la situación se reporte a la agencia estatal correspondiente.
- Si yo creo que usted está en peligro de lastimarse a usted mismo u otros, éticamente se me requiere que tome acción de protección. Estas acciones pueden incluir el contactar a familiares, buscar hospitalización para usted, notificar a cualquier víctima(s) potencial(es) y notificar a la policía.
- Una orden de la corte requiere la liberación de comunicación privilegiada.

Este es un resumen de confidencialidad y sus límites, por favor hágame saber si tiene alguna pregunta o duda.

Política de Redes Sociales: Su consejero/a no puede conectarse con usted en las redes sociales. Esta política está en vigor para proteger su confidencialidad y la relación profesional entre el cliente y el consejero/a.

Autorización para la Comunicación Electrónica

Autorización para la Comunicación Electrónica: El correo electrónico, el texto y otras formas de mensajería electrónica son métodos de comunicación convenientes. Aunque su consejero hará esfuerzos para proteger y mantener la privacidad, la mensajería electrónica no es un medio de comunicación confidencial. Por lo tanto, su consejero utilizará la comunicación electrónica solo con su permiso y sólo para fines administrativos. Si autoriza estos métodos a comunicarse con su consejero, no podemos garantizar una comunicación segura o sin errores. Puede revocar su autorización por escrito en cualquier momento.

_____ (Inicial) Autorizo a mi consejero a comunicarse conmigo por correo electrónico con fines administrativos.

_____ (Inicial) Autorizo a mi consejero a comunicarse conmigo a través de un mensaje de texto para fines administrativos.

Declaración de Reconocimiento – Yo he leído y entendido esta información y he tenido la oportunidad de aclarar cualquier duda sobre esta forma antes de revelar información acerca de mí persona.

Firmas		
Firma del Cliente	Nombre Impreso	Fecha
Firma del Representante Legalmente Autorizado (si el cliente es menor de 18 años)	Nombre Impreso	Fecha
Firma del Consejero	Nombre Impreso	Fecha

informed consent. We encourage bilingual counselors to code-switch as the client does. At times, clients might prefer the counselor to explain concepts of the informed consent form in both English and Spanish to increase their understanding or ask questions. We present a template for informed consent in Spanish in Figure. 2.5.

Please take the following considerations with the following sections of the informed consent:

- **Naturaleza de la Consejería.** As part of the informed consent, it is important to discuss what to expect from counseling and yourself, as the counselor. Latine clients may be unfamiliar with counseling services provided in the United States for several reasons. First, psychiatry and psychology are much more popular in Latin America than counseling, focusing primarily on assessment and medication. Mental health work has taken place primarily in psychiatry hospitals or community-based operations, including schools, religious organizations, and government programs. Second, there is no easy translation. Clients might not understand the direct translation, consejería and consejera(o). It tends to be correlated with consejo (advice) leading clients to believe that counselors act as advisors. As the counselor, you may also prefer a non-binary term and consejero/a struggles to attend to that need. Your clients may refer to you as doctora(a) (doctor), licenciada(o) (licensed professional), or psicóloga(o) (psychologist) as they may be more familiar with these terms. The authors' decision to use the term consejería de salud mental and consejero(a) de salud mental, despite its linguistic and cultural considerations, was twofold: (a) support the internationalization of the counseling profession and (b) help address cultural misunderstandings of the counseling profession that impact the access of mental health services to the Latine community.
- **Números de Emergencia.** Counselors should be aware that undocumented clients may hesitate to call 911 or seek emergency care due to fear of deportation. Invite the client to share any concerns about seeking emergency services and discuss safe and responsible alternatives.
- **Límites de Confidencialidad:** Clients may conceptualize harm to self or others, abuse, and neglect differently than the societal norms or expectations in the United States. This is mostly seen in corporal discipline in children or physical altercations between couples or family members. Certain aspects of discipline vary with cultural expectations of

children, beliefs about appropriate child behavior, and preferred methods of physical discipline. For example, Latine parents may discipline their children through spanking, face slaps, pinching on the arm, use of a belt or whip, or by making their children kneel with bare knees on uncooked rice (Fontes, 2002). Parents may also ask the oldest sibling(s) to take care of their younger sibling(s) during their absence, particularly when the parent(s) must work long hours to sustain the family. Counselors often feel puzzled about how to remain culturally sensitive while at the same time fulfilling their duty as mandated reporters. To begin, counselors need to understand contextual factors that may promote these behaviors. Multiple stressors of immigration including loss, dislocation, and cultural clashes make some caretakers punish their children harshly to regain control or to teach children to behave so they do not get into trouble (Johnsdotter, 2015). Parents might inflict harsh punishments with love and to keep children safe in a dangerous world, but they nevertheless exert harm and put children at risk for abuse. Moreover, exposure to individual and shared forms of trauma may lead to a higher prevalence of violence, shape experiences of safety and danger, and impact feelings about receiving "help" in affected communities (Na et al., 2016). Counselors should then inform clients about how abuse and neglect are conceptualized in the United States and that any deviation could attract unwelcome attention from authorities. Psychoeducation about the potential harms (or side effects) of these behaviors as well as suggestive alternatives can provide resources for clients.

• **Preguntas sobre Límites de Confidencialidad:** It is important to understand that some clients may not feel comfortable asking questions. The cultural value of respeto (González-Ramos et al., 1998) emphasizes obedience and dictates that children should be highly considerate of adults and should not interrupt or argue. More generally, respeto relates to "knowing the level of courtesy and decorum required in a given situation in relation to other people of a particular age, sex, and social status" (Harwood et al., 1997, p. 98). Latine children may therefore find it disrespectful to question an adult. Adult clients, particularly women, may also hesitate to question someone in authority regardless of the counselor's age. All doctors have historically held a respectful authority figure in Latine societies and countries (Dixon et al., 2008). Although counselors may not hold a doctoral degree, clients might perceive them

Figure 2.6: Requisitos de Supervisión

> **Supervisión-** Usted tiene derecho a saber el nombre de mi supervisor(es) y cómo contactar a él o ella. Posiblemente, por parte de mi entrenamiento, mi supervisor le pregunte sobre nuestras sesiones de consejería. Yo hablaré regularmente con mi supervisor y él/ella me ayudará con su cuidado. Si no se opone, yo no voy a discutir estas consultas con usted, a menos que sienta que es importante para nuestro trabajo. Tomaré nota de estas consultas como parte de mis notas clínicas.

as authority figures in mental health. Counselors should encourage questions several times while explaining informed consent.

- **Límites de Confidencialidad con Familiares:** Family boundaries with confidential information may look different in Latine families. It is not unusual that a parent may ask one of their older children or a family member to be present in the session. As such, language brokering is a common socio-cultural and linguistic practice among bilingual populations (Anguiano, 2018; Orellana, 2009). It is important to discuss with the client that this may result in the stifling of conversations about intimate issues and potentially impact the child when intimate conversations occur. Further, this may shape clients' understanding of confidentiality and parents' involvement with children in the session. If a child is present as the language broker, this may result in a transference of roles, with the child assuming the role and responsibilities of the parent. According to Orellana (2009), while there are many cognitive and affective benefits of language brokering, practices in which role reversal occurs may result in others perceiving the family as dysfunctional. Thus, the counselor needs to discuss this role reversal with the client and their families.

- **Consejero Estudiantil o en Entrenamiento:** Counselors-in-training must change, "Firma del Consejero" to "Firma del Consejero Estudiantil" or "Firma del Consejero en Entrenamiento." It is also necessary to add a separate section to explain the requirements of supervision. We provide a template in Figure 2.6.

- **Consejería a Distancia.** With any form of distance counseling, the informed consent process becomes even more paramount because clients must understand both the parameters of counseling and the further dimensions that technology adds. Bilingual counselors engaging in any form of distance counseling should add the following section illustrated in Figure 2.7 to their informed consent.

Figure 2.7: Enmienda de Consejería a Distancia

Introducción: La consejería a distancia se refiere a la prestación de servicios de consejería utilizando tecnología como audio, video, teléfono u otras comunicaciones electrónicas. La consejería a distancia ocurre entre un consejero/a y un cliente que no están en la misma ubicación física. La consejería a distancia también puede denominarse teleterapia o telesalud mental.

Naturaleza de la Consejería a Distancia: Hay beneficios y riesgos para el uso de la tecnología en la consejería. Los beneficios pueden incluir flexibilidad de programación, facilidad de acceso y disminución de los costos de transportación. Sin embargo, la naturaleza de la consejería a distancia implica ciertos riesgos de privacidad y seguridad, que se detallan a continuación.

Confidencialidad: La información relativa a sus servicios de consejería a distancia permanecerá confidencial en la mayor medida posible. Su consejero/a se encargará y tendrá en cuenta para evitar la divulgación innecesaria. Las tecnologías utilizadas en la consejería a distancia incorporan protocolos de seguridad de redes y software para proteger la confidencialidad de la información del cliente. Los registros se mantendrán en un sistema de salud electrónico y seguro.

Además de los límites de confidencialidad descritos en el consentimiento informado para la consejería, los clientes que reciben consejería a distancia entienden las siguientes consideraciones de privacidad y seguridad:

- Aunque la tecnología proporciona la apariencia de anonimato y privacidad en la consejería, la privacidad es más una preocupación con los servicios de la consejería basados en tecnología que los servicios de consejería tradicionales.
- El cliente es responsable de comprender los riesgos potenciales de confidencialidad que se incumplen a través de correo electrónico no cifrado, falta de protección con contraseña o dejar información en un equipo de acceso público. Para garantizar mejor la privacidad, le recomendamos que utilice un espacio privado, utilice solo una red WiFi segura a través de una contraseña y evite la conexión WiFi pública.
- La grabación de la sesión sin el consentimiento tanto del cliente como del consejero/a está estrictamente prohibida.
- Para las sesiones telefónicas, no podemos garantizar la confidencialidad, ya que las líneas telefónicas podrían no estar seguras.
- Los riesgos de la consejería a distancia incluyen, pero no se limitan a, fallas tecnológicas inesperadas durante las sesiones, mayor carga sobre el cliente para asegurar que las sesiones sean privadas e ininterrumpidas, y la piratería de transmisiones o almacenamiento electrónico de la información de salud mental. Además, las comunicaciones no verbales limitadas que están disponibles para el consejero/a y el cliente en persona pueden afectar el progreso o limitar la eficacia del tratamiento.

Figure 2.7: *Continued*

Métodos: Utilizaremos [nombre de la plataforma electrónica] como una plataforma de consejería a distancia. Su consejero le proporcionará instrucciones sobre cómo usar esta plataforma antes de su sesión. Los clientes necesitarán acceso a una cámara web o smartphone durante las sesiones de vídeo. Las sesiones telefónicas pueden proporcionarse como alternativa en circunstancias atenuantes.

Referencia a los Servicios en Persona: Aunque la investigación muestra que la consejería a distancia es un medio eficaz para proporcionar servicios de salud mental, algunos clientes pueden ser más adecuados para la consejería en persona. Si es necesario, la decisión de referirse a consejería en persona u otros servicios se discutirá entre usted y su consejero.

Instrumentos de Evaluación o Asesoramiento

An intricate part of the counseling process requires an accurate assessment of the client's presenting issues. Benuto's (2013) *Guide to Psychological Assessment with Hispanics* provides a thorough review of both structured and unstructured assessments available in Spanish. As you review assessments to use with Spanish-speaking clients, it is important to note that the DSM-V-TR (APA, 2022) includes several culture-bound syndromes that are specific and/or relevant to Latine. Of these syndromes, only ataques de nervios has valid and reliable assessments. For example, Livanis and Tryon (2010) developed the 31-item Adolescent Nervios Scale while Guarnaccia et al. (1989) developed an ataque de nervios scale. Thus, we encourage you to consider measures relevant to the differential diagnoses to attain an accurate diagnosis. Alternatively, you may also wish to consider culture-bound syndromes when a diagnosis cannot be made based on presenting symptoms.

Suicide attempts and completed suicide are major problems among the Latine population. In 2015, suicide was the 11th leading cause of death among Hispanics in the United States and the 3rd leading cause of death among Hispanics aged 10–34 (Centers for Disease Control and Prevention, 2017). We translated several important warning signs during suicide risk assessment recommended by the American Counseling Association's (2011) guidelines for a suicide assessment in Figure 2.8.

Figure 2.8: Evaluación del Riesgo de Suicidio

Indicaciones verbales

- Directa: "Me voy a matar"
- Indirecta: "Se va a arrepentir cuando ya no esté", "No siento que vale la pena vivir", o "Mi vida no importa".

Indicaciones psicológicas:

- Depresión
- Sentirse indefenso/a o impotente
- Sentirse desesperanzado/a
- Sentirse abrumado/a
- Sentirse triste

Indicaciones Emocionales

- Preocupación con morirse o con la muerte
- Falta de apetito/comer en exceso
- Trastornos del sueño
- Falta de concentración
- Aislamiento
- Llorando frecuentemente

Indicaciones conductuales

- Autoestima baja
- Incapacidad para realizar las tareas diarias
- Intentos previos de suicidio
- Nota de suicidio
- Participar en conductas de riesgo o impulsivas
- Rendimiento deficiente y repentino en el área escolar o laboral
- Regalar cosas importantes
- Falta de interés en cosas que antes disfrutaba
- Abstinencia repentina de actividades con la familia y amigos
- Recuperación repentina e inexplicable de la depresión

Indicaciones de contexto

- Problemas laborales o académicos
- Pérdida de trabajo/carrera
- Fallecimiento de un ser querido o conocido
- Suicidio de un ser querido o conocido
- Ruptura de una relación/separación/divorcio
- Múltiples perdidas
- Enfermedad terminal

Figure 2.8: *Continued*

Preguntas para evaluar ideas de suicidio (suicide ideation), plan de suicidio (suicide plan) e intentos de suicidio (suicide intent)
• ¿Está(s) pensando en hacerse(te) daño/suicidarse(te)?
• ¿Cuánto tiempo ha(s) estado pensando en el suicidio (frecuencia, intensidad, duración)?
• ¿Tiene(s) un plan? ¿Cuál es el plan?
• ¿Tiene(s) los medios para llevar a cabo el plan (accesibilidad de un arma, pastillas, medicamentos, etc.)?
• ¿Ha(s) intentado suicidarse(te) en el pasado?
• ¿Alguien de su(tu) familia se ha suicidado?
• ¿Hay algo o alguien que lo/a(te) detenga (creencias religiosas, niños abandonados, mascotas, etc.)?

Note: In the (), we provide the language style for a more informal conversation.

Habilidades Atencionales Básicas

Basic Counseling skills, or habilidades atencionales básicas, are fundamental counseling skills or practiced techniques that help the counselor empathically listen, invite the client to express more in-depth, and build rapport (Young, 2017). Table 2.9 discusses basic counseling skills in Spanish. We recommend Zalaquett et al's (2008) *Las Habilidades Atencionales Básicas: Pilares Fundamentales de la Comunicación Efectiva* for a more in-depth discussion of the application and consideration of these skills in Spanish.

Reflexión de Emociones

Reflecting emotions is an essential skill for counselors because it helps us, and our clients, better understand the whole person. Emotions give us a window into motivation, current mental state, behaviors, and the client's view of the world (Young, 2017). Reflecting feelings requires two steps: identifying the client's feelings and putting the emotions into words (Young, 2017). To accomplish these steps, it is important to recognize that emotions have many shades and variations, like primary colors in the light spectrum. This is true when reflecting emotions in English and Spanish. For example, a person can be upset [molesto(a)], frustrated [frustrado(a)], angry [enojado(a)], or infuriated

Table 2.9: Habilidades Atencionales Básicas: Definición, Ejemplos y Función

Basic Counseling Skills	Habilidades Atencionales Básicas	Definición, Ejemplos, y Función
Non-Verbal Behavior	Comportamiento Atencional	o Este comportamiento es individualmente y culturalmente apropiado. o Incluye contacto visual, tono de voz, lenguaje corporal, y seguimiento verbal. Función: Mostrar interés al escuchar ya que motiva a tu cliente a hablar con mayor libertad. Usar un tono empático y genuino ya que tu cliente puede no recordar lo que dijiste, pero recuerda como la/lo/le hiciste sentir.
Minimal Encourager	Motivador mínimo	o Los motivadores son respuestas breves. o Pueden ser no verbales como mover el cuerpo hacia adelante demostrando interés, asentar/negar con la cabeza, o utilizar expresiones faciales. o Pueden también ser verbales como: ¿ah?, ¿Entonces?, ¿Y?, Umm-humm, y Ah-hah, Función: Motivar a tu cliente a explorar lo que está expresando con más profundidad y claridad.
Open Question	Pregunta Abierta	o Las preguntas abiertas usualmente comienzan con: "Cómo . . .?", "Que . . .?", "Podrías . . .?". o No se recomienda empezar una pregunta abierta con "porque" ya que obliga a que los clientes busquen cuales con las razones de sus comportamientos, pensamientos y emociones y pueden poner al cliente en una posición incómoda. Ejemplo: ¿Cómo te sientes hoy? Función: Las preguntas abiertas están diseñadas para obtener una respuesta extensa sin limitaciones impuestas por el consejero ya que ayudan al cliente a explorar asuntos personales.
Closed Question	Pregunta Cerrada	o Las preguntas cerradas usualmente comienzan o utilizan conjugaciones de los verbos haber, ser, o estar como: "Hay..?", "Es . . .?", "Son..?". Ejemplo: ¿Estás pensando en suicidarte? Función: Obtener una respuesta específica, limitada, o breve compuesta de una palabra o frase.

Table 2.9: *Continued*

Basic Counseling Skills	Habilidades Atencionales Básicas	Definición, Ejemplos, y Función
Paraphrase/ Reflection of Content	*Parafraseo / Reflexión de Contenido*	o Consiste en compartir con el cliente lo que lo/a/e escuchaste decir en una manera precisa y sin repetir exactamente lo que el cliente dijo. Ejemplo: Cliente: "Esta semana ha sido muy difícil en el trabajo y en casa. No puedo seguir el ritmo de todo lo que tengo que hacer en el trabajo y, como estoy tan cansado, mi trabajo está empezando a afectar la relación con mi pareja ". Consejero: "Esta semana le ha resultado difícil porque dos áreas importantes de su vida están siendo afectadas." Función: Retroalimentar al cliente ya que reflejas la esencia de lo que se ha dicho lo cual motiva al cliente a elaborar más profundamente sobre lo que se está hablando.
Reflection of Feelings	*Reflexión de Emociones*	o Consiste en comunicar la emoción asociada con lo que tu cliente te ha comunicado. o Es importante mantener los reflejos de sentimientos cortos. Ejemplo: "Te sientes triste" Función: Identificar la emoción ya que ayuda a la exploración emocional.
Reflection of Meaning	*Reflexión de Significado Emocional*	o Consiste en comunicar el significado emocional de la experiencia de tu cliente para entender los deseos e intenciones de tu cliente. Ejemplo: Cliente: "Esta semana ha sido muy difícil en el trabajo y en casa. No puedo seguir el ritmo de todo lo que tengo que hacer en el trabajo y, como estoy tan cansado, mi trabajo está empezando a afectar la relación con mi pareja ". Consejero: "Te sientes abrumado porque estas son dos áreas importantes de tu vida que están siendo afectadas." Función: Las reflexiones de significado emocional ayudan al consejero a reafirmar el impacto personal y la importancia del evento que el cliente está describiendo. Clarificar emociones y el impacto del evento permite que tu cliente tome mejores decisiones.

(*Continued*)

Table 2.9: *Continued*

Basic Counseling Skills	Habilidades Atencionales Básicas	Definición, Ejemplos, y Función
Summary	*Resumen*	o Consiste en comunicar la esencia de lo que tu cliente ha dicho durante una parte larga de la conversación.
		o Se utiliza periódicamente para verificar nuestras percepciones con el cliente.
		Ejemplo: "Esta semana ha sido muy difícil en el trabajo y en casa. Es difícil para ti manejar las expectativas del trabajo y estar presente en casa, lo cual ha conllevado a problemas en tu relación."
		Función: Reúne todo lo que un cliente ha dicho en una breve sinopsis de la sesión hasta ese momento. El resumen vincula algunos de los principales problemas que han surgido incluyendo el contenido de lo que se ha dicho, los pensamiento y emociones del cliente, significado del problema, y planes a futuro.

[furioso(a)]. Table 2.10 shows different emotions in Spanish and different variations based on level of intensity.

Please take the following considerations when reflecting emotions in Spanish:

o For children, consider visual images that represent basic emotions. Children may not have the emotional vocabulary to identify or express basic emotions. Bilingual children may code-switch when expressing emotions.

o To form sentences about feelings and emotions in Spanish, it is necessary to understand that these adjectives undergo some variations depending on the subject of the sentence. The form of the adjective must match the noun it describes. Since moods are temporary states, we generally use the verb "estar" together with adjectives for feelings and emotions to describe how we feel at any given moment. In instances where we are using more formal Spanish, the reflexión de emociones will be, "Se siente enojado", while a more informal reflexión de emociones will be "Te sientes enojado". Since Spanish also follows a masculine/feminine

Table 2.10: Diferentes Niveles de Reflexión de Emociones

	Nivel de Intensidad		
	Leve	Moderado	Fuerte
Enojo	Consternado	Disgustado	Indignado
	Irritado	Ofendido	Enfurecido
	Molesto	Enojado	Furioso
Tristeza	Desanimado	Melancólico	Deprimido
	Desalentado	Decaído	Vacío
	Apagado	Triste	Inconsolable
Felicidad	Satisfecho	Alegre	Emocionado
	Contento	Feliz	Exaltado
	A gusto	Animado	Entusiasmado
Miedo	Precavido	Desconfiado	Paranoico
	Cauteloso	Miedoso	Aterrorizado
	Aprensivo	Asustado	Temeroso
	Preocupado	Inseguro	Nervioso
Asco	Disgustado	Asqueado	Repugnado
Sorpresa	Confundido	Impresionado	Deslumbrado
	Alarmado	Dudoso	Asombrado
	Perplejo	Sorprendido	Boquiabierto
Culpa	Responsable	Culpable	Arrepentido
Vergüenza	Descuidado	Ignorado	Rechazado
	Apenado/Incomodo	Avergonzado	Humillado
Ansiedad	Incierto	Impaciente	Desesperado
	Preocupado/ Angustiado	Ansioso	Estresado
	Cansado	Fatigado	Exhausto
Aburrimiento	Inquieto	Aburrido	Desinteresado

(Continued)

Table 2.10: *Continued*

	Nivel de Intensidad		
	Leve	Moderado	Fuerte
Amar	Interesado	Querido	Amado
	Incluido	Apreciado	Valorado
Paz	Cómodo	Tranquilo	Sereno
	Relajado	Pacifico	En Paz
Esperanza	Inspirado	Optimista	Esperanzado/ Ilusionado
	Animado	Seguro	Confiado
Valor	Determinado	Valiente	Audaz
	Atrevido	Intrépido	Sin miedo
Odio	Odio	Ira	Aborrecido
Traición	Ofendido	Lastimado	Insultado
	Celoso/Inseguro	Rencoroso	Vengativo
	Estafado	Engañado	Traicionado
	Desilusionado	Decepcionado	Defraudado
Debilidad	Ignorado	Invisible	Insignificante
	Dependiente	Incompetente	Indefenso
	Débil	Impotente	Inservible
	Vencido	Arruinado	Derrotado
Fortaleza	Hábil	Capaz	Competente
	Resistente	Fuerte	Poderoso
	Positivo	Confiado	Seguro

pronoun it would be "enojada" to describe a female and "enojado" to describe a male. Clients who identify as non-binary may struggle with these adjectives and may have a preference which we advise you to follow.

o It is common for Latine to express feelings through dichos, or sayings (Castaño et al., 2007), as well as through physical ailments like headaches or stomach aches when feeling stressed (Benuto, 2017). Expressions such as, "me siento como un cero a la izquierda" may indicate feeling neglected or invisible. "Me cuesta dormir" o "He perdido el apetito" may be indications of anxiety.

Application to Practice: Case Study

As indicated in Chapter 1, this book seeks to help bilingual counselors apply concepts and knowledge needed to develop linguistic-communicative competence. Understanding the importance of in-vivo experiences and bilingual supervision to increase counselor competency, we present the following case presentation. This case study will provide practice in translating clinical terms/concepts and instances of code-switching. These exercises also invite conversations around the client-counselor-supervisor differences in language.

Couples Counseling: Elias y Sara

Elias is a 50-year-old man and Sara a 30-year-old woman. They came to couples counseling due to marriage problems. The couple's problem consists of differences in communication, lifestyle before marriage, acculturation, and age. Elias is from the United States and Sara is from Mexico. Elias has two daughters from a previous marriage. This is Sara's first marriage. The couple met in Mexico one year before getting married. Elias is fluent in both English and Spanish and Sara is fluent in Spanish. After getting married, Sara went to live with Elias in the United States. This transition has been difficult for Sara because she is living in a new country, does not speak English, and has not acculturated to the new culture. For the first session, the counselor intends to create rapport and establish the client's communication preferences. Since one partner only speaks Spanish and the other partner speaks both English and Spanish, it is important to establish the language that will be used in the counseling session.

Consejería de Pareja: Elías y Sara

Elías es un hombre de 50 años y Sara una mujer de 30 años. Acudieron a la consejería de pareja debido a problemas matrimoniales. El problema de la pareja consiste en la comunicación, el estilo de vida diferente antes del matrimonio, la aculturación y la diferencia de edad. Elías es de los Estados Unidos y Sara de México. Elías tiene dos hijas de un matrimonio anterior. Este es el primer matrimonio de Sara. La pareja se conoció en México un año antes de casarse. Elías habla inglés y español con fluidez y Sara habla español con fluidez. Después de casarse, Sara se fue a vivir con Elías a los Estados Unidos. Esta transición ha sido difícil para Sara porque vive en un nuevo país, no habla inglés y no se ha aculturado a la nueva cultura.

Primera Sesión

For this session, the counselor intends to create rapport, o una relación basada en entendimiento, and establish the client's communication preferences.

CONSEJERO (CO):	*Hola Sr. y Señora _____; soy __. ¿Durante nuestras sesiones, ¿cómo prefieren que los llame?*
CLIENTE SARA (CL-S):	*Me puede llamar Sara*
CLIENTE ELIAS (CL-E):	*You can call me, Elías*
CO:	*Muy bien Sara y Elías. Mucho gusto en conocerlos. ¿En cuál idioma prefieren las sesiones? So that I can assist you best, what language do you feel comfortable speaking in our sessions?*
CL-E:	*I am comfortable with either English or Spanish, but we can speak Spanish.*
CL-S:	*Yo prefiero español.*
CO:	*Ok, ya que los tres podemos hablar en español creo que es mejor que usemos ese idioma durante nuestras sesiones. Si en algún momento queremos decir algo en inglés también podemos hacer eso. Esto nos va a permitir tener un entendimiento mutuo y generar confianza. ¿Qué les parece?*
CL-E/CL-S:	*Está bien.*
CO:	*Ok, entonces platiquenme de su situación. ¿En que los puedo ayudar?*
CL-E:	*Las cosas con mi esposa no van bien y ella me dijo que quiere dejarme. Nunca fue así cuando iba a visitarla a México.*
CL-S:	*Mi esposo nunca me escucha y estoy cansado de eso. Desde que nos casamos y me mudé a los Estados Unidos siento que él es una persona diferente. Es como si ni siquiera lo conociera.*
CO:	*Parece que para los dos su relación en México era diferente a su relación aquí.*
CL-E:	*Yes, tiene razón.*
CO:	*¿Qué es lo que más ha cambiado en su relación?*
CL-E:	*Ahora mi esposa quiere controlar todo lo que hago y nunca quiere hacer las cosas sola. Yo tengo que trabajar y mis hijas de mi otro matrimonio también están aquí, así que las visité y no tienen una relación con mi esposa. My*

	daughters solo hablan inglés, por lo que les resulta difícil comunicarse con mi esposa. They just can't speak or understand Spanish, you know?
CL-S:	*Pues yo crecí en una casa donde apenas teníamos dinero y cuando te veo gastando tanto dinero quiero controlar nuestras finanzas. No conozco a nadie aquí en los Estados Unidos, pero tú ya tienes toda tu vida aquí hecha. Me siento fuera de lugar. Ni siquiera quería mudarme aquí, pero tuvimos que hacerlo para estar con tus hijas.*
CO:	*Entonces, antes de casarse, cada uno de ustedes tenía diferentes estilos de vida, vivían en diferentes países y hablaban diferentes idiomas. Y ahora que están casados les ha sido difícil debido a estas diferencias.*
CL-E:	*Así es.*
CO:	*¿Cuáles son algunas de las cosas que ambos comparten en común?*

Time to Reflect

- In this case, since the counselor is fluent in both languages, Spanish would be the common language amongst the three. However, the counselor needs to have this conversation with the couple and not assume their language preference.
- Since Elías speaks both English and Spanish, the counselor wants to provide him with the space to switch languages to better describe specific events.
- One of the couple's identified problems is communication issues, so the counselor needs to observe the communication style when the couple discusses the presenting problem and allow for space for them to code-switch when needed for clarification or amplification. The counselor can also restate what the couple is discussing, "so what I hear you saying is" to assist in the communication and to build trust for one another.

Reflective Questions:

1. Why is asking clients what they prefer to be called important?
2. Why is using the clients' language preference or modality important?
3. What are some other suggestions to address language preference in session?
4. How does Elías's code-switching affect how Sara feels?

Segunda Sesión:

For this session, the counselor intends to focus on how the couple communicates with one another. Both Sara and Elías need things from one another. For this relationship to work, these needs must be communicated with one another and understood.

CO: *¿En qué idioma se hablan? What language do you speak with each other?*

CL-S: *Pues, Elías me habla en español, pero habla en inglés con todos los demás y con sus hijas, nunca se lo que dicen.*

CO: *Según lo que me dices, te sientes aislada porque no hablas inglés.*

CL-S: *Sí, todo el tiempo . . . ni me puedo defender cuando sus hijas están hablando mal de mí. Estoy en un mundo diferente. De soltera, era muy independiente y ahora tengo que depender en Elías para hacer mis trámites o ir de compras.*

CO: *Elías, ¿sabías cómo se siente Sara?*

CL-E: *She always talks about it. Things with my wife are not good and she told me she wants to leave me. It was never like this when I went to visit her in Mexico. En esos tiempos era diferente.*

CO: *Entonces Elías, ¿cómo era diferente antes?*

CL-E: *Pues antes yo iba a visitar a Sara en México y hablábamos en español pues por el ambiente y ahora que estamos en los Estados Unidos pues se habla en inglés—la situación es diferente. Y porque hay estos sentimientos, entonces hay problemas entre Sara y yo. Es difícil para ella porque ella es la única en la casa que no habla inglés.*

CO: *¿Qué podrían hacer diferente?*

CL-E: *Pues entender creo. Entender lo difícil que es para ella y ser más considerado. Ayudar a traducir y ayudarla a que aprenda.*

CL-S: *Pues si la verdad es que sé que tengo que aprender, pero es bien difícil. Me da tanta pena y por eso me doy por vencida.*

CL-E: *Podemos practicar en casa.*

CL-S: *Eso me ayudaría mucho.*

Time to Reflect

- It is important to note the effect of language differences on an individual. In this case, Sara's language difference affects her sense of belonging.
- Here Sara is starting a new identity as a wife in a new country with a language she does not speak. Elías is starting a new identity as a husband in a country he is familiar with, with a language he knows.

Reflective Questions:

1. What other activities can Sara and Elías do together to bring them closer and improve their communication?

Tercera Sesión:

For this session, the counselor intends to explore how the couple's communication issues affect their relationship.

CO: *En la última sesión hablamos sobre el problema de comunicación entre ustedes y como el idioma impacta su relación. ¿Qué ha ocurrido desde la última vez que nos vimos?*

CL-E: *So, so . . . allí vamos. Hemos estado practicando con Sara en casa.*

CL-S: *Si allí voy. Pero me falta mucho. Eso es lo que más me desespera que tengo tanto que aprender y por mientras tengo que depender de él. La vez pasada fui al super y quería comprar un kilo o libra de carne y no me acordaba de como decir libra . . .*

CL-E: *Pounds*

CL-S: *Pues sí, pero en ese momento no me acordaba. Entonces la gente me queda viendo raro y ya me siento mal y avergonzada.*

CO: *Puedo ver que eso la hace sentir frustrada.*

CL-S: *Claro y el problema es que él se molesta conmigo porque no quiero salir a hacer cosas sin él. Él me dice que vaya sola, pero me pongo super nerviosa.*

CL-E: *Pero honey, tienes que aventarte. Es la única forma de aprender.*

CL-S: *Yo entiendo eso, pero es horrible no entender ni poder comunicarte en algo tan sencillo como ir al super. Yo antes era una persona bien independiente y sé que eso es lo que a él no le gusta, que me he vuelto bien dependiente de él. Entonces él se enoja y yo me resiento con él. Me dan ganas de irme.*

CL-E: *La verdad que si te entiendo. No ha de ser fácil y por eso trato de tener paciencia para ayudarte.*

CL-S: *Si es cierto, has cambiado un poco desde que hemos hablado de esto con la doctora.*

CL-E: *¡Ya ve, I've improved!*

CO: *¡Qué bueno que así se sienten! Entonces de lo que escucho te sientes más apoyada por Elias, pero todavía es bien difícil para ti estar acá sin poder hablar el idioma.*

CL-S: *Sí, es muy difícil.*

CO: *Al principio hablaron de que sentían que eran personas diferentes que cuando se conocieron. ¿Cómo se sienten hoy?*

CL-E: *¿Creo que ha mejorado, no honey?*

CL-S: *Si ha mejorado. Lo que me cuesta más es cuando él habla en inglés. No entiendo para nada lo que dice. Y si eres bien diferente acá, pero creo que es la cultura. Solo te enfocas en el trabajo, no paras. Pero acá todo es diferente. Yo también siento que he cambiado por el ambiente en el sentido que ando siempre a la carrera. Ni me siento a comer. Como parada o enfrente de la tele.*

CL-E: *Si acá es más difícil tomarse un tiempo para estar juntos.*

CO: *¿Ayudaría hacer un tiempo para ustedes o incorporar hábitos de México en sus vidas acá en los Estados Unidos?*

CL-E: *Si, la verdad que sí. Tal vez podemos hacer el esfuerzo de sentarnos a la mesa a cenar o desayunar los fines de semana en la mesa. What you think?*

CL-S: *¡Si eso me gustaría mucho!*

Time to Reflect

- Not being able to communicate their needs created miscommunication between the couple. In this case, Sara feels excluded, dependent, and misses the independence of her life in Mexico. Whereas Elías misses how their relationship was when they met in Mexico and wants her to become independent in the United States.
- The counselor tries to find a commonality between them to make efforts to bring them together. What other activities or suggestions could promote communication and closeness within the couple?

Reflective Questions

1. Reflect on an emotional life experience. What do you remember? In what language did these incidents occur? Why are life memories and associated emotions often expressed in the language in which the incident occurred?
2. When writing up the counseling session notes, in addition to examining what the client is saying, why is it important to note the language modality used?
3. What linguistic/communication differences do you note between the husband and wife?
4. How will you ensure that you will have the bilingual competency to work with bilingual clients?
5. Are there cultural differences that you note between Sara and Elias? How can you as a counselor assist here?
6. What other questions would you ask to incorporate multicultural counseling skills?

Implications for Clinical Practice, Bilingual Training, and Research

Language is an essential tool during the counseling process. As previously mentioned, bilingual clients will remember life events and associated emotions in the language in which these experiences occurred (Santiago-Rivera et al., 2009). Counselors should be aware of how language preferences and modality may affect the counseling relationship. To do so, the counselor must explore their self-awareness of language modalities and see language as a critical component of the counseling relationship.

For counselor educators, CACREP (2016) standards encourage programs to address the multicultural characteristics of diverse client groups, the growing need of Spanish-speaking clients, and regional social justice concerns impacting this population (Ratts et al., 2016). Training counselors in bilingual counseling concurrently with their standard counseling curriculum can help counselor education programs minimize challenges and feelings of incompetence experienced by bilingual counselors (Castaño et al., 2007; Ivers & Villalba, 2015; Trepal et al., 2019; Verdinelli & Biever, 2009).

We will discuss bilingual supervision in a subsequent chapter (see Chapter 4). Nevertheless, the role of the supervisor is to guide bilingual counselors to become aware of the multicultural and language factors that may affect the counseling relationship, such as language preferences and modality (use of English vs. Spanish, code-switching), body movements, facial expressions, and the ways certain words are used. While supervising bilingual counselors it is also important to identify and discuss the bilingual counselor's language use and level of self-awareness.

More research is needed on identity development and bilingualism within the counseling field. Additional counseling research must focus on specific age, gender, generation, immigration, and language differences to assess and understand within-group differences relevant to working with bicultural-bilingual populations.

Conclusion

In this chapter, given the ever-changing linguistic landscape of the United States, we have highlighted the critical role of bilingual counselors in recognizing and valuing the language preferences and modalities of their clients.

We have also discussed the importance of considering language as a multi-cultural factor in counseling. Moreover, we have demonstrated the need for bilingual counselors to attain bilingual competency as well as counseling skills to be culturally efficacious counselors. We have provided resources that can be used during intake and counseling sessions. To ensure that bilingual clients achieve their therapeutic goals, the culturally efficacious counselor creates the conditions that allow for clients to freely express themselves. Lastly, we have provided recommendations for preparing bilingual counselors and for needed research to fill the current gap that exists in the field of counseling.

Points to Remember

- The Latine population is not monolithic; it is heterogeneous depending on their age, gender, generational, immigrational, and language differences.
- The heritage or native language is often used to express emotions because life events are encoded in our memories.
- The bilingual counselor must have the full repertoire of bilingual language competency (including Spanish professional terms) to assist the bilingual client and match the client's language preference and modality.
- The bilingual client has the right to receive counseling in their preferred language modality and it is the culturally efficacious bilingual counselor who is attentive to linguistic needs and considerations to support the clients' therapeutic goals.

Resources

American Psychological Association. (2013). *Guia de Consulta de Los Criterios Diagnósticos del DSM-5(TM)*. Author

Bender, D. E. (2006). *Spanish for Mental Health Professionals: A step by step handbook*. University of New Mexico Press.

Benuto, L. T. (2017). *Toolkit for counseling Spanish speaking clients: Enhancing behavioral health services*. Springer.

Bernal, G., & Domenech Rodríguez, M. M. (Eds.). (2012). *Cultural adaptations: Tools for evidence-based practice with diverse populations*. American Psychological Association.

Buki, L., & Piedra, L. M. (Eds.). (2011). *Creating infrastructures for Latino mental health*. Springer.

Council for Accreditation of Counseling and Related Educational Programs. (2016). *CACREP 2016 standards*. http://www.cacrep.org/wp-content/uploads/2017/08/2016-Standards-with-citations.pdf

Ivey, A. E., Ivey, M. B., Zalaquett, C. P., & Chatters, S. (2017). *Basic attending skills* (5th ed.). Microtraining Associates.

Swazo, R. (2013). *The Bilingual Counselor's guide to Spanish: Basic vocabulary and interventions for the non-Spanish speaker*. Routledge.

Washburn Center for Children. (2015). *Spanish clinical language and resource guide*. https://washburn.org/wp-content/uploads/2023/08/Spanish_Clinical_Language_and_Resource_Fall-2015.pdf

Zalaquett, C. P., Ivey, A. E., Gluckstern-Packard, N., & Ivey, M. B. (2008). *Las habilidades atencionales básicas: Pilares fundamentales de la comunicación*. Microtraining Associates.

References

Adelsope, O. O., Lavin, T., Thompson, T., & Ungerleider, C. (2010). A systematic review and meta-analysis of the cognitive correlates of bilingualism. *Review of Educational Research*, 80(2), 207–245. https://doi.org/10.3102/0034654310368803

Altarriba, J. (2014). Emotion, memory, and bilingualism. In R. Heredia, & J. Altarriba (Eds.), *Foundations of bilingual memory* (pp. 185–203). Springer.

Alvarado, M., Lerma, E., & Vela, J. C. (2019). Experiences of Spanish speaking counseling students: Implications for the profession. *The Journal of Counselor Preparation and Supervision, 12*(4). https://digitalcommons.sacredheart.edu/cgi/viewcontent.cgi?article=1264&-context=jcps

American Counseling Association. (2014). *ACA code of ethics*. https://www.counseling.org/resources/aca-code-of-ethics.pdf

American Counseling Association. (2011). *Suicide assessment*. https://www.counseling.org/docs/trauma-disaster/fact-sheet-6---suicide-assessment.pdf?sfvrsn=2

American Psychiatric Association. (2022). *Diagnostic and statistical manual of mental disorders – Text Revision* (5th ed.). Author.

Anguiano, R. (2018). Language brokering among Latino immigrant families: Moderating variables and youth outcomes. *Journal of Youth and Adolescence, 47*(1), 222–242. https://doi.org/10.1007/s10964-017-0744-y

Anzaldúa, G. (1987). *Borderlands/La frontera: The new mestiza*. Aunt Lute Books.

Anzaldúa, G. (2002). Preface: (Un)natural bridges, (Un)safe spaces. In G. Anzaldúa & A. Keating (Eds.), *This bridge we call home* (pp. 1–5). Routledge.

Artiga, S., Young, K., Conrachione, E., & Garfield, R. (2015). The role of language in health care access and utilization for insured Hispanic adults. *Disparities Policy*. https://www.kff.org/report-section/the-role-of-language-in-health-care-access-and-utilization-for-insured-hispanic-adults-issue-brief/

Benuto, L. T. (2013). *Guide to psychological assessment with Hispanics*. Springer Science + Business Media. https://doi.org/10.1007/978-1-4614-4412-1_1

Benuto, L. T. (2017). *Toolkit for counseling Spanish speaking clients: Enhancing behavioral health services*. Springer.

Bialystok, E., Craik, F. I., Green, D. W., & Gollan, T. H. (2009). Bilingual minds. *Psychological Science in the Public Interest, 10*(3), 89–129. https://doi.org/10.1177/1529100610387084

Borden, R. S. (2014). The English only movement: Revisiting cultural hegemony. *Multicultural Perspectives, 16*, 229–233. https://doi.org/10.1080/15210960.2014.956607

Brown, H. D. (1994). *Principles of language learning and teaching* (3rd ed.). Prentice Hall Regents.

Canale, M., & Swain, M. (1980). Theoretical bases of communicative approaches to second language teaching and testing. *Applied Linguistics, 1*(1), 1–4.

Castaño, M. T., Biever, J. L., González, C. G., & Anderson, K. B. (2007). Challenges of providing mental health services in Spanish. *Professional Psychology: Research and Practice, 38*(6), 667–673. https://doi.org/10.1037/0735-7028.38.6.667

Center for Applied Linguistics. (2017). *Dual language program directory.* http://webapp.cal.org/duallanguage/

Centers for Disease Control and Prevention. (2017). Web-based injury statistics query and reporting system (WISQARS). *Leading causes of death reports, 1981–2015.* www.cdc.gov/ncipc/wisqars.

Chomsky, N. (1965). *Aspects of the theory of syntax.* The MIT Press.

Clandinin, D. J., & Rosiek, J. (2007). Mapping a landscape of narrative inquiry: Borderland spaces and tensions. In D. J. Clandinin (Ed.), *Handbook of narrative inquiry: Mapping a methodology* (pp. 35–75). SAGE Publication.

Delgado-Romero, E., De Los Santos, J., Raman, V., Merrifield, J., Vazquez, M., Monroig, M., Cárdenas Bautista, E., & Durán, M. (2018). Caught in the middle: Spanish-speaking bilingual mental health counselors as language brokers. *Journal of Mental Health Counseling, 40*(4), 341–352. https://doi.org/10.17744/mehc.40.4.06

Dixon, S. V., Graber, J. A., & Brooks-Gunn, J. (2008). The roles of respect for parental authority and parenting practices in parent-child conflict among African American, Latino, and European American families. *Journal of Family Psychology (Division 43), 22*(1), 1–10. https://doi.org/10.1037/0893-3200.22.1.1

Eaton, M. (1994). Patently confused, complex inequality and Canada v. Mossop. 1 Rev. Cons. Stud.

Flores, B. B., & Clark, E. R. (2017). Despertando el ser: Awakening the ethnic identity and consciousness of Latino teachers. In B. B. Flores & E. R. Clark (Eds.), *Despertando el ser: Transforming Latino teachers' identity, consciousness, and beliefs* (pp. 3–23). Peter Lang Publishers.

Fontes, L. A. (2002). Child discipline and physical abuse in immigrant Latino families: Reducing violence and misunderstandings. *Journal of Counseling & Development, 80*(1), 31–40. https://doi.org/10.1002/j.1556-6678.2002.tb00163.x

Freedman, J. (2018). The uses and abuses of 'vulnerability' in EU asylum and refugee protection: Protecting women or reducing autonomy? *Papeles del CEIC 2019/1, Papel 204*, 1–15. https://doi.org/10.1387/pceic.19525

Fuertes, J. N. (2004). Supervision in bilingual counseling: Service delivery, training, and research considerations. *Journal of Multicultural Counseling and Development*, 32(2), 84–94. https://doi.org/10.1002/j.2161-1912.2004.tb00363.x

Gallardo-Cooper, M., Arredondo, P., Delgado-Romero, E. A., & Zapata, A. L. (2014). *Culturally responsive counseling with Latinas/os*. John Wiley & Sons.

González, L. M., Ivers, N. N., Noyola, M. C., Murillo-Herrera, A., & Davis, K. M. (2015). Supervision in Spanish: Reflections from supervisor–trainee dyads. *The Clinical Supervisor*, 34(2), 184–203. https://doi.org/10.1080/07325223.2015.1058208

González-Ramos, G., Zayas, L. H., & Cohen, E. V. (1998). Child-rearing values of low-income, urban Puerto Rican mothers of preschool children. *Professional Psychology: Research and Practice*, 29(4), 377. https://doi.org/10.1037/0735-7028.29.4.377

Guarnaccia, P. J., Rubio-Stipec, M., & Canino, G. (1989). Ataques de nervios in the Puerto Rican diagnostic interview schedule: The impact of cultural categories on psychiatric epidemiology. *Culture, Medicine and Psychiatry*, 13(3), 275–295.

Haley, H., Romero Marin, M., & Gelgand, J. C. (2015). Language anxiety and counseling self-efficacy. *Journal of Multicultural Counseling and Development*, 43(3), 162–172. https://doi.org/10.1002/jmcd.12012

Harwood, R. L., Miller, J. G., & Irizarry, N. L. (1997). *Culture and attachment: Perceptions of the child in context*. Guilford Press.

Interiano-Shiverdecker, C. G., Robertson, D. L., Zambrano, E., Contreras, J., & Morgan, A. (2021). Development and implementation of a bilingual counseling curriculum. *Teaching and Supervision in Counseling*, 3(3), Article 3. https://doi.org/10.7290/tsc030303

Ivers, N. N., & Villalba, J. A. (2015). The effect of bilingualism on self-perceived multicultural counseling competence. *The Professional Counselor*, 5(3), 419–430, https://doi.org/10.15241/nni.5.3.419

Johnsdotter, S. (2015). European Somali children dumped? On families, parents, and children in a transnational context. *European Journal of Social Work*, 18(1), 81–96. https://doi.org/10.1080/13691457.2013.844682

Kissil, K., Davey, M., & Davey, A. (2013). Therapists in a foreign land: Acculturation, language proficiency and counseling self-efficacy among foreign-born therapists practicing in the United States. *International Journal for the Advancement of Counseling*, 35(3), 216–233. https://doi.org/10.1007/s10447-012-9178-0

Livanis, A., & Tryon, G. S. (2010). The development of the Adolescent Nervios Scale: preliminary findings. *Cultural Diversity and Ethnic Minority Psychology*, 16(1), Article 9. https://doi.org/10.1037/a0014905

McCaffrey, A., & Moody, S. J. (2015). Providing equitable services: Implementing bilingual counseling certification in counselor education programs. *VISTAS online*, Article 33, 1–11. https://www.counseling.org/docs/default-source/vistas/article_33625c21f16116603ab cacff0000bee5e7.pdf?sfvrsn=fc4a412c_8

Miranda, A. O., & Umhoefer, D. L. (1998). Acculturation, language use, and demographic variables as predicators of career self-efficacy of Latino career counseling clients. *Journal of Multicultural Counseling and Development*, 26(1), 39–51. https://doi.org/10.1002/j.2161-1912.1998.tb00182.x

Moradi, B., & Grzanka, P. R. (2017). Using intersectionality responsibly: Toward critical epistemology, structural analysis, and social justice activism. *Journal of Counseling Psychology*, 64(5), 500–513. https://doi.org/10.1037/cou0000203

Na, S., Ryder, A. G., & Kirmayer, L. J. (2016). Toward a culturally responsive model of mental health literacy: Facilitating help-seeking among East Asian immigrants to North America. *American Journal of Community Psychology*, 58(1–2), 211–225. https://doi.org/10.1002/ajcp.12085

Norton, B. (2012). *Identity and second language acquisition*. The encyclopedia of applied linguistics. Wiley Online. https://onlinelibrary.wiley.com/doi/abs/10.1002/9781405198431.wbeal0521

Orellana., M. F. (2009). *Translating childhoods: Immigrant youth, language, and culture*. Rutgers University Press. Print.

Palmer, D., Zúñiga, C., & Henderson, K. I. (2015). A dual language revolution in the United States? On the bumpy road from compensatory to enrichment education for bilingual children in Texas. In W. E. Wright, S. Boun, & O. Garcia (Eds.), *Handbook of bilingual and multilingual education* (pp. 447–460). Wiley-Blackwell.

PEW Research Center. (2018). *Key facts about young Latinos, one of the nation's fastest-growing populations*. https://www.pewresearch.org/fact-tank/2018/09/13/key-facts-about-young-latinos/

PEW Research Center. (2019). *Key facts about U.S. Hispanics and their diverse heritage*. https://www.pewresearch.org/fact-tank/2019/09/16/key-facts-about-u-s-hispanics/

Rafieyan, V., Orang, M., Bijami, M., Nejad, M. S., & Eng, L. S. (2013). Language learners' acculturation attitudes. *English Language Teaching*, 7(1), 114–119. 114–119. https://doi:10.5539/elt.v7n1p114

Ramos, D. C., & Sayer, P. (2017). Differentiated linguistic strategies of bilingual professionals on the US-Mexico border. *Critical Inquiry in Language Studies*, 14(1), 25–57. https://doi.org/10.1080/15427587.2016.1228457

Ratts, M. J., Singh, A. A., Nassar-McMillan, S., Butler, S. K., & McCullough, J. R. (2016). Multicultural and social justice counseling competencies: Guidelines for the counseling profession. *Journal of Multicultural Counseling and Development*, 44(1), 28–48. https://doi.org/10.1002/jmcd.12035

Reyes, I. (2004). Functions of code-switching in schoolchildren's conversations. *Bilingual Research Journal*, 28(1), 77–98. https://doi.org/10.1080/15235882.2004.10162613

Rudolph, N. (2016). Negotiating borders of being and becoming in and beyond the English language teaching classroom: Two university student narratives from Japan. *Asian Englishes*, 18(1), 1–17. https://doi.org/10.1080/13488678.2015.1132110

Santiago-Rivera, A. L., & Altarriba, J. (2002). The role of language in therapy with the Spanish-English bilingual client. *Professional Psychology: Research and Practice*, 33(1), 30–30. https://doi:10.1037//0735-7028.33.1.30

Santiago-Rivera, A. L., Altarriba, J., Poll, N., González-Miller, N., & Cragun, C. (2009). Therapists' views on working with bilingual Spanish–English speaking clients: A qualitative investigation. *Professional Psychology: Research and Practice*, 40(5), 436. https://doi.org/10.1037/a0015933

Sonnenschein, S., Metzger, S. R., Dowling, R., & Baker, L. (2017). The relative importance of English versus Spanish language skills for low-income Latino English language learners' early language and literacy development. *Early Child Development and Care, 187*(3–4), 727–743. https://doi.org/10.1080/03004430.2016.1219854

Suarez, D. (2002). The paradox of linguistic hegemony and the maintenance of Spanish as a heritage language in the United States. *Journal of Multilingual and Multicultural Development, 23*(6), 512–530. https://doi.org/10.1080/01434630208666483

Tigert, J., Groff, J., Martin-Beltán, M., Peercy, M. M., & Silverman, R. (2019). Exploring the pedagogical potential of translanguaging in peer reading interactions. In J., MacSwan & C. J. Faltis (Eds.), *Codeswitching in the classroom: Critical perspectives on teaching, learning, policy, and ideology*, (pp. 65–87). Center for Applied Linguistics. Routledge.

Trepal, H., Ivers, N., & Lopez, A. (2014). Students' experiences with bilingual counseling. *The Journal for Counselor Preparation and Supervision, 6*(2), 21–34. http://dx.doi.org/10.7729/62.1096

Trepal, H., Tello, A., Haiyasoso, M., Castellon, N., Garcia, J., & Martinez-Smith, C. (2019). Supervision strategies used to support Spanish-speaking bilingual counselors. *Teaching and Supervision in Counseling, 1*(1), 3. https://doi.org/10.7290/tsc010103

U.S. Census Bureau. (2019). *State and county Quickfacts*. Data derived from population estimates, American community survey, census of population and housing, county business patterns, economic census, survey of business owners, building permits, census of governments. https://www.census.gov/quickfacts/fact/table/US/HSG010218

Verdinelli, S., & Biever, J. L. (2009). Experiences of Spanish/English bilingual supervisees. *Psychotherapy: Theory, Research, Practice, Training, 46*, 158–170. https://doi.org/10.37/a0016024

Young, M. (2017). *Learning the art of helping building blocks and techniques* (7th ed.). Pearson.

Zalaquett, C. P., Ivey, A. E., Gluckstern-Packard, N., & Ivey, M. B. (2008). *Las habilidades atencionales básicas: Pilares fundamentales de la comunicación*. Microtraining Associates.

· 3 ·

CULTURAL CHOQUES AND ACCULTURATION: SOCIOCULTURAL CONSIDERATIONS FOR SERVING THE COUNSELING NEEDS OF THE LATINE POPULATIONS

In this chapter, we consider the cultural choques (clash/tensions) that Latine, bicultural clients often experience, positioned as a minoritized/colonized group. Often, these cultural choques are reflective of the individual's acculturation level or degree of biculturalism. As previously noted in Chapter 2, Latine clients may have experienced language loss because of hegemonic discourse or laws which prohibited them from speaking or learning in their native or heritage language. The cultural choques that are experienced within a hegemonic, dominant society impact the psychological well-being of the bilingual client (Morand, 2003; Ngo, 2008). Researchers such as Ngo (2008) identified cultural clash as a common experience in the stories of immigrant families residing in the United States. He stated, "more often than not, these stories highlight the *clash of cultures* or the ways that immigrant youth are torn or caught between two worlds . . ." (p. 4). A cultural clash can create a range of mixed emotions in the individual (Ngo, 2008). They may feel tension because of strong ties to the native or heritage culture as opposed to the adopted country or dominant U.S. culture. Having a constant interaction with new cultural values may inhibit the person's cultural values and create identity conflicts. Ngo (2008) stated that "the experiences of immigrant families frame the choices and struggles of culture and identity within East/West or immigrant/nonimmigrant binaries" (p. 8). In other words, when making life decisions and establishing their identity, people's thought processes involve a cultural frame. Bilingual counselors need to approach counseling from a social justice lens and have a deep understanding of the acculturation process and the resultant acculturative stress that occurs when Latine clients experience conflict or choques with their cultural values, generational status, and gender identification.

Social Justice Theoretical Framework

No one theory exists that can conceptualize Latine as a whole and therefore, counselors must critique each theory for multicultural effectiveness in practice (Singh et al., 2020). "Although social justice theories have a long history in counseling, they are often treated as 'additional' theoretical perspectives rather than as foundational groundings for counseling practice" (Singh et al., 2020, p. 262). Counselors may do well to also consider adapting classical theories that were not created with the mission of dismantling systems of oppression or taking a stance of social justice (Singh et al., 2020). Grounding in theories with feminist and multicultural frameworks is essential to understand Latine's experiences, including their mental health and wellness. The following are examples of how one might utilize different counseling frameworks through a social justice lens. Table 3.1 also presents a glossary on some theoretical concepts and interventions in both English and Spanish to expand the counselor's professional terminology.

Las Teorías Psicoanalíticas o Psicodinámicas

Psychodynamic or psychoanalytic theories emphasize unconscious patterns of behavior (patrones de comportamiento subconscientes) and interpretation to help clients change (Sommers-Flanagan & Sommers-Flanagan, 2018). Traditional psychoanalytic practice centers its knowledge on internal psychological processes that tend to neglect social and cultural influences. Progress in including external factors of analysis has been slow, leaving clients of color feeling excluded and marginalized.

In addition, counselors should consider employing an expanded flexible approach to psychodynamic treatments with a flexible focus on the relationship (Gelman, 2004). For example, counselors may consider the context of the client as an individual person as well as the impact of their social/cultural realities.

Table 3.1: *Spanish Glossary of Therapeutic Interventions, Concepts, and Techniques*

English Term	Términos en Español
Psychoanalytic/Psychodynamic Approaches	*La Perspectiva Psicoanalítica o Psicodinámica*
Unconscious Patterns of Behavior	*Patrones de Comportamiento Subconscientes*
Interpretation	*Interpretación*
Insight	*Introspección*
Self-disclosure	*Autorrevelación o Divulgación Voluntaria*
Free Association	*Asociación Libre*
Catharsis	*Catarsis*
Repression	*Represión*
Denial	*Negación*
Projection	*Proyección*
Rationalizing	*Racionalizar*
Displacement	*Desplazar*
Psychosexual development stages	*Etapas del Desarrollo Psicosexual*
Oral Stage	*Etapa Oral*
Anal Stage	*Etapa Anal*
Phallic Stage	*Etapa Fálica*
Latent Period	*Período de Latencia*
Genital Stage	*Etapa Genital*
Humanistic Therapy	*Terapia o Psicología Humanística*
Adlerian Therapy	*Terapia o Psicología Adleriana*
Person-centered therapy	*Terapia Centrada en la Persona*
Self-realization	*Autorrealización*
Congruency or congruent	*Congruencia o Congruente*
Empathy	*Empatía*
Unconditional Positive Regards	*Consideración Positiva Incondicional*
Ideal Self	*El "yo" ideal*
Real Self	*El "yo" real*
Holistic/Integrated/Postmodern Therapeutic Approaches	*Perspectivas de Terapia Holísticas/Integradas/Postmodernas*
Narrative Therapy	*Terapia o Psicología Narrativa*
Metaphors	*Refranes*
Dominant Story	*Historia Dominante*
Counterstories	*Historia Contrarrestante*
Acculturation	*Aculturación*
Heritage-culture maintenance	*Mantenimiento de Patrimonio Cultural*
Receiving-culture participation	*Participación en Cultura Receptora*

Table 3.1: *Continued*

English Term	Términos en Español
Assimilation	*Asimilación*
Separation	*Separación*
Marginalization	*Marginalización*
Integration	*Integración*
Behavioral acculturation	*Aculturación en el Plano de Conductas*
Value acculturation	*Aculturación en el Plano de Valores*
Identity acculturation	*Aculturación en el Plano de Identidad*
Acculturative stress	*Estrés por Aculturación*
Ethnic Pride	*Orgullo Étnico*
Bicultural or Integrated identity	*Identidad Bicultural o Integrada*
Cognitive-Behavioral Therapy	*Terapia Cognitiva Conductual*
Rational Emotive Behavioral Therapy	*Terapia Racional Emotiva Conductual*
Reality Therapy	*Terapia de la Realidad*
Automatic Thought	*Pensamiento Automático*
Core Belief	*Creencias Fundamentales*
Thinking Errors	*Errores de Procesamiento Cognitivo*
Schema	*Esquemas*
Activating Event	*Evento de activación*
Distortions	*Pensamientos Distorsionados*
Mindfulness	*Conciencia Plena*
Eye Movement Desensitization and Reprocessing (EMDR)	*Desensibilización y reprocesamiento por medio de movimiento ocular*
Motivational Interviewing	*Intervenciones Motivacionales*
Dialectical Behavioral Therapy	*Terapia dialéctica-conductual*
Trauma Focused Cognitive Behavioral Therapy	*Terapia cognitiva conductual enfocada en el tratamiento de trauma*
Coping Mechanisms	*Mecanismos o técnicas de afrontamiento*
Defense Mechanisms	*Mecanismos o técnicas de Defensa*
Breathing Techniques	*Técnicas de Respiración*
Grounding Techniques	*Técnicas para Centrarse*
Rupture	*Ruptura*
Termination	*Terminación*

There is also an understanding of "special transferential and countertransferential dynamics that can potentially arise from an intra-ethnic therapeutic dyad presupposes self-awareness, a fundamental aspect of cultural sensitivity" (Gelman, 2004, p. 73). Counselors must acknowledge their ingrained biases and prejudices, including in the theories they employ, to maintain cultural sensitivity and assist clients.

When executing psychodynamic techniques, such as interpretation or insight, counselors may find it helpful to exercise self-disclosure with Latine individuals as compared to other clients. The use of self-disclosure will help to establish a connection and therapeutic alliance that is central to Latine culture (Gelman, 2004). At the same time, counselors should avoid over-identification with clients to ensure that they are confronting issues that need to be addressed. Denial of pathology and collusion may occur when counselors focus solely on socioeconomic and cultural factors. Specifically, Latine counselors must maintain a balanced perspective so as not to automatically assume commonalities between them and their clients based on background and culture.

Teorías Humanísticas

Humanistic theories of counseling such as Person-centered and Adlerian theories focus on individual perspectives for treatment. When employing techniques from an individualistic approach, counselors must consider how this may impact Latine clients with collectivistic values. Understanding how clients function within the context of their families is essential for developing treatment plans that fit their needs.

In Adlerian theory, Alfred Adler made assumptions about demands placed on an individual's life, including challenges faced in things such as work, social relationships, love, self, spirituality, and parenting/family (Sommers-Flanagan & Sommers-Flanagan, 2018). Although there is validity in his conceptualization of these tasks, it dismisses cultural variables such as the effects of acculturation in culturally diverse populations such as Latine. Although Adlerian theory does well to promote a holistic, wellness-oriented approach, an adaptation of concepts is necessary for helping culturally diverse individuals.

Carl Rogers (1977) described the value of a person-centered counselor as aiming to understand a client's journey in the world and to see them from the inside without imposing values onto their experiences. In addition, a person-centered counselor's hope for their clients is that they can access and exercise their full range of potentialities in their environments. This view aligns directly with social justice advocacy efforts and a counselor's duty to voice concerns on how systems or discriminatory actions harm people. On a client level, counselors using a person-centered approach will validate client experiences and clarify their feelings within the context of a safe, trusting, and accepting relationship (Swan & Cebellos, 2020). Furthermore, societal advocacy from a person-centered perspective requires counselors to become agents of change through reform of public policy and legislative decisions, increasing client access to services, combating the stigma of mental health, and emphasizing social justice initiatives within organizations (Singh et al., 2020; Swan & Cabellos, 2020).

Teorías Cognitivas Conductuales

Cognitive-behavioral theories include rational emotive behavior therapy (REBT), reality therapy, and cognitive behavior therapy (CBT; Corey, 2018). Cognitive-behavioral approaches tend to be structured, psychoeducational, and goal-directed (Sharf & Sharf, 2012). This lens of viewing client change is based on the assumption that problems are learned, and people can learn and implement new ways of being (Fenn & Byrne, 2013). Cognitive and behavioral theories can be multiculturally sensitive, however, there are a few considerations for counselors to keep in mind when working with Latine clients. Although theories in this framework are structured, counselors should individualize treatment based on the needs of each client.

As mentioned above, cognitive and behavioral approaches are directive, often utilizing homework, and psychoeducational. This teaching approach to therapy has been demonstrated to help Latine clients who come from backgrounds where mental health stigma is prevalent (Organista, 2019). A lot of work in this framework is examining core beliefs and helping individuals identify thinking errors (Sharf & Sharf, 2012). A culturally efficacious counselor will be mindful not to assume that healthy functioning adults are those whose values and thinking patterns fall into traditional Eurocentric or American culture (Organista, 2019).

Terapia de Juego Centrada en el Niño

Child-centered play therapy (CCPT) recognizes the relationship as the primary healing agent in the counseling process. CCPT has a long-standing relationship with counselors who have utilized practical and effective interventions for elementary-aged children experiencing diverse challenges (Ray et al., 2015). By providing a safe and supportive environment through natural play, children feel more comfortable sharing their emotions and thoughts with counselors. Autonomy is designated through self-directed play and counselor observation, so that children may gain confidence in themselves and their abilities. In addition, CCPT is conscious of diverse cultural experiences, such as language, ability, and socioeconomic status, and how these might become apparent in the world of play. CCPT is a responsive intervention shown to be effective with diverse populations, including Latine children (Ceballos & Bratton, 2010; Lin & Bratton, 2015). Latine children benefit from an open space to navigate issues such as parent deportation, acculturation, language acquisition, or discrimination. CCPT may help the child to increase their sense of self, safety, and trust during a difficult time when they feel uncertain about their place in the world. Through this avenue, children may recognize their protective factors of resilience, bilingualism, and biculturalism.

Terapias Holísticas/Integradas/Postmodernas

Several scholars recommended that counselors consider holistic/integrated/postmodern theories when working with the Latine population to provide multiculturally sensitive services (Farrel & Gibbons, 2019; Taylor et al., 2006). This is largely in part because postmodern frameworks take a step-down approach to counseling which is highlighted by Taylor et al. (2006):

> Postmodernism sustains the idea that when the therapist is aware of his/her own assumptions, values, and biases, and understands the worldview of the culturally different client, he/she can embrace the social-cultural-political dimension of the problems presented in the therapeutic room and see beyond the privatization of culture (p. 432).

By taking a step-down approach, these approaches encourage counselors to engage in continued reflection that multiple truths exist at one time (Combs & Freedman, 2012). Holistic/integrated/postmodern approaches are cited as the most popular approach with Latine because of their focus on family and social contrasts (Farrel & Gibbons, 2019).

Narrative therapy has emerged as a helpful tool (Farrel & Gibbos, 2019; Henry et al., 2005). Latine culture is rich in storytelling using cuentos, dichos, and consejos, which will be elaborated on in the cultural values section. Therefore, the power of stories in narrative-based therapy is a natural way to incorporate Latine values. One of the first steps in implementing narrative therapy is to identify dominant stories. For Latine individuals, dominant stories may be "family comes first", "la ropa sucia se lava en la casa", or "therapy es para los locos" (Henry et al., 2005). Whatever dominant story has brought individuals to counseling, the counselor aids with deconstructing and reauthoring this story with a focus on understanding core values, worldviews, and various identities (Farrel & Gibbons, 2019). Narrative therapists work alongside their clients to offer alternative counterstories to the problem story. It also uses stories as metaphors to externalize problems and avoid framing the person as the problem. Combs and Freedman (2012) described it as, "all narrative work is social justice work in that it always has the intent of countering and undermining the marginalization that can happen in pathology-based approaches to mental health" (p. 1041). This theory is in line with the goals of social justice and antiracist practice in therapy because it denies neutrality in place of resistance. It considers intersectionality as critical in conceptualization which is beneficial to a pan-ethnic population such as the Latine people.

Latino/a/x Critical Race Theory (LatCrit)

LatCrit is grounded in the power of Critical Race Theory in its purpose to challenge traditional methodologies centering on racist ideologies and white supremacy. Further LatCrit aims to examine the intersectionalities of the Latino/a/e racialized, gendered, and classed experiences as oppressive structures that serve to marginalize them (Solorzano & Yosso, 2001). Focused attention is given to unique experiences that Latine people face including multilingualism, immigration, and transcultural identities that are more than the white/black binary (Mizell, 2022). LatCrit seeks to address how mental health professions have historically oppressed clients of color and how that might impact the counseling dynamic. Through a counseling perspective, mental health practitioners use their power to provide culturally sensitive therapy that counters Western epistemologies guiding common practice. Moreover, LatCrit calls counselors further to respond to and disrupt White hegemonic structures through centering social transformation and spotlighting counter-narratives.

When working with Latine clients experiencing racism, xenophobia, and related intolerance, emotions of anger, frustration, and despair may arise. Counselors need to cultivate a counter-space of resistance for clients to acknowledge and validate their stories. Although LatCrit is not considered a counseling theory, bilingual counselors may do well to use the framework to provide clients

with a space of healing and empowerment (Rodríguez, 2010). Using this framework, a counselor might consider applying Borderlands Theory with Latine clients to explore issues related to identity and address sociopolitical experiences
tied to oppression and discrimination.

Borderlands Theory

Borderlands Theory speaks to the existence of the experiences of transgres-
sive identities reaching far beyond the United States. Developed by Gloria
Anzaldúa in her work *Borderlands/La Frontera: The New Mestiza* (1987), her
conceptualization of marginalized peoples transformed cultural concepts and
became one of the most influential works in Latine studies. Most importantly,
it exposed the gaps within traditional feminist theories where the focus on
interracial, intercultural, transnational, and queer women of color was invisible. Anzaldúa called for a new mestiza, one that centered intersecting identities
and new ways of learning/knowing, a new consciousness (Anzaldúa, 1987).
Moreover, she exposed the difficulties of having to navigate the complexity
of these cultural identities and finding strength within oneself. Her theory is
composed of four realms that many counselors might consider using to better understand their clients' cultural lived experiences when they are facing
adversity and acculturation conflicts (Hinojosa & Carney, 2016). Clients may
experience one or all the realms, moving freely through them, or skipping and
circling back. The process is meant to be fluid and dynamic, changing according to the individual's experience and walk-through life.

The first stage is *nepantla*, or the space of in-between which describes one's
inner conflict when faced with oppression or privilege (Moraga & Anzaldúa,
2015). A bilingual client who identifies himself as Afro-Latino may speak
about his recent experience with racism within Hispanic cultures and reflect
on their ethnic identity. This journey may lead the client into the second
realm or *coatlicue*, a space of new knowledge and knowing. This concept is
often described as a difficult one due to the person processing painful aspects of
their experiences. For example, the Afro-Latino client may come to acknowledge his contradictory identities of race and find himself pulling away from one
identity to support the other. He may have feelings of resentment and guilt for
having to develop protective measures for himself. After battling this internal struggle, the client may move forward in reconstructing a new identity, to
integrate and heal all parts of self, also referred to as *coyolxhauqui*. The final
realm is *la concienca de la mestiza*, the space where a client will tolerate ambiguity and contradictions (Anzaldúa, 1987). Here there is an understanding

that although this new consciousness sprouted from pain, the individual has transformed this to create their language, culture, and identity. This synthesis is always changing, in motion, and the individual is learning and growing with it. Borderlands theory can co-create meaning with clients in safe spaces using culturally appropriate interventions.

Pláticas y testimonios. An intervention through a LatCrit and Borderlands lens may look like a counselor being called to use pláticas within their session. For example, a counselor working with a bilingual older client recalls his history of working as a bracero, including his experiences with discrimination and racism. Throughout their session, the counselor relies on pláticas or charlas to reinforce mutuality and reciprocity through a cultural alliance. Pláticas, in this way, are used as a way of gathering cultural and family knowledge through passed-down stories (Fierros & Delgado Bernal, 2016). During their conversations, the door is opened to create a testimonio, or an oral narrative, which is passed down through spoken word. Testimonios hold power in their implications for Latine generations to understand the sociopolitical histories of their ancestors and create shared meaning within their communities. The counselor acknowledges the client's experiences with oppression through validation and honoring his past. By co-creating a sacred space of healing from the client's vulnerabilities, the counselor is acknowledging the client's reality using culturally sound practice.

Cultural Considerations

To approach counseling from a social justice lens, the bilingual counselor must consider the cultural values of the group, how cultural choques result from the acculturation process, and how acculturative stress is manifested at various life junctures. We introduce these concepts to further extend our understanding of the Latine population. We explore generational and/or mixed immigrant family status, and gender identification.

Cultural Values

Latinidad encompasses over 20 different countries, each with its distinct histories and culture. The Latine culture emphasizes upholding interpersonal relationships and is often referred to as collectivistic in its values. Cultural values such as familismo, personalismo, simpatía, religiosity, and fatalismo are evident in Latine families and impact their ways of being. Although these cultural values are cited in the literature as a cultural commonality, it is important to consider within-group differences, such as education level, acculturation level, and generational status (Sue et al., 2022). In the subsequent paragraphs, we discuss these Latine cultural values in relation to the counseling setting.

Familismo places family as a priority and involves family obligations, perceived support, and being a role model for family members (Miranda et al., 2006). Familismo is a Latine value that can impact the therapeutic process. This cultural value can aid or inhibit help-seeking behavior based on familial dynamics (Chan et al., 2013). Chan et al. (2013) found that the higher familial cohesion present for Latine individuals, the more likely the family is to meet wellness needs and the less likely they would seek mental health services. Counselors can broach topics regarding family expectations and experiences, while also discussing how Latine families can still be accessed for emotional support.

Personalismo is the value of building and investing in relationships with others (Locke, 2017). Respect, interdependence, and cooperation are highly emphasized (Sue et al., 2022). Personalismo can be difficult to grasp in health settings where there is a clear distinction of power, which is held by the medical or mental health professionals. Counselors can counteract these power relationships by connecting with Latine clients and becoming visible in their communities. For example, counselors can connect with local churches, organizations, and schools and provide informational groups.

Like personalismo and familismo, simpatía is another cultural value emphasizing interpersonal relationships. Simpatía refers to harmonious, agreeableness, politeness, and a pleasant persona (Triandis et al., 1984). Additionally, it is viewed as prioritizing others over the individual (Rodríguez-Arauz et al., 2019). Rodríguez-Arauz et al. (2019) noted behavioral evidence of Latina mothers' simpatía as they prioritized politeness and emphasized others' well-being, feelings, or positionality in their daily interactions. Hence, counselors can better serve their Latine clients when they take into consideration manifestations of simpatía in the treatment approach (Rodríguez-Arauz et al., 2019).

Religiosity plays a prominent role among many Latine families. Many Latine individuals report religious affiliation or upbringing, with the majority identifying as Catholic (Pew Research Center, 2019). Religion has been cited as a source of wellness and resiliency building. Many Latin women, especially immigrant women, report utilization of religious resources for mental health issues (Choi et al., 2019; Moreno et al., 2017). Research shows a negative correlation between religiosity and help-seeking behaviors (Choi et al., 2019; Moreno et al., 2017). Thus, Latine with strong religious beliefs are less likely to seek support from counselors. Counselors may do well to consider advocating the benefits of counseling through networking at local church events and building relationships with clergy and staff.

Fatalismo is associated with spirituality and religion with the emphasis that life events are caused by divine will (Sue et al., 2022). If time is not taken to understand this cultural value, counselors risk misinterpreting this value for passivity. However, fatalismo's connection to religion can be a source of resiliency for many Latine (Tello & Lonn, 2017). Counselors can help promote well-being by taking into consideration how fatalism can influence Latine's view on adversity.

Ethnolinguistic Practices

Consejos, dichos, cuentos, and refranes are linguistic expressions that convey cultural values and as such should be considered when counseling Latine clients. The use of these linguistic expressions also signifies the individual language preference and/or modality (see Chapter 2). Espinoza-Herold (2007) makes the distinction between dichos and consejos describing them as sayings and guidelines, respectively. The author describes dichos as popular proverbs or idioms and states that this verbal practice is how Latine families pass on cultural wealth. These ethnolinguistic practices are a way of passing on ancestral wisdom and reinforcing values that tie together generations (Delgado-Romero et al., 2017). Godinez (2006) found that Mexicanas explain consejos as life lessons passed down by their parents and grandparents. The Mexicanas reflected on the way consejos impacted their ways of being and thinking and thus identity. Although Godinez's participants were Mexican women, individuals from Latin American backgrounds engage in this type of passing of knowledge as well (Delgado-Romero et al., 2017). Counselors working with Latine clients can gain understanding by tapping into this level of informal and community learning. Although some dichos and consejos are unique to certain regions or nationalities, counselors can take a step-down approach and invite clients to explain. Inviting discussion on cultural values can thus reinforce a strengths-based approach and instill a sense of ethnolinguistic pride and cultural strength.

Acculturation Process

The concept of acculturation is an attempt to explain the cultural exchange that occurs when two cultures interact. The first scientists to study acculturation were sociologists and anthropologists Redfield et al. (1936). They defined acculturation as the (p. 149):

> Phenomena which result when groups of individuals having different cultures come into continuous first-hand contact, with subsequent changes in the original cultural patterns of either or both groups.

Redfield and colleagues (1936) believed that these changes were cultural, social, and psychological in nature. Social and cultural changes refer to immigrants' adaptation to the societal practices and norms of the host country, whereas psychological changes refer to the individual's mental receptiveness and willingness to identify with the new culture (Berry et al., 2006). These changes occur to find a balance between two dimensions: heritage-culture maintenance and receiving-culture participation (Berry, 1997). Heritage-culture maintenance determines the extent to which a person retains connection and involvement in their culture of origin. On the other hand, receiving-culture participation measures the degree to which a person adopts the attitudes, behaviors, and values of the host culture (Berry et al., 2006).

Early conceptualizations of acculturation were unidimensional and assumed that acculturation took place along a single continuum; where acquiring aspects of the receiving culture would automatically result in the loss of heritage cultural values and practices (Gordon, 1964). In the late 20th century, scholars (e.g., Berry, 1980, 1997; Szapocznik et al., 1980) began to recognize acculturation as a bi-dimensional phenomenon as immigrants entering the United States from different parts of the world were unable to discard their heritage culture. Szapocznik and colleagues (1980) described it as necessary for persons participating in two cultures to learn and retain "separate sets of rules" to successfully navigate within and between the cultures (p. 354). This shift led to a conceptualization of acculturation where the acquisition of receiving culture no longer required the individual to relinquish their heritage culture (Berry, 1980, 1997; Szapocznik et al., 1980). Instead, heritage-culture and receiving-culture orientations operated as separate dimensions where individuals could endorse practices from both cultures (Benet-Martínez & Haritatos, 2005; Szapocznik et al., 1980).

Psychologist John W. Berry (1997) introduced the most popular and widely used model of acculturation. His model consisted of four acculturation strategies: (a) assimilation, (dismissal of heritage culture and acceptance of receiving culture), (b) separation (retention of heritage culture and rejection of receiving culture), (c) marginalization (rejection of both cultures), and (d) integration (successful balance of heritage-cultural maintenance and participation in the receiving culture). Berry's integration category is often associated with the most favorable psychosocial outcomes (e.g., higher self-esteem, lower depression; Benet-Martínez, & Haritatos, 2005; Guo et al., 2009).

However, in the past decade, researchers pointed out several important limitations of Berry's model (Schwartz et al., 2010, 2015). First, researchers question the validity of marginalization as an acculturative strategy (Schwartz et al., 2010). The likelihood that a person will develop a cultural sense of self without adopting either the heritage or receiving cultural contexts is likely, not possible. Indeed, empirical studies found little to no marginalization groups and scales that attempt to measure marginalization typically have poor reliability and validity measure in comparison to scales that measure the other categories (Schwartz et al., 2014a, 2014b; Szapocznik et al., 1980).

A further criticism is that Berry's model adopts a "one size fits all" approach (Schwartz et al., 2010, p. 240). It considers four acculturation categories that provide only four acculturative strategies. Therefore, all migrants, regardless of the type of migrant, the countries of origin and settlement, and the host country's attitudes towards their ethnic group, fall into one of those four categories. Researchers (Rudmin, 2009; Schwartz et al., 2014a, 2014b) contended that even when individuals fall into the same acculturative strategy (i.e., integration) each person's acculturation process is unique. People do not migrate equally and similarly between the receiving culture and the migrant's heritage culture impacts their ability to adapt to the receiving culture. When research points towards integration as the healthiest acculturation strategy, it is unclear to what extent non-native individuals should (a) acquire the culture of the host country or (b) preserve their culture of origin (Schwartz et al., 2010). Defining acculturation as a singular process that identifies an individual as acculturated or not, is, therefore, an oversimplification of a very complex phenomenon (Schwartz et al., 2010).

Schwartz and colleagues (2010) reconceptualized the concept of acculturation by evaluating Berry's (1997) four possible acculturation strategies and independently measuring these changes across three domains. The first domain referred to behavioral acculturation, the ability to engage in cultural practices such as language use, culinary preferences, choice of friends, and use of media (Schwartz et al., 2010). For example, within the United States, cultural assimilation included an overall tendency to speak English, eat American foods, associate with American friends and romantic partners, and read American newspapers, magazines, and websites. For Latine clients, the opposite end would consist of speaking primarily in Spanish, eating Latin foods, associating with Latine friends and romantic partners, and reading or watching entertainment in Spanish. Both the client and the counselor adopt a particular behavioral acculturation, either falling completely in one end or being somewhere in the middle. How could differences or similarities in behavioral acculturation impact the counseling relationship? One example would be the client's desire to speak primarily in English or Spanish or code-switch between one language or the other.

The second domain, value acculturation, refers to beliefs and values about the relative importance of collectivism (subjugation of individual wishes and desires to the needs of the family or other social group) and individualism (focus on one's identity, desires, and priorities; Schwartz et al., 2010). Members of the Latine community tend to embrace collectivistic values. However, acculturation to the United States may change an individual's perspective to consider individualistic values that provide more freedom to pursue personal needs. Differences in value acculturation may create conflict between family members. For example, parents born in Central America who hold on to collectivistic values (e.g., respeto, familismo) may struggle to relate to their children born in the United States who value individualistic values (e.g., pursuing personal dreams regardless of the impact on their family).

The third domain, identity acculturation, evaluates solidarity and commitment to one's ethnic group. On one hand, clients might identify solely with their native or heritage culture (e.g., Mexican, Latine), while others might identify as American. Some might choose a bicultural identity (e.g., Mexican-American). Schwartz et al. (2010) argued that acculturative changes at each domain do not occur at the same rate or in the same direction. For example, they found that changes in language use may occur at a different rate and may have no impact on changes in cultural values and identification (Schwartz et al., 2006a; Schwartz et al., 2007; Wang et al., 2010). Some migrants who speak English and who socialize with Americans may not value competition and independence or may not think of themselves as Americans (Schwartz et al., 2014). Similarly, studies with Asian American and Latine adolescents showed that although they were not proficient in their native language, they still identified strongly with their countries of origin and retained many of their heritage values (Schwartz et al., 2007). Immigrants also integrated heritage and receiving-culture practices or values more easily than their ethnic identity (Schwartz et al., 2006b). Schwartz et al. (2013) found that adopting American practices and customs was not problematic in family relationships between Latine adolescents and their parents, as long as Latine values and identities remained intact.

Acculturative Stress

The process of acculturation can result in acculturative stress in which individuals feel caught between two worlds. There are various life junctures in which acculturative stress impacts the psychological well-being of the Latine client. In Holleran's (2003) ethnographic study of Mexican-American youth, he observed:

> The participants in the study are torn between allegiance to their ethnic roots and assimilation to the majority culture ... the actions and attitudes of the Mexican American youth in this study illustrate not only a lack of solidarity but also a relationship steeped in domination and subordination defined along particularly racial lines and emphasizing the interests and values of the dominant, Eurocentric group. In essence, they are fighting against the dichotomy posed by their own unique bicultural identity (pp. 365–366).

Acculturative stress is connected to at-risk behaviors, delinquency, substance abuse (Barrera et al., 2004), depression, suicide, and anxiety among Latine clients (Revollo et al., 2011; Zvolensky et al., 2016). First-generation college students of color, such as Latine, have also been shown to experience higher levels of acculturative stress (Franklin et al., 2014; Torres et al., 2012). Moreover, exposure to different values, attitudes, and behavioral expectations can result in acculturation-based problems among families with different degrees of acculturation (Bemak & Chung, 2015). In many Latine families, children and adolescents attend school and acculturate more quickly to U.S. culture, whereas the parents and older family members tend to adhere to heritage cultural values (Sue et al., 2022). Latine youth experiencing acculturation may struggle with language barriers, societal and peer pressures, and adapting to new cultural norms. More specifically, they might find themselves experiencing emotional, behavioral, and academic problems (Pasch et al., 2006). Parent-child acculturation discrepancies can also result in strained relationships, a sense of alienation between family members, and changes in family dynamics (Bemak

& Chung, 2015; Deng & Marlowe, 2013). Due to language differences, many parents often rely on their children for resource access and communication (Deng & Marlowe, 2013). Traditional ways of parenting, child-rearing, discipline, and punishment may contradict legal practices in the resettlement country, creating additional frustration and stress (Bemak & Chung, 2015; Deng & Marlowe, 2013). As a result, children may lose confidence, trust, and respect for their parents as they witness them transform from autonomous and culturally competent caretakers to individuals who are overwhelmed with trying to learn a new language and customs (Bemak & Chung, 2015; Deng & Marlowe, 2013). Therefore, many Latine families seek counseling services when parent-child acculturation discrepancies lead to intergenerational conflicts or produce psychological symptoms among members of the family.

Counselors should view clients' cultural processes through a circular lens with an emphasis on biculturalism as a protective factor. Biculturalism emphasizes the individual's strength and ability to navigate multiple cultures, by maintaining their culture of origin while acquiring a second (Bacallao & Smokowski, 2005). Conversations with clients may include discussion on navigating multiple roles and identities, bilingualism, and coping skills they have developed (Trueba, 2002). Having parents process acculturation issues as they arise within themselves and their children, can "help to build empathy and a heightened understanding of each other's experiences" (Bacallao & Smokowski, 2005, p. 504).

One major factor that influences the degree of acculturative stress is the magnitude of cultural differences between one's culture of origin and the new culture such as language, the status of women and underrepresented populations, work norms, individualism and collectivism, and orientation to time (Berry et al., 1992; Chirkov et al., 2005). These studies suggest that when the discrepancy between the receiving culture and the heritage culture is greater, their adjustment is likely to be more stressful. For example, Asian immigrants in the United States who have greater cultural differences (e.g., language, the structure of relationships, and collectivism vs. individualism) between their culture of origin and the U.S. culture, have higher levels of adjustment difficulties compared with European immigrants in the United States (Yeh & Inose, 2003). In social situations, they tend to experience more difficulties with direct expression of feelings and assertive expression of opinions (Yeh & Inose, 2003). In contrast, European immigrants are less likely to experience a stressful acculturation process since they are more likely to come from a cultural context that shares fundamental values with the dominant culture in American society that encourages independence and individual expression (Yeh & Inose, 2003).

It is also worth noting that the receiving context may significantly influence the level of acculturative stress that individuals may experience (Schwartz et al., 2006b). For instance, large, culturally diverse cities such as New York, Los Angeles, San Francisco, Miami, and Texas have long histories of receiving foreign-born populations (Constantine et al., 2004; Olivas & Li, 2006). They are more likely to have heritage-cultural communities that represent sources of support (Schwartz et al., 2006b). More rural or monocultural areas may be less racially and ethnically diverse, presenting stronger pressures to adopt the heritage culture (Guo et al., 2009; Wang et al., 2010). It is also important to note that the reception of contexts has changed over time. An increase in government rhetoric that demonizes or belittles immigrants and refugees has increased fear and anxiety among these groups. Euro and ethnocentric perspectives fostered harmful and untrue beliefs about foreign-born groups such as all Latine being "illegal" and Muslims being "terrorists" (Interiano-Shiverdecker et al., 2021). These collective perspectives and widespread beliefs about immigrant groups seem to instill native-born Americans with a desire to support and voice anti-immigrant policies (Interiano-Shiverdecker et al., 2021).

Chung and colleagues (2011) coined the term *political countertransference* to describe a counselor's negative reaction or perception towards foreign-born population clients. Without their choice, counselors in America are surrounded by the same host attitudes that promote falsehoods and myths about migrant populations. Therefore, awareness of political views and beliefs concerning immigration laws and other charged issues is fundamentally essential. Without self-awareness and cultural humility, counselors may struggle to accept the reality of covert discrimination and even their contribution to oppressive beliefs and behaviors towards foreign-born groups. This may prevent counselors from addressing intrapersonal dynamics of privilege and power within the therapeutic relationship, recognizing social, economic, and political stressors impacting assessment, diagnosis, and interventions, and advocating outside of the session against discriminatory behaviors, rhetoric, and public policies affecting this population

Ethnic Pride

Ethnic pride is also an important cultural consideration when working with Latine populations. Due to cultural clashes, individuals may experience acculturative stress in which they feel torn, but ethnic pride may serve as a protective factor. According to Dinh et al. (2009):

> Although research on the relationship of ethnic pride to physical and mental health outcomes is limited, especially for Latina samples, existing studies with other ethnic minority or youth populations suggest the beneficial effects of ethnic pride on certain psychosocial and behavioral outcomes. (p. 4).

Clauss-Ehlers (2004) demonstrated that having a bicultural identity, in which individuals see themselves as part of two distinct cultures, assists psychological well-being, acts as a resiliency buffer, and increases the capacity to experience success. In investigating Latina bilingual education teacher candidates, Flores et al. (2008) posit that identity formation, which encompasses acculturation level, can mediate cognitive, psychological, and behavioral approaches and ways of being. This is supported by other studies and models that describe the relationship between integrative identity development with reduced psychological stress and higher well-being (Anzaldúa, 1987; Berry, 1980; Sue et al., 2022)

Understanding Generational and Mixed Immigration Status Families

As mentioned in the previous chapter, the Latine population is not homogeneous; there are generational, immigration, cultural, and linguistic differences. The largest group of Latine living within the U.S. are of Mexican heritage, with the majority born in the United States (Pew Research Center, 2019). Within the Latine Mexican heritage population, there is much heterogeneity, in that some can trace their family roots to colonial times when the territories of the southwest of the United States, including present-day Arizona, California, Colorado, Nevada, Texas, and Utah were originally ruled by Spain, later France, and eventually Mexico. It was not until the Treaty of Guadalupe Hidalgo when Mexico ceded claims to the territories north of the Rio Grande that these territories became part of the United States. This colonization "resulted in near genocide" (Holleran, 2003, p. 353) of the Mexican population, and their language and cultural practices were considered inferior. The Mexican descendants, regardless of whether they were U.S.-born or immigrants, were subjected to oppressive treatment, discrimination, and prejudice through Jim Crow laws and other laws which prohibited the teaching of Spanish and segregated schooling of Mexican descendent children (Montejano, 1987). The subjugation of Mexican descendants resulted in a lack of educational, employment, and housing opportunities. In our present day, these types of microaggressions continue to be evident in which individuals of Mexican descent are treated as second-class citizens. This long history of subjugation can impact the psychological well-being of the Latine population and result in acculturative stress or cultural choques, in which they feel torn between two cultures.

Other considerations for culturally sensitive counseling include considering immigration history, documentation status in the country, and generational differences. Nearly 11.4 million undocumented immigrants live in the United States with Mexico, Guatemala, El Salvador, and Honduras representing the top four places of birth of these individuals (U.S. Department of Homeland Security, 2019). Mixed-status families have family members with various immigration documentation statuses. A news report from the University of Southern California's Center for the Study of Immigrant Integration estimates that there are approximately 16.7 million individuals living in mixed-status families (Mathema, 2017). Undocumented legal status impacts immigrants on a psychosocial level, and literature has linked, anxiety, depression, post-traumatic stress disorder, and substance use disorder as mental health consequences (Benuto, 2013; Benuto & Leany, 2017).

After the 2016 presidential election, immigrant children and adolescents reported increased anxiety and questioned their and their family's security in the country (Sondel et al., 2018). Fear of deportation and family separation impacts the mental health of family members. As clinicians continue to work with immigrant and mixed-status families, they must consider the socio-political factors impacting wellness. For example, Dreby (2012) described the psychological trauma that ensues when children witness a parent's deportation and the instability that follows. In addition, Dreby (2012) reported how fear of deportation acts as a barrier to access to healthcare, including mental health care. Immigrants may choose not to access healthcare even when documentation status is not solicited (Dreby, 2012). Counselors must consider how documentation status impacts access to treatment and the development of trust in the therapeutic relationship. Counselors can explore the hesitancy and openness of the client, but trust must be firmly established by discussing any deportation or documentation concerns. Counselors should also seek to stay informed about public policies that impact immigrants and refugees.

Latine Lesbian, Gay, Bisexual, Trans, and Queer Clients

Psychological distress is compounded when race and ethnicity are taken into account. Research on mental health in this community suggests that LGBTQ+ individuals experience higher levels of psychological distress, violence, and suicidality when compared to their heterosexual counterparts (Eisenberg et al., 2006; Fish, 2008). Counselors working within the Latine LGBTQ+ community must consider ways they may experience further discrimination even within their LGBTQ+ spaces. Concepts such as skin color, normative beauty standards, age, or other individual differences can influence one's experience in the world. Intersectionality, which describes the compounded experience of multiple identities, is a helpful framework that can be implemented across theoretical practice (Fish, 2008).

Latine LGBTQ+ who are also immigrants may experience acculturative stress in which there is grief and loss associated with their pre- and post-migration journey (Lonn & Dantzler, 2017). There may also be internal and external conflict due to a clash of cultural values/traditions or integrating their identity within a new system (Messih, 2016). Many Latine LGBTQ+ immigrants have sought refuge in the United States from their home countries (Morales, 2013). The United Nations High Commissioner for Refugees does not track statistics on LGBTQ+ status and therefore exact percentages are unavailable. However, The Heartland Alliance has estimated that between 3.8% and 4.6% of refugees identify as LGBTQ+ (US Department of Health and Human Services, 2011). The Heartland Alliance highlights LGBTQ+ immigrants and refugees experiencing double marginalization and are frequently prone to isolation due to fear of non-acceptance of their immigrant and sexual minority status. Counselors should be aware that marginalization experience is intensified by intersections of their identity and plays as a barrier to health services.

Application to Practice: Case Study

Rey's case study illustrates an adolescent's transcultural experience and how he must navigate complex issues such as immigration, acculturation, and unique family dynamics. Over the course of four sessions, the school counselor works with Rey to develop healthy coping mechanisms and provide family support. The following are samples from their sessions.

Rey's Case Study: A Case of Acculturation and Transnational Identity

Rey, a 3rd-grade student, presented to meet with the school counselor during his English class. The counselor requested for Rey to receive counseling services after a teacher noted that he often refused to participate in class. Due to three consecutive cancelations to meet at a parent-teacher conference, the counselor intervened. The counselor set up some toys (train, bear, car, action figures, puppets) in a play space that might stimulate conversation. However, Rey is not drawn to the play space.

Estudio De Caso De Rey: Un Caso De Aculturación e Identidad Transnacional

Rey, un estudiante de 3er grado, se presentó para reunirse con el consejero escolar durante su clase de inglés. El consejero solicitó que Rey recibiera servicios de consejería después de que un maestro notó que a menudo se negaba a participar en clase. Debido a tres cancelaciones consecutivas para reunirse en una conferencia de padres y maestros, intervino el consejero. El consejero colocó algunos juguetes (tren, oso, automóvil, muñecos de acción, marionetas) en un espacio de juego que podría estimular la conversación. Sin embargo, Rey no se siente atraído por el espacio de juego.

Primera Sesión

COUNSELOR (CO):   *Hola Rey, I have a special place in my office that sometimes helps children talk about their feelings. ¿Quieres jugar? Would you like to play with some of my toys?*

REY (CL-R):   *Looks at the play space, but remains quiet, and looks down.*

CO: *I know you just moved to this school. Can you share with me about your family? Me gustaría platicar contigo sobre tu familia.*

Rey spoke very little in the session although he did mention that he and his mother were currently living with his aunt because his father was taken from their home and deported back to Venezuela. When asked further questions, Rey immediately shut down and refused to speak further.

Time to Reflect

- Sometimes children need some time to assess the playroom and to get to know the client. Do not be concerned if the client takes time to open up.
- Children from Latine backgrounds may also remain quiet and/or avoid contact as a sign of respect to someone older.
- It is important to have toys that are representative of your client and their lives.

Reflective Questions:

1. What are some cultural considerations you may be able to identify within this case?
2. What are some strategies that the counselor can use so that Rey can feel comfortable speaking?
3. What might the counselor try differently to help Rey feel comfortable to talk more about his experience?

Segunda Sesión:

The counselor brings Rey to her office, and she has selected some Latine children's literature (e.g., Yuyi Morales, Duncan Tonatiuh; see below for additional resources) that speaks about immigration issues to help Rey express his feelings. She asks Rey to select one of the books and after reading the book, she asks Rey to complete a genogram family tree. She set up assorted colors of construction paper, markers, colored pencils, stickers, paint, and other craft supplies so that Rey may choose his art tools. During the session, Rey shared that his dad has been living in Venezuela since he was deported a year ago. He also spoke about his new experience sharing a room with his cousin Hector, who often picked on him for being short and having a strong Venezuelan accent. Since moving away from Florida, following his dad's deportation, Rey has lived in Texas with their extended family who was of Mexican descent. Rey shared that they spoke differently from him, and they introduced him to new foods he enjoyed. He discussed the love he had for his family even when he felt out of place or missing home. Later in the session, Rey disclosed that he missed his "papi".

CO: *I'm wondering who this relative is that you drew here next to your mami. ¿Quién es esta persona?*

CL-R: *Oh, that's my papi. Trabaja en las piscas. He is a migrant worker and works very hard for me and my mami. We had a small house and my pet turtle, Jake. I miss him a lot.*

CO: *Tú quieres a tu papi y lo extrañas. He is very important to you and your mami huh?*

CL-R: *Yes, I wish we could go back to our house, but mami says that we have to wait for papi to come back home when it is safer for him. There are many people not wanting him here, mean people.*

CO: *You must be really worried for your papi.*

CL-R: *Sometimes I get scared, but I remember how strong he is and how strong my mami and me are too.*

CO: *You are a very brave, Rey. I bet your papi is really proud of you, and Jake too!*

Time to Reflect

- Utilizing books that are representative of the client's situation and family background the counselor normalizes his experience.
- Consider having books in both English and Spanish to accommodate the client's preferred language for reading.

Reflective Questions:

1. As Hector gains confianza in the counseling relationship, how might the counselor continue their work to solidify their trust and openness?
2. What are some skills the counselor utilized in this session based on the dialogue above?

Tercera Sesión:

The counselor sees Rey after a particularly difficult day in class. The teacher sent Rey's behavior chart which displays information about Rey yelling at another peer in class. The counselor decides to use play therapy to help Rey process some of the feelings he was harboring in class today. When entering the play space, Rey gravitates to the action figures on the shelf and immediately starts a conflict between two of the figures. He shares that one of the figures hurt the other figures' feelings and they were very angry. He yells that the figure should stop being a "bully" and be nicer to him, even if he doesn't have a daddy right now. The counselor continues tracking Rey through play and eventually closes the session with Rey. At the end of the session, Rey shares that he is angry with his papi for being gone and wants things to go back to "the way they were".

CO: *You are angry with your papi for not being here right now. It's hard because you miss him very much. Let's pretend that your anger was alive, that we could see it, hear it, and feel it. What do you think that anger would look like?*

CL-R: *Oh, that's easy! My anger would be a huge monster! With big green eyes and sharp teeth! *Stomps around* RAAAAWWR! ¡Soy un monstruo gigante!*

CO: *¡Si! ¡Eres enorme! ¿De qué color eres?*

CL-R: *Probably red.*

CO: *Mmm. And what about its skin?*

CL-R: *Weeeelll, probably scaly, he would feel cold if you touched him.*

CO: *Oh yeah, so he's jumbo size with a rough and cold body. He has huge green eyes and razor-sharp teeth!*

CL-R: *Yeah! And my name is Beast!*

CO: *Well, Beast, it's nice to meet you.*

CL-R: *Grrr.*

CO: *I can tell you're pretty upset, Beast, it's okay to feel angry because we all have those tough feelings sometimes.*

The counselor and Rey end the session with some discussion about Beast and when he may have shown up in his past week. Rey played through a scenario where Beast appeared and used some deep belly breaths to calm down and tell someone he trusted that he needed a break.

Time to Reflect

- By externalizing his anger, the counselor and the client can discuss the client's anger without shaming the client.

Reflective Questions:

1. Understanding more about the client's whole context, how might you move forward as the counselor? How might you include Rey's family in his treatment plan?
2. What do you see as Rey's needs? What are some resources you might need as a counselor? As a parent? As a teacher?

Cuarta Sesión:

The counselor was able to make contact with Carmen, Rey's mother, to join them for a family session. Carmen had previously shared that it had been difficult for her to make contact with Rey's teachers due to her having to work until late in the evenings. In their meeting without Rey, she shared some stressors she had such as saving money to send back to her husband and making sure she was also contributing to the household in which she and Rey were staying. Carmen expressed her gratitude for helping Rey at school and working to manage some of his overwhelming emotions. She also discussed Rey's inability to sleep, and how his nightmares woke them up at different times in the night. Carmen explained that Rey was home when her husband was taken by Immigration and Customs Enforcement (ICE), and he disclosed being scared he was next, despite her reassurance that would not happen. The counselor also gave Carmen several resources for pro bono counseling and legal services for immigrant families.

In the session, the counselor had Carmen and Rey play his favorite game, Uno. Rey assigned different rules to each of the colors, such as naming a favorite food for choosing green, sharing a time they were angry during the week for red, and acting out a silly dance for yellow. During the interaction, the counselor pointed out positive strengths in both Carmen and Rey's interaction together, such as taking turns and being a good sport when the other person was winning. They closed the session with one thing they learned about the other person and themselves. Carmen was happy to learn about Beast and how he expresses his feelings of anger safely.

CL-C: *Creo que aprendí lo valiente que es Rey y cómo continúa mejorándose. ¡También aprendí que amo a mi familia y a los chilaquiles! *Everyone laughs**

CO: *Ves todo lo bueno que Rey está haciendo en la escuela y estás muy orgulloso de él. *Carmen nods**

CL-R: *I learned that my mami is a great uno player and she loves the game as much as I do! Also, that Beast is doing his best, even when he gets mad, he tries to make it better.*

CO: *Yeah, this game is so much fun huh? We see all the effort Beast puts in and you have been so helpful in teaching him how to accept his anger in a safe way.*

CL-R: *He's a good listener and he loves chocolate! *All laugh**

Time to Reflect

- Counselors treating children and their families navigating cultural choques must recognize the impact of unique issues such as acculturation stress, family separation, and discrimination, and how these challenges present differently across Latine cultures.

• Knowledge and skill acquisition, in addition to recognizing biases within ourselves, is a lifelong practice that counselors strive for.

• As you reflect on Rey's case in future work, consider how you might approach sessions with him, including incorporating family sessions and consultations with his teachers.

Reflective Questions:

1. Rey appears to be making progress in session and the classroom, although his mother reports he is struggling at home. What are some possible factors that could be contributing to his behaviors?

2. How might you work with Rey's mother to discuss Rey's acculturation issues and the impacts of trauma while remaining cognizant of her own experiences?

Implications for Clinical Practice, Bilingual Training, and Research

This chapter discussed important socio-cultural considerations for serving the counseling needs of the Latine populations. Consideration of appropriate mental health terms and therapeutic techniques in Spanish helps facilitate a therapeutic relationship with clients. Moreover, an important piece of the counseling profession is multiculturalism and advocacy. Counselors have a responsibility to Latine clients who typically underutilize mental health services that are impacted by sociopolitical factors and unfavorable experiences. This chapter provides students with crucial knowledge on cultural and social justice issues that may negatively impact their clients' well-being or become barriers to growth. When working with children, the use of play therapy and children's literature can assist in creating a trusting environment in which the child feels comfortable to speak and share feelings.

Counselors are likely to render mental health services to the diverse Latine population, some of whom are native-born and others who are immigrants. Both groups are likely to experience micro and macro-aggressions, such as ethnic/linguistic discrimination and oppression. Several researchers suggest that the U.S. English-only movement involves racist initiatives (i.e., Baker &

Wright, 2017) that result in individuals feeling alienated or oppressed. Note-worthy, as opposed to the U.S.-born Latine population, the experience of immigrants does differ. As counselors, it is crucial to be aware of the client's emotional side effects for leaving their native country. Additionally, the client's legal status also adds to their emotional state, we must recognize the anxiety and stress experienced by the client and family members.

There is a need for future research that examines the use of counseling theories with the Latine population, with special attention to the varying eth-noracial groups. It would also be important to explore if strategies employed with one group are effective with other Latine groups. Furthermore, special issues within Latine groups such as LGBTQ+, immigrants, and disability pop-ulations should be considered. For example, counselors may assess the accept-ability and adaptability of gender-neutral terms such as "elle" within LGBTQ+ Latine groups to promote the visibility of gender-diverse people (Di Stefano et al., 2021). Research is also sparse on immigrant Latine transgender popula-tions, including intersectional experiences of oppression (Abreu et al., 2021).

Lastly, due to the complexity and diversity of the Latine experience, men-tal health counseling interventions ought to move beyond a Westernized lens. Alternative cultural paradigms such as testimonios, pláticas, and more indige-nous practices embody Latine traditions and ways of knowing (Consoli et al., 2022; Fierros & Delgado Bernal, 2016). Mental health professions ought to move beyond only cultural adaptations of therapies, assessments, and diagno-ses and include other non-traditional, non-western ways of healing.

Conclusion

In working with bilingual clients, counselors must have a clear understanding of the cultural values and practices of the group. As discussed in the previous section, sociocultural considerations also include the ethnolinguistic practices of the group, such as dichos and refranes. Incorporating oral communication tied to Latine culture has the potential to further identify values and norms created by families, improving treatment planning and goals.

For many Latine bilingual clients, mental health and well-being vary widely. Clients may benefit from a high bicultural identity integration, which may help to minimize acculturative stress (Benet-Martínez et al., 2002; Benet-Martínez & Haritatos, 2005). Latine clients may have a difficult time interweaving cultures in ways they desire. Counselors may consider ways to recenter their client's stories through acknowledgment of the complexities of the Latine experience and the ways it is impacted by historical, sociopolitical, cultural, and individual factors.

Points to Remember

- The Latine community is not a monolithic group; as an ethnoracial group, there may be some common cultural practices, but it is important to note that they represent differences and practices.
- The individual's ethnic/racial identity may be tied to their heritage cultural group. Some clients may identify themselves using a pan-ethnic identity such as Latine, but others may prefer other identity markers, such as Mexican American, Puerto Rican, Caribbean, Afro-Latino, etc. Thus, counselors allow the client to use their preferred identity label.
- Acculturation is the process of acquiring new cultural perspectives and practices within the majority or host culture.
- Latine may experience acculturative stress in which they feel marginalized from the majority/host group because of their cultural values.
- Other sources of acculturative stress can result from differing within-group cultural values. For example, the traditional gender role expectations versus the individual's gender identity.

Resources

- Anzaldúa, G. (1987). *Borderlands/La Frontera: The new mestiza.* Aunt Lute Books.
- Avila, E. & Parker, J. (2000). *Woman who glows in the dark: A curandera reveals traditional Aztec secrets of physical and spiritual health.* Tarcher.
- Carver, C. S., & Sheier, M. F. (2014). *Teorías de la personalidad* (7ma Ed.). Pearson.
- Flores, Y. (2013). *Chicana and Chicano mental health: Alma, corazón y mente.* University of Arizona.
- Gorski, P.C. and Goodman, R. D. (2015). *Decolonizing "multicultural" counseling through social justice.* Springer.

- Hernandez-Wolfe, P. (2013). *A borderlands view on Latinos, Latin Americans, and decolonization: Rethinking mental health.* Jason Aronson.
- Ibrahim, F.A. and Heuer, J.R. (2016). *Cultural and social justice: Client-specific interventions.* Springer.
- Menakem, R. (2017). *My grandmother's hands.* Central Recovery Press.
- Suarez-Orozco, C., Abo-Zena, M.M., and Marks, A.K. (2015). *Transitions: The development of children of immigrants.* New York University Press.

Children's Literature

- Flora Ada, Alma
  - *¡Sí! Somos Latinos*, Alfaguara (Madrid, E.S.P.) 2014.
  - *I love Saturdays y domingos*, (New York, N.Y.) 2004.
- Loma Garza, Carmen
  - *In My Family/En Mi Familia*, Children's Book Press (New York, N.Y.) 2000.
- Tonatiuh, Duncan
  - *Dear Primo: A Letter To My Cousin*, Abrams Books for Young Readers (New York, N.Y.) 2010.

Children's Literature on Immigration
Compiled By Claudia Treviño Garcia, Ph.D.
University of Texas at San Antonio
2021

Age Group	Title	Author
5–8	Dreamers	Yuyi Morales
	Mango Moon	Diane De Anda
	Apple Pie Fourth of July	Janet S. Wong
	La Mariposa	Francisco Jimenez
	My Diary From Here to There	Amanda Irma Perez

Age Group	Title	Author
5–8 Cont'd	Pancho Rabbit and the Coyote: A Migrant's Tale	Duncan Tonatiuh
	Tea with Milk	Allen Say
	Mango, Abuela, and Me	Meg Medina and Angela Dominguez
	Mamá the Alien	Rene Colato Lainez
	Two White Rabbits	Jairo Buitrago and Rafael Yockteng
8–12	Blue Jasmine	Kashmira Sheth
	I Lived on Butterfly Hill	Marjorie Agosin
	The Land of Forgotten Girls	Erin Entrada Kelly
	Return To Sender	Julia Alvarez
	Esperanza Rising	Pam Muñoz Ryan
	La Frontera: El Viaje con papá	Deborah Mills, Alfredo Alva, and Claudia Navarro
Middle School	Shooting Kabul	N.H. Senzai
	Einstein: The Fantastic Journey of a Mouse in Space and Time	Torben Kuhlman
	Inside Out and Back Again	Thanhha Lai
	It Ain't So Awful Falafel	Firoozeh Dimas
	Turtle of Oman	Naomi Shihab
	The Only Road	Alexandra Diaz
High School	Living Beyond Borders: Growing Up Mexican in America	Lupe Ruiz-Flores and Carolyn Dee Flores
	The Poet X	Elizabeth Acevedo
	The Astonishing Color of After	Emily X. R. Pan
	The Closest I've Come	Fred Aceves

References

Abreu, R. L., Gonzalez, K. A., Capielo Rosario, C., Lockett, G. M., Lindley, L., & Lane, S. (2021). "We are our own community": Immigrant Latinx transgender people community experiences. *Journal of Counseling Psychology*, 68(4), 390–403. https://doi.org/10.1037/cou0000546

Anzaldúa, G. (1987). *Borderlands/La Frontera: The new mestiza*. Aunt Lute Books.

Bacallao, M. L., & Smokowski, P. R. (2005). "Entre Dos Mundos" (Between Two Worlds): Bicultural skills training with Latino immigrant families. *The Journal of Primary Prevention*, 26(6), 485–509. https://doi.org/10.1007/s10935-005-0008-6

Baker, C., & Wright, W. E. (2017). *Foundations of bilingual education and bilingualism* (6th ed.). Multilingual Matters.

Barrera, Jr. M., Gonzales, N. A., Lopez, V., & Fernandez, A. C. (2004). Problem behaviors of Chicana/o and Latina/o adolescents: An analysis of prevalence, risk, and protective factors. In R. Velasquez, L. M. Arellano & B. W. McNeill (Eds.), *The handbook of Chicana/o psychology and mental health* (pp. 83–109). Erlbaum.

Bemak, F., & Chung, R. C.-Y. (2015). Critical issues in international group counseling. *Journal for Specialists in Group Work*, 40(1), 6–21. https://doi.org/10.1080/01933922.2014.992507

Benet-Martínez, V., & Haritatos, J. (2005). Bicultural identity integration (BII): Components and psychosocial antecedents. *Journal of Personality*, 73(4), 1015–1050. https://doi.org/10.1111/j.1467-6494.2005.00337.x.

Benet-Martínez, V., Leu, J., Lee, F., & Morris, M. W. (2002). Negotiating biculturalism: Cultural frame switching in biculturals with oppositional versus compatible cultural identities. *Journal of Cross-cultural Psychology*, 33(5), 492–516. https://doi.org/10.1177/0022022102033005005

Benuto, L. T. (2013). A guide to psychological assessment with Hispanics: An introduction. In L. Benuto (Ed.), *Guide to psychological assessment with Hispanics*. Springer.

Benuto, L. T., & Leany, B. (2017). Evidence-based practices for conducting therapy with Spanish-speaking clients. In L. T. Benuto (Ed.), *Therapist's guide: A toolkit for working with Spanish-speaking clients*. Springer.

Berry, J. W., Poortinga, Y. H., Segall, M. H., & Dasen, P. R. (1992). *Cross cultural psychology: Research and applications*. Cambridge University Press.

Berry, J. W. (1980). Acculturation as varieties of adaptation. In A. M. Padilla (Ed.), *Acculturation: Theory, models, and some new findings* (pp. 9–25). Westview.

Berry, J. W. (1997). Immigration, acculturation, and adaptation. *Applied Psychology: An International Review*, 46(1), 5–68. https://doi.org/10.1111/j.1464-0597.1997.tb01087.x.

Berry, J. W., Phinney, J. S., Sam, D. L., & Vedder, P. (2006). *Immigrant youth in cultural transition*. Erlbaum.

Ceballos, P., & Bratton, S. (2010). Empowering Latina/o families: Effects of a culturally responsive intervention for low-income immigrant Latina/o parents on children's behaviors and parental stress. *Psychology in the Schools*, 47(8), 761–775. https://doi.org/10.1002/pits.20502

Chan, J., Natsuaki, M. N., & Chen, C. N. (2013). The importance of family factors and generation status: Mental health service use among Latino and Asian Americans. *Cultural Diversity and Ethnic Minority Psychology, 19*(3), 236. https://doi.org/10.1037/a0032901

Chirkov, V. I., Ryan, R. M., & Willness, C. (2005). Cultural context and psychological needs in Canada and Brazil: Testing a self-determination approach to the internalization of cultural practices, identity, and well-being. *Journal of Cross-Cultural Psychology, 36*(4), 423–443. https://doi.org/10.1177/0022022105275960

Choi, N., Bern, M., Elias, D. O., McGinley, R. H., Rosenthal, M. F., & Hebets, E. A. (2019). A mismatch between signal transmission efficacy and mating success calls into question the function of complex signals. *Animal Behaviour, 158,* 77–88. https://doi.org/10.1016/j.anbehav.2019.09.017

Chung, R. C.-Y., Bemak, F., & Grabosky, T. K. (2011). Multicultural-social justice leadership strategies: Counseling and advocacy with immigrants. *Journal for Social Action in Counseling and Psychology, 3*(1), 86–102. https://doi.org/10.33043/JSACP.3.1.86-102

Clauss-Ehlers, C. S. (2004). A framework for school-based mental health promotion with bicultural Latino children: Building on strengths to promote resilience. *International Journal of Mental Health Promotion, 6*(2), 26–33. https://doi.org/10.1080/14623730.2004.9721928

Combs, G., & Freedman, J. (2012). Narrative, poststructuralism, and social justice: Current practices in narrative therapy. *The Counseling Psychologist, 40*(7), 1033–1060. https://doi.org/10.1177/0011000012460662

Consoli, A. J., López, I., & Whaling, K. M. (2022). Alternate cultural paradigms in Latinx psychology: An empirical, collaborative exploration. *Journal of Humanistic Psychology, 62*(4), 516–539. https://doi.org/10.1177/00221678211051797

Constantine, M. G., Okazaki, S., & Utsey, S. O. (2004). Self-concealment, social self-efficacy, acculturative stress, and depression in African, Asian, and Latin American international college students. *American Journal of Orthopsychiatry, 74*(3), 230–241. https://doi.org/10.1037/0002-9432.74.3.230

Corey, G. (2018). *The art of integrative counseling.* John Wiley & Sons.

Delgado-Romero, E. A., Unkefer, E. N., Capielo, C., & Crowell, C. N. (2017). El que oye consejos, llega a viejo: Examining the published life narratives of US Latino/a psychologists. *Journal of Latina/o Psychology, 5*(3), 127–141. https://doi.org/10.1037/lat0000071

Deng, S. A., & Marlowe, J. M. (2013). Refugee resettlement and parenting in a different context. *Journal of Immigrant & Refugee Studies, 11*(4), 416–430. https://doi.org/10.1080/15562948.2013.793441

Di Stefano, M., Almazán-Vázquez, A., Yepes-Amaya, W., & Britton, E. R. (2021). "Tu lucha es mi lucha": Teaching Spanish through an equity and social justice lens. *Foreign Language Annals, 54*(3), 753–775. https://doi.org/10.1111/flan.12578

Dinh, K. T., Castro, F. G., Tein, J. Y., & Kim, S. Y. (2009). Cultural predictors of physical and mental health status among Mexican American women: a mediation model. *American Journal of Community Psychology, 43*(1–2), 35–48. https://doi.org/10.1007/s10464-008-9221-9

Dreby, J. (2012). *How today's immigration enforcement policies impact children, families, and communities.* https://cdn.americanprogress.org/wp-content/uploads/2012/08/DrebyImmigrationFamiliesFINAL.pdf

Eisenberg, Marla E., & Resnick, Michael D. (2006). Suicidality among gay, lesbian and bisexual youth: The role of protective factors. *Journal of Adolescent Health*, 39(5), 662–668. https://doi.org/10.1016/j.jadohealth.2006.04.024

Espinoza-Herold, M. (2007). Stepping beyond Sí Se Puede: Dichos as a cultural resource in mother-daughter interaction in a Latino family. *Anthropology and Education Quarterly*, 38(3), 260–277. https://doi.org/10.1525/aeq.2007.38.3.260

Farrell, I. C., & Gibbons, M. M. (2019). Using narrative therapy to assist college-age Latino immigrants. *Journal of College Counseling*, 22(1), 83–96. https://doi.org/10.1002/jocc.12116

Fenn, K., & Byrne, M. (2013). The key principles of cognitive behavioral therapy. *InnovAiT: Education and Inspiration for General Practice*, 6(9), 579–585. https://doi.org/10.1177/1755738012471029

Fierros, C. O., & Delgado Bernal, D. (2016). Vamos a platicar: The contours of pláticas as Chicana/Latina feminist methodology. *Chicana/Latina Studies*, 15(2), 98–121.

Fish, J. (2008). Navigating queer street: Researching the intersections of lesbian, gay, bisexual and trans (LGBT) identities in health research. *Sociological Research Online*, 13(1), 104–115. https://doi.org/10.5153/sro.1652

Flores, B. B., Clark, E. R., Guerra. N., & Sánchez, S. (2008). Acculturation among Latino bilingual education teacher candidates: Implications for teacher preparation institutions. *Journal of Latinos and Education*, 7(4), 288–304. https://doi.org/10.1080/15348430802143550

Franklin, J. D., Smith, W. A., & Hung, M. (2014). Racial battle fatigue for Latina/o students. *Journal of Hispanic Higher Education*, 13(4), 303–322. https://doi.org/10.1177/1538192714540530

Gelman, C. (2004). Toward a better understanding of the use of psychodynamically-informed treatment with Latinos: Findings from clinician experience. *Clinical Social Work Journal*, 32(1), 61–77. https://doi.org/10.1023/B:CSOW.0000017514.64368.86

Godinez, F. E., (2006) Braiding cultural knowledge into educational practices and policies. In S. Villenas, D. D. Bernal, F. E. Godinez, & C. A. Elenes (Ed.), *Chicana/Latina education in everyday life: Feminista perspectives on pedagogy and epistemology*. Suny Press.

Gordon, M. (1964). *Assimilation in American life*. Oxford University Press.

Guo, X., Suarez-Morales, L., Schwartz, S. J., & Szapocznik, J. (2009). Some evidence for multidimensional biculturalism: Confirmatory factor analysis and measurement invariance analysis on the Bicultural Involvement Questionnaire-Short version. *Psychological Assessment*, 21(1), 22–31. https://doi.org/10.1037/a0014495.

Henry, H. M., Stiles, W. B., & Biran, M. W. (2005). Loss and mourning in immigration: Using the assimilation model to assess continuing bonds with native culture. *Counseling Psychology Quarterly*, 18(2), 109–119. https://doi.org/10.1080/09515070500136819

Hinojosa, T. J., & Carney, J. V. (2016). Mexican American women pursuing counselor education doctorates: A narrative inquiry. *Counselor Education and Supervision*, 55(3), 198–215. https://doi.org/10.1002/ceas.12045

Holleran, L. K. (2003). Mexican American youth of the Southwest borderlands: Perceptions of ethnicity, acculturation, and race. *Hispanic Journal of Behavioral Sciences*, 25(3), 352–369. https://doi.org/10.1177/0739986303256913

Interiano-Shiverdecker, C. G., Hahn, C., McKenzie, C., & Kondili, E. (2021). Refugees, discrimination, and barriers to health. *Journal of Professional Counseling: Practice, Theory & Research, 48*, 91–105. https://doi.org/10.1080/15566382.2021.1947106

Lin, Y., & Bratton, S. C. (2015). A meta-analytic review of child-centered play therapy approaches. *Journal of Counseling & Development, 93*(1), 45–58. https://doi.org/10.1002/j.1556-6676.2015.00180.x

Locke, A. F. (2017). *Latino doctoral students in counseling programs: Navigating professional identity within a predominantly White American profession.* Montclair State University.

Lonn, M. R., & Dantzler, J. Z. (2017). A practical approach to counseling refugees: Applying Maslow's hierarchy of needs. *Journal of Counselor Practice, 8*(2), 61–82. https://doi.org/10.22229/olr789150

Mathema, S. (2017). *Keeping families together: Why all Americans should care about what happens to unauthorized immigrants.* https://www.americanprogress.org/article/keeping-families-together/

Messih, M. (2016). Mental health in LGBT refugee populations. *American Journal of Psychiatry Residents' Journal, 11*(7), 5–7. https://doi.org/10.1176/appi.ajp-rj.2016.110704

Miranda, A., Bilot, J., Peluso, P., Berman, K., & Van Meek, L. (2006). Latino families: The relevance of the connection among acculturation, family dynamics, and health for family counseling research and practice. *The Family Journal: Counseling and Therapy for Couples and Families, 14*(3), 268–273. https://doi.org/10.1177/1066480706287805

Mizell, J. D. (2022). Testimonios and picturebooks: An Afro-Latino adolescent's exploration of immigration stories through the lens of LatCrit and testimonios. *Middle School Journal, 53*(1), 4–15. https://doi.org/10.1080/00940771.2021.1997533

Montejano, D. (1987). *Anglos and Mexicans in the Making of Texas, 1836–1986.* University of Texas Press.

Moraga, C., & Anzaldúa, G. (Eds.). (2015). *This bridge called my back: Writings by radical women of color* (Fourth). SUNY Press.

Morales, E. (2013). Latino lesbian, gay, bisexual, and transgender immigrants in the United States. *Journal of LGBT Issues in Counseling, 7*(2), 172–184. https://doi.org/10.1080/15538605.2013.785467

Morand, D. A. (2003). Politeness and the clash of interaction orders in cross-cultural communication. *Thunderbird International Business Review, 45*(5), 521–540. https://doi.org/10.1002/tie.10089

Moreno, O., Nelson, T., & Cardemil, E. (2017). Religiosity and attitudes towards professional mental health services: Analysing religious coping as a mediator among Mexican origin Latinas/os in the southwest United States. *Mental Health, Religion & Culture, 20*(7), 626–637. https://doi.org/10.1080/13674676.2017.1372735

Ngo, B. (2008). Beyond "culture clash" understandings of immigrant experiences. *Theory into Practice, 47*(1), 4–11. https://doi.org/10.1080/00405840701764656

Olivas, M., & Li, C. (2006). Understanding stressors for international students in higher education: What college counselors and personnel need to know. *Journal of Instructional Psychology, 33*(3), 217–222.

Organista, K. C. (2019). Cognitive behavior therapy with Latinxs. In G. Y. Iwamasa & P. A. Hays (Eds.), *Culturally responsive cognitive behavior therapy: Practice and supervision* (pp. 79–104). American Psychological Association.

Pasch, L. A., Deardorff, J., Tschann, J. M., Flores, E., Penilla, C., & Pantoja, P. (2006). Acculturation, parent-adolescent conflict, and adolescent adjustment in Mexican American families. *Family Process, 45*(1), 75–86. https://doi.org/10.1111/j.1545-5300.2006.00081.x

PEW Research Center. (2019). *Key facts about U.S. Hispanics and their diverse heritage.* https://www.pewresearch.org/fact-tank/2019/09/16/key-facts-about-u-s-hispanics/

Ray, D. C., Armstrong, S. A., Balkin, R. S., & Jayne, K. M. (2015). Child-centered play therapy in the schools: Review and meta-analysis. *Psychology in the Schools, 52*(2), 107–123. https://doi.org/10.1002/pits.21798

Redfield, R., Linton, R., & Herskovits, M. J. (1936). Memorandum for the study of acculturation. *American Anthropologist, 38*(1), 149–152. https://doi.org/10.1525/aa.1936.38.1.02a00330.

Revollo, H. W., Qureshi, A., Collazos, F., Valero, S., & Casas, M. (2011). Acculturative stress as a risk factor of depression and anxiety in the Latin American immigrant population. *International Review of Psychiatry, 23*(1), 84–92. https://doi.org/10.3109/09540261.2010.545988

Rodríguez, D. (2010). Storytelling in the field: Race, method, and the empowerment of Latina college students. *Cultural Studies? Critical Methodologies, 10*(6), 491–507. https://doi.org/10.1177/1532708610365481

Rodríguez-Arauz, G., Ramírez-Esparza, N., García-Sierra, A., Ikizer, E. G., & Fernández-Gómez, M. J. (2019). You go before me, please: Behavioral politeness and interdependent self as markers of Simpatía in Latinas. *Cultural Diversity and Ethnic Minority Psychology, 25*(3), 379–387. https://doi.org/10.1037/cdp0000232

Rogers, C. (1977). *Carl Rogers on personal power: Inner strength and its revolutionary impact.* Delacorte Press.

Rudmin, F. W. (2009). Constructs, measurements and models of acculturation and acculturative stress. *International Journal of Intercultural Relations, 33*(2), 106–123. https://doi.org/10.1016/j.ijintrel.2008.12.001.

Schwartz, S. J., Benet-Martínez, V., Knight, G. P., Unger, J. B., Zamboanga, B. L., Des Rosiers, S. E., Stephens, D. P., Huang, S., & Szapocznik, J. (2014a). Effects of language of assessment on the measurement of acculturation: Measurement equivalence and cultural frame switching. *Psychological Assessment, 26*(1), 100–114. https://doi.org/10.1037/a0034717

Schwartz, S. J., Des Rosiers, S., Huang, S., Zamboanga, B. L., Unger, J. B., Knight, G., . . . Szapocznik, J. (2013). Developmental trajectories of acculturation in Hispanic adolescents: Association with family functioning and adolescent risk behavior. *Journal of Child Development, 84*(4), 1355–1372. https://doi.org/10.1111/cdev.12047.

Schwartz, S. J., Montgomery, M. J., & Briones, E. (2006a). The role of identity in acculturation among immigrant people: Theoretical propositions, empirical questions, and applied recommendations. *Human Development, 49*(1), 1–30. https://doi.org/10.1159/000090300

Schwartz, S. J., Pantin, H., Sullivan, S., Prado, G., & Szapocznik, J. (2006b). Nativity and years in the receiving culture as markers of acculturation in ethnic enclaves. *Journal of Cross-Cultural Psychology, 37*(3), 345–353. https://doi.org/10.1177/0022022106286928

Schwartz, S. J., Unger, J. B., Des Rosiers, S. E., Lorenzo-Blanco, E. I., Zamboanga, B., Huang, S., . . . Szapocznik, J. (2014b). Domains of acculturation and their effects on substance use and sexual behaviors in recent Hispanic immigrant adolescents. *Society for Prevention Research, 15*(3), 385–396. https://doi.org/10.1007/s11121-013-0419

Schwartz, S. J., Unger, J. B., Zamboanga, B. L., Córdova, D., Mason, C. A., Huang, S., . . . & Szapocznik, J. (2015). Developmental trajectories of acculturation: Links with family functioning and mental health in recent-immigrant Hispanic adolescents. *Child Development, 86*(3), 726–748. https://doi.org/10.1111/cdev.12341

Schwartz, S. J., Unger, J., Zamboanga, B., & Szapocznik, J. (2010). Rethinking the concept of acculturation: Implications for theory and research. *American Psychologist, 65*(4), 237–251. https://doi.org/10.1037/a0019330

Schwartz, S. J., Zamboanga, B. L., & Jarvis, L.H. (2007). Ethnic identity and acculturation in Hispanic early adolescents: Mediated relationships to academic grades, prosocial behavior, and externalizing symptoms. *Cultural Diversity and Ethnic Minority Psychology, 13*(4), 364–373. http://dx.doi.org/10.1037/1099-9809.13.4.364

Sharf, R. S., & Sharf, R. S. (2012). *Theories of psychotherapy and counseling, concepts and cases, fifth edition, Richard S. Sharf: Student manual.* Brooks/Cole.

Singh, A. A., Appling, B., & Trepal, H. (2020). Using the multicultural and social justice counseling competencies to decolonize counseling practice: The important roles of theory, power, and action. *Journal of Counseling & Development, 98*(3), 261–271. https://doi.org/10.1002/jcad.12321

Solorzano, D. G., & Yosso, T. J. (2001). Critical race and LatCrit theory and method: Counter-storytelling. *International Journal of Qualitative Studies in Education, 14*(4), 471–495. https://doi.org/10.1080/09518390110063365

Sommers-Flanagan, J., & Sommers-Flanagan, R. (2018). *Counseling and psychotherapy theories in context and practice: Skills, strategies, and techniques.* John Wiley & Sons.

Sondel, B., Baggett, H. C., & Dunn, A. H. (2018). "For millions of people, this is real trauma": A pedagogy of political trauma in the wake of the 2016 US Presidential election. *Teaching and Teacher Education, 70*, 175–185. https://doi.org/10.1016/j.tate.2017.11.017

Sue, D. W., Sue, D., Neville, H. A., & Smith, L. (2022). *Counseling the culturally diverse: Theory and practice.* John Wiley & Sons.

Swan, A., & Ceballos, P. (2020). Person-centered conceptualization of multiculturalism and social justice in counseling. *Person-Centered & Experiential Psychotherapies, 19*(2), 154–167. https://doi.org/10.1080/14779757.2020.1717981

Szapocznik, J., Kurtines, W., & Fernández, T. (1980). Bicultural involvement and adjustment in Hispanic-American youths. *International Journal of Intercultural Relations, 4*(3–4), 353–365. https://doi.org/10.1016/0147-1767(80)90010-3

Taylor, B. A., Gambourg, M. B., Rivera, M., & Laureano, D. (2006). Constructing cultural competence: Perspectives of family therapists working with Latino families. *The American Journal of Family Therapy, 34*(5), 429–445. https://doi.org/10.1080/01926180600553779

Tello, A. M., & Lonn, M. R. (2017). The role of high school and college counselors in supporting the psychosocial and emotional needs of Latinx first-generation college students. *Professional Counselor, 7*(4), 349–359. https://doi.org/10.15241/AMT.7.4.349

Torres, L., Driscoll, M. W., Voell, M. (2012). Discrimination, acculturation, acculturative stress, and Latino psychological distress: A moderated mediational model. *Cultural Diversity and Ethnic Minority Psychology, 18*(1), 17–25. https://doi.org/10.1037/a0026710

Triandis, H. C., Marin, G., Lisansky, J., & Betancourt, H. (1984). Simpatía as a cultural script of Hispanics. *Journal of Personality and Social Psychology, 47*(6), 1363. https://doi.org/10.1037/0022-3514.47.6.1363

Trueba, H. T. (2002). Multiple ethnic, racial, and cultural identities in action: From marginality to a new cultural capital in modern society. *Journal of Latinos and Education, 1*(1), 7–28. https://doi.org/10.1207/S1532771XJLE0101_2

US Department of Health and Human Services. (2011). *Rainbow Welcome Initiative: An assessment and recommendations report on LGBT refugee resettlement in the United States.* https://rainbowwelcome.org/uploads/pdfs/ORR%20Report%20MASTER%20COPY_01.2012.pdf

U.S. Department of Homeland Security. (2019). *Estimates of the Unauthorized Immigrant Population Residing in the United States: January 2015–January 2018.* https://www.dhs.gov/sites/default/files/publications/immigration-statistics/Pop_Estimate/UnauthImmigrant/unauthorized_immigrant_population_estimates_2015_-_2018.pdf

Wang, S. C., Schwartz, S. J., & Zamboanga, B. L. (2010). Acculturative stress among Cuban American college students: Exploring the mediating pathways between acculturation and psychosocial functioning. *Journal of Applied Social Psychology, 40*(11), 2862–2887. https://doi.org/10.1111/j.1559-1816.2010.00684.x.

Yeh, C. J., & Inose, M. (2003). International students' reported English fluency, social support satisfaction, and social connectedness as predictors of acculturative stress. *Counseling Psychology Quarterly, 16*(1), 15–28. http://dx.doi.org/10.1080/0951507031000114058.

Zvolensky, M. J., Jardin, C., Garey, L., Robles, Z., & Sharp, C. (2016). Acculturative stress and experiential avoidance: Relations to depression, suicide, and anxiety symptoms among minority college students. *Cognitive Behaviour Therapy, 45*(6), 501–517. https://doi.org/10.1080/16506073.2016.1205658

· 4 ·

BILINGUAL SUPERVISION
FOR DEVELOPING AND GUIDING
CULTURALLY EFFICACIOUS COUNSELORS

In this chapter, we discuss one of the most important aspects of bilingual train-ing: supervision. Supervised clinical practice is a requirement for adequate training and ethical practice in counseling programs. Existing professional mandates assert that supervisors must attend to multicultural issues, including language and cultural competence. The American Counseling Association's (ACA, 2014) *Code of Ethics* clearly states the need for counselors and super-visors to attend to multicultural issues in both counseling and supervision. According to sections A.2.c. and E.8., counselors should accommodate clients' language preferences to maintain cultural sensitivity, ensure comprehension, and account for client diversity in areas such as assessment and informed con-sent. While the ACA's *Code of Ethics* mentions the importance of counselors attending to the language preferences of clients, bilingual counselors typically receive supervision in English, despite the language used in session (Gallardo et al., 2014; Trepal et al., 2019). In these instances, bilingual counselors trans-late their work with Spanish-speaking clients into English, creating a poten-tial ethical issue as the supervisor entrusts the supervisee with the adequate translation of the session. Bilingual counselors also report many difficulties and frustrations as training programs are unable to meet their specific needs, leaving them feeling incompetent (Castaño et al., 2007; Johal, 2017; Ivers &

Villalba, 2015) or isolated and stressed while providing services in another language (Trepal et al., 2014,2019; Verdinelli & Biever, 2009b). Scholars (Interiano-Shiverdecker et al., 2021; McCaffrey & Moody, 2015) recommended supervision and in-vivo experiences in practicum and internship as opportunities for counselors-in-training to apply cultural and language competency, integrate culturally specific techniques, engage in case conceptualizations, and learn through other experiential activities. To supplement these opportunities practicum and internship sites that both work with Spanish-speaking clients and have bilingual supervisors are critical elements for this component of bilingual training.

Social Justice Theoretical Framework

Schwartz et al. (2010) stated, "the idea that an intern should simply be able to translate sessions into English for the purpose of supervision reflects an ethnocentric view" (p. 212). Schwartz et al. (2010) imply that ethnocentric mentality inhibits the growth of supervisors' multicultural awareness. Aside from this, translating a counseling session from Spanish to English requires certain skills and language mastery. Consequently, the supervisor may fully trust the beginner bilingual supervisee to counsel in a language unknown to the supervisor, and covertly assign the supervisee as the expert in translating and counseling in Spanish. We believe that bilingual supervision not only attends to ethical conduct in supervision but also advocates for the end of ethnocentric views in counselor training and supervision. Following social justice recommendations, bilingual supervision seeks to produce conditions that allow for equal access and opportunity for bilingual counselors, reduce or eliminate disparities in education and resources, and encourage supervisors and supervisees to consider micro, meso, and macro levels in the assessment, diagnosis, and treatment of clients and client systems.

Bilingual Supervision in Counselor Education

Researchers have stressed the need for more bilingual counselors to serve the growing Spanish-speaking, Latine population (Biever et al., 2002, 2011; Delgado-Romero et al., 2018; Santiago-Rivera et al., 2009). Despite the demand for developing bilingual counselors, limited research guides bilingual counselor training and supervision (Seto & Forth, 2020). Students who do not receive adequate training may struggle with their perceptions of self-efficacy (Alvarado et al., 2019; Martinez-Smith, 2018), deficient supervision (González et al., 2015), and educating supervisors on Latine experiences (Verdinelli & Biever, 2009b). Conversely, benefits of training and supervision included strong bonds with bilingual supervisors (González et al., 2015), pride in serving their community (Lopez & Torres-Fernandez, 2019), enhanced resourcefulness, and advocacy skills (Interiano-Shiverdecker et al., 2023; Verdinelli & Biever, 2009a).

Bernard and Goodyear (2018) described supervision as "an intervention provided by a more senior member of a profession to a more junior member or members of that same profession" (p. 7). They elaborated that the three primary elements of this relationship are: (a) its evaluative and hierarchical nature; (b) its extension over time; and (c) its simultaneous purpose of enhancing the professional functioning of the more junior person, monitoring the quality of professional services, and serving as a gatekeeper for those who are to enter the profession. Supervisors serve as teachers, consultants, coaches, and mentors. As *teachers*, they assist in the development of counseling knowledge and skills by identifying learning needs and transmitting knowledge for practical use and professional growth. Bernard and Goodyear (2018) incorporated the supervisory *consulting role* to monitor performance, provide oversight of counselor work to achieve mutually agreed-upon goals, and professional gatekeeping for the organization and discipline. As a *coach*, supervisors provide morale-building, assess strengths and needs, suggest varying clinical approaches, model, cheer-lead, and prevent burnout. For entry-level counselors, the supportive function is critical. Finally, the experienced supervisor serves as a *mentor* to teach the supervisee through role modeling, facilitate the counselor's overall professional development and sense of professional identity, and train the next generation of supervisors.

In bilingual supervision, supervisors must protect client welfare, promote trainee skill development, create an effective supervisory alliance, and simultaneously attend to the impact of culture and language in counseling and supervision (Fuertes, 2004; González et al., 2015). Additional components of bilingual supervision include (a) differences in background, acculturation, or sociocultural realities between counselor and client (González et al., 2015); (b) language switching in session; and (c) conveying complex emotional concepts in another language that may not always directly translate (McCaffrey & Moody, 2015). In our experiences of bilingual supervision, we have also noticed the importance of speaking to racial identity development between supervisors, counselors, and clients. It is for this reason that we present several important areas of bilingual supervision to guide bilingual counselors through-out their supervision journey.

Ethics

An ethical dilemma arises as ethical codes call for counselors to practice within their training experience (ACA, 2014, C.2.a & F.7.b) while also nudging them to expand their services to reach underserved populations. According to the ACA (2014) *Code of Ethics*, a lack of training resources and a low supply of services raise potential ethical concerns. We discuss several ACA codes and assist with how to address each one of them.

- *Section A. Roles and Relationships at Individual, Group, Institutional, and Societal Levels* under *A.7.a Advocacy*, stated that it is the counselor's responsibility to advocate "when appropriate" to address potential or existing barriers, impacting access or growth of clients, at an individual, group, institutional, and societal levels. At an individual level, bilin-gual counselors may have to advocate for not only services in Spanish but also make sure that all documentation is offered in both languages. Clinical sites may lack informed consent, intake forms, or other assess-ments in Spanish. In Chapter 2 we provide several examples for each of these documents to help bilingual counselors create their own to fit the site in which they are working. Bilingual counselors should advo-cate against the use of any documentation in English when clients pre-fer Spanish or have limited English proficiency. This may impede their ability to provide informed consent or provide accurate information during intake or assessments. As previously stated in Chapter 2, pro-viding all services in the client's preferred language may also increase rapport building between the counselor and client. Counselors should consult with professional translators to ensure accuracy during this pro-cess. With language considerations, we also encourage bilingual coun-selors to consult with counselors, psychologists, or other mental health professionals in Spanish-speaking countries that may have accurate translations for some mental health terms or concepts. Although the responsibility of translation may fall on the counselor, we also strongly believe that this responsibility should not fall on bilingual counselors, as they have not been trained as translators. Agencies and organizations should consider hiring professional translators for this task.

- Section C. *Professional Responsibility* provided guidelines for professional responsibility: (a) *C.2.a Boundaries of Competence* in which counselors should *only* practice within their professional competence level; (b) *C.2.b. New Specialty Areas of Practice* where counselors only exercise new areas of specialty after "appropriate education, training, and supervised experience" (ACA, 2014, p. 8); (c) *C.2.c Qualified for Employment* in which counselors should accept a position only if they are qualified; (d) *C.2.d Monitor Effectiveness* and the importance of constant evaluation of counselors' performance; (e) *C.2.e. Consultation on Ethical Obligations* expect counselors to engage in consultation with other counselors; and (f) *C.2.f Continuing Education* as a way to maintain competence in the professional field. As we have discussed throughout this book only 10 CACREP-accredited counseling programs offer specialized training for bilingual counseling to both clinical mental health and school counselors. Therefore, many bilingual counselors find themselves offering services in Spanish without training or supervision. Providing services in Spanish is a way to advocate for quality and access to services. However, it is important to assess your level of comfortability and proficiency in Spanish. Bilingual counselors should not categorize themselves as "bilingual" when their proficiency level is minimal. Instead, share with clients an honest description of your Spanish proficiency, such as "I understand Spanish well, but I am not as proficient when speaking it". More proficient Spanish speakers may still have to clarify their level of proficiency to clients. For example, "Crecí hablando en español con mi abuela y mi mamá, pero a veces me cuesta la gramática en español", "Te hablo en español, pero a veces se me olvidan ciertas palabras y pueda que tenga que pensar o buscar la traducción". Bilingual counselors are also encouraged to consult with more experienced bilingual counselors regarding any ethical issues around the topic of competence.

Perry (2016) also found that non-Latine clinical supervisors of bilingual counselors can struggle to understand the lived experiences of Latine Spanish-speaking clients. For example, clinical supervisors with little cultural competence can experience difficulties in grasping the impact of immigration status on clients' lives. Beyond immigration status, supervisors with limited cultural competence and knowledge of Latine clients can fail to interpret presenting problems, such as ataque de nervios, in a culturally appropriate manner. Supervisors should recognize that ataque de nervios is a nonpathological, culturally bound cluster of symptoms commonly occurring in response to a stressful event (American Psychiatric Association [APA], 2013).

Counselor Self-Efficacy

Counselor self-efficacy is described as a clinician's beliefs about their ability to effectively counsel clients and perform counseling-related behaviors (Larson et al., 1992). Counselor self-efficacy is positively associated with perceived problem-solving effectiveness, higher therapy outcome expectancies, and career satisfaction (Kozina et al., 2010). Cristina Martinez-Smith, now Cristina Thornell, is one of the authors of this book and her dissertation (2018) focused on this particular area among bilingual counselors-in-training based on numerous reports that bilingual counselors experienced low counselor self-efficacy. Throughout her qualitative study, she presented the stories of several students throughout their bilingual counseling training. Many of them struggled with the shifting from Spanish to English and vice versa, while also remaining present with the client. At times, some felt overwhelmed, overthinking things to the extent that they at times missed half of what was being said. One of the participants, Ofelia, shared her first experience counseling in Spanish.

> I remember just feeling nervous before I went in to sit with them. I had a little bit of difficulty reading confidentiality to them in Spanish. Just because I was not used to that language but then I had to remind myself like, they are going to share their story like anybody else. And just remembering the importance of listening and being present with that client and then remembering my skills and translating that to Spanish in the aspect of listening, reflecting feeling, and kind of summarizing. Like those translated to Spanish. So that is kind of how I took it from there, I just took it session by session . . . The language I was concerned [about], I was concerned that they would view me as unprepared . . . not as professional if I stumbled with a word because I could not think of something. If I did not know how to translate that in session, then I believed that they would view me [as] less competent to be working with them. (p. 50)

One of the main reasons why many bilingual counselors experience low counselor self-efficacy is because of the lack of opportunity to practice in Spanish before working with real clients. Scholars suggest that acquiring and communicating clinical terminology in Spanish is not only one of the biggest challenges for bilingual counselors but also one of the main reasons they may experience low self-efficacy when providing services in Spanish. As discussed throughout Chapter 2, even fluent bilingual counselors may struggle to provide services in Spanish without an understanding of how to translate concepts ingrained within our profession. Martinez-Smith (2018) shared how bilingual counselors-in-training, even those who felt very fluent in Spanish, experienced many challenges. Ofelia did not know how to translate "different interventions with Spanish speakers or even some of the terminology that we use as counselors" (Martinez-Smith, 2018. p. 51). Terry, another bilingual counselor-in-training, shared that providing services in Spanish required so much more work because he was learning new clinical terminology in Spanish,

> I was already super nervous in English, like, I mean, I remember sweating through my cardigan and everything, and then it was just like, that was just English, and I think I had, like, one or two sessions before that. So, I had two sessions in English, and then my third session that day was in Spanish, and I was just like, "ok." Everything I just did in Spanish, it just felt overwhelming, like it just felt like I had so much more to do. And so, I was, like, trying to talk to people, like, giving them support. Like, asking questions, like, I was, like, "hey does this sound right if I say it this way?" "Yes. Oh, that is fine." Or "maybe do not use that word because it sounds too technical" (Martinez-Smith, 2018. p. 58).

If you agree with Terry's point that providing services in Spanish requires additional work, you are right! Bilingual supervisees do not readily fit into traditional counseling and supervision paradigms (Perry, 2016; Trepal et al., 2014; Verdinelli & Biever, 2009b). Bilingual supervisees often find themselves burdened by professional responsibilities beyond their traditional counterparts (Trepal et al., 2014). For example, bilingual students find themselves, at times, educating colleagues or even supervisors about the Latine community. The role of the educator is particularly difficult for counselors-in-training since it is not aligned with the role of the student (Verdinelli & Biever, 2009b). This role inversion may alienate students from peers and supervisors, upset cultural norms associated with authority figures, and create dissonance for the student (Perry, 2016).

Moreover, most bilingual counselors do not possess formal training as interpreters, yet many report serving as interpreters, and are therefore perceived as such by their colleagues (Verdinelli & Biever, 2009b). Such dual roles create an ethical conundrum for bilingual counselors. Interpreting for clients, co-counselors, and supervisors is an added responsibility, leaving bilingual supervisees with the burden of performing additional work beyond counseling (Verdinelli & Biever, 2009b).

Finally, providing services in Spanish requires an instant translation from one language to another, while remaining attuned to the client, integrating multicultural considerations, and attending to other counseling aspects (i.e., assessment, diagnosis, treatment planning). It is for this reason that we recommend as many in-vivo practices as possible throughout a bilingual counselor's training. Providing in-vivo practice in clinical courses such as Counseling Skills, Practicum, and Internship could provide a space for bilingual students to engage with each other through supervision, case conceptualizations, case presentations, observations, feedback, and clinical practice. This can allow growth in personal and professional awareness, and vicarious learning regarding culture-specific concerns, translations, techniques, skills, language incongruences, and cultural nuances of Spanish-speaking populations.

Throughout this book, we also provide numerous translations of clinical terminology that can help build your clinical vocabulary in Spanish. However, we recognize that our discussion is not extensive and may therefore require additional research from bilingual counselors. We recommend searching among Spanish psychology books for clinical terminology rather than a Google search, since the latter may not represent an accurate translation.

At the same time, recognize that certain words/concepts may simply not translate from one language to the other without losing their essence or accurate meaning. In Martinez-Smith (2018), Sergio, another bilingual counselor-in-training, provided a suggestion when struggling to translate his words in counseling "cuando no encuentro la palabra adecuada . . .. nada más trato de explicarme trato de visualizar mi emoción darle una imagen y tratar de describir esa imagen con las palabras que tengo en mi cerebro del otro idioma" (p. 78). Think of using creative ways to translate the meaning of the concept or term. For example, the word self-care may not easily translate to Spanish since "auto cuidarse" o "cuidado personal" does not carry the same meaning. However, we can translate the meaning with metaphors. For example, a "full cup" o "una copa llena" can represent an energized individual, while a "drained cup" o "una copa vacía" may represent burnout or exhaustion.

It is also important to mention that regardless of our limitations, providing services in Spanish is a form of advocacy. Sonia, another bilingual counselor-in-training introduced in Martinez-Smith's dissertation (2018), described how her ability to speak Spanish served as a form of advocacy for Spanish-speaking clients and thus boosted her confidence to provide services in Spanish. She shared,

Tomé la decisión en aceptar gente en español, pues primero porque hablo el español, y segundo pues, viví yo varios años en México, aunque no nací en México, viví allá diez años. En ese caso me sentí con algo como— no obligación, pero si como mi deber; aunque iba ser más trabajo para mí, me sentí mal. Vi el señor en la sala de espera y dije si necesita la ayuda y si no acepto a verlo le van a pedir que espere al siguiente semestre. Esos fueron los motivos por los cuales me animé a regresar con clientes en español . . . La niña que aconsejé [primer cliente en español] . . . le encantaba el aspecto de que podía ella utilizar español o inglés, lo que ella se sintiera más cómoda. La mamá de ella y el papá estaban súper contentos conmigo, se sintieron mal cuando tuve que terminar, hasta me dijeron: "Oh, si ya estás terminando, ¿dónde vas a poner tu práctica y te la llevamos para allá?" . . . Entonces, los papás se sentían muy cómodos. El poder sentarse y hablar con alguien que entendía de dónde venían, el hecho de que son también inmigrantes. (p. 76)

Similarly, Tamara realized that her ability to speak Spanish facilitated a connection with the client thus reducing her anxiety when translating,

I think that just as sessions went by, I got used to it. I learned more from myself after the session that we were having. I was able to, you know, all of my clients spoke a different Spanish, so as I got to know them, I got to know how they, what word they were using [and] what those words meant for them. And I think with that, we also just got more comfortable with each other to where I was not too much in my head about, "oh my God am I translating this right?" because at this point, they knew, they knew that my Spanish was different. They knew that if they did not understand something that I said that they would ask me for clarification and vice versa. If they said something that I did not understand I would ask them for clarification. It was just building that relationship that really helped me overcome the fear of translating things in my head. (Martinez-Smith, 2018, p. 54)

These stories highlight that although many bilingual counselors may experience low counselor self-efficacy due to limited training in Spanish and the additional work required to translate the work from one language to another, their services are crucial to developing mental health services for the Latine community.

Supervisor-Supervisee-Client Relationship and Identity

Striking similarities exist between the process of counseling and clinical supervision. Perhaps the most pronounced of these is the centrality and role of the interpersonal relationship. Just as a positive and productive relationship is critical to successful counseling, so too is a positive and productive relationship critical to successful supervision (Bernard & Goodyear, 2018; Ramos-Sánchez et al., 2002). Understanding relationship variables that affect the supervisory and client relationship is of utmost importance in all forms of supervision, including bilingual supervision. The influence of cultural factors on the supervision relationship has always received sustained attention. Killian (2001) stated that

> Since we all inhabit various social locations on ecosystemic axes of race, gender, class, and culture, to name but a few, and these locations intersect in unique and sometimes contradictory ways, we are all multicultural and our interactions with others must necessarily be so as well (p. 63).

Social justice literature underscores the fact that the helping professions are sociopolitical in nature (Goodman et al., 2004; Ibrahim & Heuer, 2016; Sue et al., 2019). By ignoring cultural differences, the dominant culture neglects much injustice done to non-dominant cultures. Supervision is vulnerable to reflecting dominant cultural norms and ignoring the enormous and evasive effects of power and privilege. All supervision is not only cultural but also political. Because supervisors have positions of power, they, by definition, weigh in on one side or the other of the many cultural struggles that define one's place in society.

Supervision of bilingual counselors, whether provided in English or Spanish, by a White or non-White supervisor, adheres to these dynamics. When receiving supervision from non-Spanish and/or non-Latine supervisors, many bilingual counselors encounter numerous challenges. At times, they describe being perceived as a translator, not a valued professional counselor (Perry, 2016). Bilingual supervisees also report feelings of frustration when their supervisors are unable to speak or read Spanish and lack cultural competence (Perry, 2016). Bilingual counselors may find themselves having to educate colleagues and/or supervisors about the Latine culture. Moreover, this supervision dynamic creates some practical problems, such as not being able to review tapes or progress notes without translation (Perry, 2016; Verdinelli & Biever, 2009a).

Therefore, most bilingual counselors prefer to receive supervision in Spanish. Although we have wholeheartedly supported this concept throughout this book, we recognize that this dynamic also brings its own set of factors. To believe that the supervisor, supervisee, and client all share the same life experience because they are Spanish-speaking Latine, would be erroneous. As we discussed in Chapter 3, as a group the Latine community defies simplistic categorization, and does not easily fit into the models of race and identity that have historically prevailed in the United States. The concept of race is particularly challenging when applied to Latine in the United States, who, according to the Census, "can be of any race." These patterns vary depending on national origin, state of residence, and a variety of other demographic characteristics. For many Latine, their identity as such incorporates racial elements, while for many others, race is a different type of identity not addressed by their identification as Latine, Latinx, Latino/a, or Hispanic. Even the term "Latinx" brings considerable discussion for although many prefer its non-binary characteristics, a large number may struggle to identify with this term.

Therefore, even within bilingual supervision, it is important to consider and assess differences in identity development. Ferdman and Gallegos (2001) *Latino* identity development discuss (a) how *Latino* is used as an umbrella term to identify similar-looking cultural groups and people of mixed heritage and (b) suggest Latinos develop orientations or lenses based on experiences with social institutions including the family, education system, peer groups, and U.S. cultural racial constructs. These lenses are included in Table 4.1 and include:

(a) *Latino Integrated,* understanding of racial constructs and ability to challenge them,
(b) *Latino Identified,* acceptance of the races Latino and White, and identification with Latino,
(c) *Subgroup Identified,* identification of multiple Latino races and identification with a regional subgroup,
(d) *Latino as Other,* identification as a generic Latino due to mixed heritage,
(e) *Undifferentiated,* color blindness, adherence to the dominant culture, and tendency to attribute failure to the individual rather than racial constructs, and
(f) *White Identified,* acceptance of White and Latino races, and identification with White and rejection of Latino.

It is important to understand that although identity development models help us understand a person's journey and how it may differentiate or resemble another person's identity development, they are to be considered guidelines. Identity development is not linear, and a person may find themselves experiencing symptoms of different identity development levels at once.

We invite you to take some time to evaluate your identity development as part of the Latine community. What has your journey been like? Where are you now? Where would you like to be? How do you differentiate yourself from other people in your life?

Table 4.1: Latinos and Racial Identity Development

Orientation	Lens	Identify As/Prefer	Latinos are Seen	Whites Are Seen	Framing of Race
Latino-integrated	Wide	Individuals in a group context	Positively	Complex	Dynamic, contextual, socially constructed
Latino-Identified (Racial/Raza)	Broad	Latinos	Very positively	Distinct; could be barriers or allies	Latino/not Latino
Subgroup-Identified	Narrow	Own Subgroup	My group is OK, others maybe	Not central (could be barriers or blockers)	Not clear or central; secondary to nationality, ethnicity, culture
Latinos as Other	External	Not White	Generically, fuzzily	Negatively	White/not White
Undifferentiated/ Denial	Closed	People	"Who are Latinos?"	Supposed color-blind (accept dominant norms)	Denial, irrelevant, invisible
White-Identified	Tinted	Whites	Negatively	Very positively	White/Black, either/or, one-drop or "mejorar la raza"

Throughout bilingual counseling and supervision, you will also notice differences between yourself, your clients, their family members, your colleagues, and your supervisors. Counselors should evaluate how identity development impacts the counseling relationship as well as the supervision relationship. Martinez-Smith (2018) shared how Fatima, a bilingual counselor-in-training, felt a strong calling to provide counseling services in Spanish to help clients feel proud of their language. She shared,

> I realized a lot of people, like, second-generation, Mexicans that have shame in speaking Spanish. It is kind of like denying my roots, and I really did not want that for me, like, I wanted to [speak Spanish] because I know my family, and I, we came from Mexico and when we first got here many years ago, we did not know any English. And anybody who would help us, we really appreciated that. So, it made me, like, you know, this is a profession where you want to help people, and so why not help them [and] also [provide help] for those who do not speak English. (p. 64)

Based on this excerpt we could say that Fatima is Latino-identified. She is proud of her heritage and her language. How could her identity impact her relationship with clients both positively and negatively? How could her identity impact her experiences in supervision with either a Spanish-speaking supervisor or an English-speaking supervisor?

Resources for Bilingual Supervision

The use of transcripciones (transcripts), conceptualizaciones de caso (case conceptualizations), planes de tratamiento (treatment plans) is regarded by many to be core clinical tools for training of clinical mental health and school counselors (Kendjelic & Eells, 2007; Sheperis & Sheperis, 2015).

Trascripciones

Las transcripciones y grabaciones de audio (audio recordings) provide an opportunity for supervisors to obtain direct access to the work of supervisees and for supervisors to provide feedback on strengths and areas of concern (Sheperis & Sheperis, 2015). Bernard & Goodyear (2018) also emphasized that digitally recording counseling sessions has many advantages, including the ability to see and/or hear the complexity of the interaction between counselor and client, and the ability to notice congruency between verbal and nonverbal communication. Another advantage listed by Bernard and Goodyear is that counselors can see or hear themselves in the role of the helper. Transcripts are oftentimes a tool used to accompany audio and/or digital recordings of a counseling session, especially for novice counselors (Arthur & Gfoerer, 2002). They mentioned that the advantages of transcribing the sessions were the ability to review the whole counseling session rather than just a snapshot of it, and the review gave concrete examples of what the supervisees needed to work on as well as a visual or audio reminder of the sessions. Therefore, we suggest that bilingual supervision should include at least one audio recording accompanied by transcriptions. These can be produced in Spanish when the supervisor speaks Spanish. We recommend that for English-speaking supervisors, counselors consider including a video recording, if possible, and a transcription in English. For a transcription in Spanish, we provide the following guidelines and template in Figure 4.1.

Figure 4.1: Direcciones Para la Selección y Formato de Transcripción

---

Las transcripciones deben ser 20 minutos consecutivos de interacción entre el consejero/a/e y el cliente. Elija una sección que incluya un mínimo de 10 respuestas del consejero. Las respuestas como sí, hmm, de acuerdo, etc., no cuentan como una respuesta de consejero; una respuesta contada del consejero debe ser más sustancial. (Nota: Debe tener un mínimo de 10 respuestas sustanciales del consejero, pero no evalúe sólo 10, debe evaluar TODAS las respuestas sustantivas del consejero.)

*La sección transcrita de 20 minutos de la grabación de audio/video, incluirá TODAS las respuestas del consejero y del cliente, debe ser literal y consecutiva en secuencia de tiempo. NO PUEDE utilizar un servicio de transcripción debido a la confidencialidad del cliente. Recomendamos que envié su grabación de audio y transcripción a su supervisor.

Instrucción:

1. Incluya **el seudónimo del cliente, la edad, el sexo, la fecha, el número de sesión, el modelo teórico y las técnicas empleadas.** Comience con la declaración del cliente y luego siga con su respuesta (consejero estudiantil).

2. Siga estos criterios para la evaluación de todas las respuestas de los consejeros (excepto los mínimos):

(a) Identifique la habilidad demostrada en la respuesta del consejero (por ejemplo, pregunta abierta, reflexión de emociones).
(b) Indique la intención de su respuesta.
(c) Evalúe la eficacia de la respuesta en función de su intención.

Figure 4.1: *Continued*

(d) Identifique una respuesta alternativa que podría haber sido más útil. SIEMPRE proporcione una respuesta alternativa. Por lo general, las respuestas identifican los sentimientos, pensamientos y/o comportamientos del cliente, y están basados en teoría. Busque maneras en las que podría haber reflejado mejor los sentimientos, pensamientos o comportamientos del cliente. También busque maneras de hacer más preguntas abiertas o reflexiones en vez de preguntas cerradas. Tenga en cuenta cuántas preguntas está haciendo sin incluir reflexiones de sentimiento y contenido. Incluso si cree que su respuesta original fue adecuada, obligue a identificar otras alternativas. Identifique la habilidad de su respuesta alternativa como en el paso anterior (a). Las habilidades no se limitan a las habilidades básicas y pueden incluir habilidades avanzadas o basadas en teoría.

La siguiente es una muestra de una transcripción.
Seudónimo del cliente, edad, sexo, fecha de sesión, número de sesión, modelo teórico y técnicas empleadas.

Respuesta de consejería	Habilidad demostrada (a) e Intención Teórica (b)	Crítica c) y Respuesta Alternativa (d)
¿Cuáles son sus razones para venir hoy?	(a) Pregunta abierta. (b) Invitar al cliente a profundizar en el problema.	(c) Creo que esta habilidad fue eficaz para ayudar al cliente a abrirse más sobre sus preocupaciones. d) "Pareces ansioso y aliviado por venir hoy" Reflexión de Sentimientos
Cliente: Desde el funeral del abuelo, no puedo dejar de llorar. Sabía que iba a morir, pero no esperaba que me golpeara tan fuerte.		
Te sientes herido.	Reflexión del Sentimiento. -mostrar que estoy escuchando y conectando con el cliente y validar sentimientos.	Creo que un reflejo del sentimiento era apropiado, pero podría haber usado palabras de sentimiento más descriptivas e incluir un reflejo del significado "Trataste de prepararte, pero ahora te sientes abrumado por la tristeza y el dolor porque tu abuelo era una parte tan importante de tu vida". Reflexión del significado

---

Conceptualización de Caso

Eels (2022) defined case conceptualizations, o conceptualizaciones de caso, as a way of viewing the origin of, etiology of, and conditions that sustain a client's presenting problem. Conceptualizaciones de caso have numerous benefits including, (a) making numerous and complex problems more manageable helping the counselor accurately identify the causes and effects involved in the client's presenting problems, (b) normalizing the client's presenting problems, and (c) serving as a guide for the selection of interventions, and help establish a strong therapeutic relationship between client and counselor (Sheperis & Sheperis, 2015). Based on this a case conceptualization should include the following elements (Ingram, 2006; Persons, 2008): (a) a description of all the client's symptoms, disorders, and problems, (b) information about the precipitating, predisposing, perpetuating, and protective factors of the current problems, (c) a hypothesis based on the above factors and a theoretical framework that provides an explanation, and (d) decisions about specific treatment interventions. In bilingual supervision, most counselors find themselves presenting case conceptualizations in English, despite working with Spanish-speaking clients. This may prevent bilingual counselors from developing critical analysis and professional writing and presentation of the client in Spanish. Therefore, we provide a template in Figure 4.2 for a case conceptualization that can serve to create written and oral case presentations of the client in Spanish.

Figure 4.2: Conceptualización de Caso

Conceptualizaciones de caso
Los consejeros bilingües pueden utilizar el formato para una conceptualización escrita del caso y/o una presentación oral en la clase.

I Identificación de datos

1. Datos personales relevantes, incluyendo edad, raza, género
   a. Nombre disfrazado
2. Nivel de trabajo o grado
3. Fuente de referencia

II Datos de antecedentes relevantes y estado actual
1. Información familiar: antecedentes, cultura, historia, dinámica, creencias espirituales
2. Información relacionada con el trabajo/escuela: Nivel educacional, empleo
3. Información médica: historia, salud general, problemas de salud física o mental
4. ¿Qué llevó al cliente a buscar consejería en este momento?
5. Número de sesiones con este cliente

Figure 4.2: *Continued*

III Su conceptualización del caso

1. Fortalezas / recursos personales del cliente y debilidades / desafíos
2. Evaluación y Diagnóstico
3. Describa cómo determinó este diagnóstico en función a la presentación de sintomatología, quejas y comportamientos del cliente y cualquier diagnóstico diferencial que haya considerado.
4. Declaración del problema (por ejemplo, afectiva, cognitiva, conductual)

   a. Presentado
   b. Tratamiento actual

IV Objetivo(s)/Metas para el Cambio de Cliente

1. Cliente
2. Del consejero/a/e

V Proceso de asesoramiento (Describa brevemente su enfoque para trabajar con este cliente)

1. Base teórica utilizada
2. Describa cómo abordó los problemas multiculturales con el cliente o cómo los problemas culturales pueden haber afectado a su cliente. Específicamente, describa cómo aplicó las competencias multiculturales a la consejería clínica de salud mental que implica la conceptualización de casos, diagnóstico, tratamiento, derivación y prevención de trastornos mentales y emocionales.
3. Desarrollo de la relación de consejería
4. Flujo del proceso de consejería
5. Logros hasta la fecha
6. Cualquier factor que complique la relación o el proceso de consejería.
7. Cualquier actividad creativa: genograma, actividades artísticas y expresivas, etc.
8. Describa cómo modeló la defensa de justicia social, promovió una salud mental óptima para el cliente y promovió el desarrollo humano óptimo, el bienestar y la salud mental a través de actividades de prevención, educación y promoción.
9. Describa cómo refirió a su cliente a recursos adicionales dentro de la comunidad y describa estos recursos (por ejemplo, grupos de adicción, tratamiento médico, etc.).
10. Describa cómo reconoció sus propias limitaciones como consejero clínico de salud mental y buscó la supervisión o la referencia de los clientes cuando sea apropiado.
11. Resultado
12. Seguimiento (real/planificado)

VI. Solicitar Comentarios/ sugerencias

1. ¿Qué dificultades particulares está teniendo con este caso?
2. ¿Qué tipo de ayuda le gustaría de sus colegas o supervisor?

Figure 4.3: Plan de Tratamiento

Plan de tratamiento	
Problema 1:	El cliente presenta dificultad con manejar síntomas de ansiedad que prevalecen en varios aspectos de su vida.
Diagnóstico Provisional	300.02 Trastorno de ansiedad generalizada
Meta:	Desarrollar técnicas para manejar sus síntomas de ansiedad.
Objetivo 1:	Identificar factores que generan o alteran (triggers) su ansiedad.
Objetivo 2:	Reducir la frecuencia e intensidad de sus síntomas de ansiedad.
Intervenciones:	Utilizar habilidades para calmar (Ejercicios de Respiración, Relajación Muscular, Meditación), examinar el pasado, y explorar formas alternativas de expresión (Ejercicio, Arte, Música).

Plan de Tratamiento

A treatment plan, o plan de tratamiento, flows out of the case conceptualization. A treatment plan can be defined as a process of developing a plan for the progression of counseling (Sheperis & Sheperis, 2015). It is a blueprint of the clinical mental health counselor and the client to map how the client's presenting concerns will be addressed and what the likely outcome will be (Seligman, 1993). Treatment plans should be individualized to fit the client based on their unique needs, abilities, goals, lifestyle, socioeconomic realities, work history, educational background, and culture (Stilen et al., 2007). We provide a template and example for a treatment plan in Figure 4.3.

Application to Practice: Case Study

The following case example highlights common issues and possible solutions experienced in bilingual supervision.

Bilingual Supervision

Victoria is 41 years old, female, brown-skinned, and a second-generation Mexican American. She is a professional clinical supervisor with over 20 years of clinical experience. She supervises Practicum and Internship students of varying ethnic and cultural backgrounds. Isabel is 25 years old, a master's student completing her internship at a behavioral health department at a clinic serving mostly Spanish-speaking clients. Isabel is a white-skin Latine born in Guatemala, who immigrated to the United States two years ago. Both speak Spanish and English fluently, with Spanish as their first language. However, Victoria spoke Spanish primarily at home, while Isabel spoke Spanish all the time in her home country. Isabel recently started working with Gabriela. Gabriela is brown-skinned, 35 years old, married, has two children, and was born in Mexico. She immigrated to the United States a year ago. Gabriela is seeking counseling for several reasons. She reported that her oldest son, who is 10 years old, has not adjusted well and is acting out by talking back and refusing to complete the chores assigned. She also explains that her oldest son's behavior is creating relationship issues. Her husband becomes upset when their son does not obey and when she and her son start arguing. She explains he makes her feel guilty because their behavior is her responsibility. Isabel decides to further discuss this case with Victoria.

Supervisión Bilingüe

Victoria tiene 41 años, es mujer, de piel morena y es México-Americana de segunda generación. Es supervisora clínica con más de 20 años de experiencia clínica. Ella supervisa a los estudiantes de prácticas y pasantías de diferentes orígenes étnicos y culturales. Isabel tiene 25 años, es una estudiante de maestría que completa su pasantía en un departamento de salud conductual en una clínica que atiende principalmente a clientes de habla hispana. Isabel es una latina de tez blanca nacida en Guatemala, que emigró a los Estados Unidos hace dos años. Ambas hablan español e inglés con fluidez, con el español como su primer idioma. Sin embargo, Victoria hablaba español principalmente en casa, mientras que Isabel hablaba español todo el tiempo en su país de origen. Isabel recientemente comenzó a trabajar con Gabriela. Gabriela es de piel morena, tiene 35 años, está casada, tiene dos hijos y nació en México. Ella emigró a los Estados Unidos hace un año. Gabriela está buscando consejería por varias razones. Ella informó que su hijo mayor, que tiene 10 años, no se ha adaptado bien y está actuando mal al responder y negarse a completar las tareas asignadas. También explica que el comportamiento de su hijo mayor está creando problemas en su relación matrimonial. Su esposo se molesta cuando su hijo no obedece y cuando ella y su hijo comienzan a discutir. Ella explica que él la hace sentir culpable porque su comportamiento es su responsabilidad. Isabel decide discutir más a fondo este caso con Victoria.

First supervision session:

SUPERVISOR VICTORIA (SUP-V):	*Hello Isabel, what client would you like to discuss today?*
COUNSELOR ISABEL (CO):	*Hello Victoria, so there is one client that I would like to talk about. There are a number of things that she discusses, and I also have an ethical question about this client.*
SUP-V:	*Ok, let's listen to it.*
CO:	*Ok. [Isabel plays audiotape]*
CO:	*¿Cuénteme Doña Gabriela en que le puedo ayudar?*
GABRIELA (CL-G):	*Pues mire mijita necesito ayuda porque desde que nos mudamos desde México, mi hijo mayor no se porta bien para nada.*
CO:	*Ok, cuénteme más a que se refiere con que no se porta bien.*
CL-G:	*Se ha convertido completamente en un desobediente y malcriado. Yo le digo que él tiene que ayudarnos y portarse bien. Es su responsabilidad ayudar a esta familia. Lo único que le pido es que me ayude en la casa, que me ayude a limpiar los platos después de comer, que lave su ropa, y que limpie su cuarto. Yo le digo que necesitamos su ayuda en esta familia, que su papá y yo no podemos solos. Pero cuando le digo algo, él no me hace caso y me empieza a gritar. La vez pasada me empezó a gritar y decirme unas groserías. Me enojé tanto que le di una cachetada. Yo sé que no debo hacer eso, pero él tiene que aprender a respetar a sus mayores, y a respetarme a mí. Yo soy su mamá. Él tiene que aprender que él tiene que obedecer lo que yo diga. Lo he tenido que hacer varias veces porque ya no sé qué hacer. Y le grito porque estoy tan cansada. Extraño a mi familia. Y lo peor es que mi esposo no ayuda para nada. Él llega de trabajar cansado y se enoja conmigo porque el niño no obedece. Yo le digo a mi hijo, mira lo que estás haciendo con tu comportamiento para que entienda. Este niño hasta está causando problemas en mi relación. Desde que venimos mi esposo y yo estamos bien distantes y es culpa de este niño.*
CO:	*Puedo ver que se siente muy molesta por toda esta situación.*
CL-G:	*¡Claro que sí mijita! Y desesperada. Ya no sé qué hacer. Por eso decidí venir para que usted me ayude con mi hijo. La verdad pensé en traerlo a él porque necesito que usted me ayude a que obedezca.*
CO:	*¿Usted quiere que él reciba servicios de consejería o usted?*
CL-G:	*Pues me gustaría que nos viera a los dos, pero separados.*
CO:	*Ya veo. Vamos a ver cómo le podemos ayudar. Déjeme consultar con mi supervisora porque usualmente no se recomienda que trabajemos con miembros de una sola familia por separado por conflictos éticos. ¿No sé si prefiere que pregunte y vemos o le ofrezco terapia familiar con su hijo?*

CL-G: *Pues yo prefiriera separado porque así cada quien tiene chance de platicar lo suyo, pero si no se puede terapia de familia está bien.*

CO: *Ok, déjeme averiguar más y lo platicamos la siguiente semana. En cuanto a lo que me estaba contando, me mencionó el comportamiento de su hijo y también las dificultades matrimoniales. También la escuche mencionar que extraña su familia y su país.*

CL-G: *Ay si mija, es que todo se me ha acumulado. Pues la verdad que lo más primordial es lo de mi hijo, ya no sé qué hacer la verdad con él.*

CO: *Puedo ver que está muy preocupada por su hijo.*

CL-G: *La verdad que sí.*

CO: *También mencionó que su comportamiento ha ocasionado que usted se moleste al grado que lo ha cacheteado y le ha gritado.*

CL-G: *¡Ay sí, es que viera cómo me molesto! Cuando yo le iba a gritar o contestar así a mi mamá. Y mi esposo me dice que es mi culpa. Que lo estoy malcriando. Que él nunca le contestó así a su mamá y que yo le permito demasiado. Por eso lo cacheteo para que él entienda, pero también para que mi esposo mire que no lo permito.*

CO: *Ya veo. Puedo ver que usted siente mucha presión para que su hijo se porte bien.*

CL-G: *¡Claro mija! ¿Usted es mamá?*

CO: *No*

CL-G: *Ya. Es que ese es el trabajo de una mamá. Él no me puede contestar así. Él tiene que obedecerme en todo y ayudarle a esta familia.* [The recording stops]

CO: So, I have several questions about this client. The first is do I have to report this?

SUP-V: When she says it is often, what does she mean by that?

CO: I am not sure. I did not ask. I know that it is common in Latin cultures. My grandmother slapped me a couple of times when I was younger when I was disrespectful to her. My concern is why she is doing it. I feel that she is very stressed and taking it out on her son. I am also concerned about how she holds her 10-year-old responsible for adult behavior. Sometimes when you are the oldest child or the only child you are expected to help your family. My mother was the oldest and she had to pretty much help her single mother raise her three younger siblings. She was probably like 6 or 7 when she had to start helping.

SUP-V: These are important points but we do have to assess if this is common behavior.

CO: I also wanted to get your thoughts on her question about me as a parent. Was it ok to answer it? I think she felt I was not competent to guide her.

SUP-V: Do you feel like that?

CO: I do feel competent, but I know that she may not feel like that. We tend to get our "consejos" from family members that do have children.

SUP-V: You may not have children, but you have been trained to work with all clients with all different issues.

Reflection Questions

1. What are some cultural elements important to consider between counselor-supervisor? Client-Counselor?
2. What ethical considerations must the supervisor consider to best advise Isabel?
3. What other issues may have been important to consider here for Isabel to discuss with the client?

Second Supervision Session:

SUP-V: *Hello, how are you doing?*

CO: *I am doing well. I would like to talk to you about the client I talked to you about last week. It didn't go so well.*

SUP-V: *Ok, tell me more.*

CO: *Well, I can play it for you. [Isabel plays recording]*

CO: *Hola, Doña Gabriela. ¿Cómo está hoy?*

CL-G: *Pues no estoy bien mija. Mi hijo está peor que nunca. No quiere hacer caso. No hace nada en la casa solo quiere pasar chateando en ese teléfono. Yo necesito que él me ayude en los quehaceres de la casa. Pero el cómo que si no es con él. Yo le grito y él solo me grita más y me tira la puerta. Le tuve que pegar muy duro el otro día.*

CO: *¿Cuándo dice que le tuve que pegar, a que se refiere con eso?*

CL-G: *Pues que le pegue. Le dije que limpiara los platos y no me hacía caso, entonces agarré la faja y le pegué varias veces. Tenía cólera.*

CO: *Ya entiendo. ¿Esto es común que ocurra?*

CL-G: *¿Qué cosa?*

CO: *¿Tener que castigar a su hijo con el uso de la faja?*

CL-G: *¡Pues cuando se porta mal, claro que sí! No es que lo maltrato ni nada de eso. Pero a veces me enojo tanto con el que le doy con la faja por cómo me contesta. Le deje una marca en la pierna con la faja por andar de malcriado. Ya le dije que a mí no me va a faltar el respeto, que soy su mamá. Póngale que cada dos semana nos agarramos así donde le tengo que pegar con la faja.*

CO: *Puedo ver que eso le molesta mucho. También para usted el respeto es sumamente importante.*

CL-G: *¡Claro que sí! Yo no voy a criar a un malcriado.*

CO: *¿Habrá otra forma en la que podamos mantener ese respeto sin el uso de la faja?*

CL-G: *¿Como así?*

CO: *La razón por la cual pregunto Doña Gabriela es porque me preocupa que usted pueda enfrentar ciertos problemas en los Estados Unidos al utilizar el castigo corporal. En los Estados Unidos, el uso frecuente del castigo corporal puede ser considerado abuso.*

CL-G: *¡Pero yo no estoy abusando de mi hijo! ¡Aquí exageran!*

CO: *Entiendo que ese no es el propósito para usted. Sin embargo, sé que en los Estados Unidos eso se puede percibir de forma distinta.*

CL-G: *¿Y qué es lo que quieren que haga? Por eso es que aquí los muchachos son malcriados o andan con babosadas porque no se enseña la disciplina. ¡El problema no soy yo! ¡Yo vine para que usted me ayudara con mi hijo y ahora me dice que la solución es dejar de castigarlo! ¡No mijita! ¿Y qué, entonces esto me va a meter en problemas?*

CO: *Puedo ver que mi recomendación le molesto.*

CL-G: *¡Claro que sí! (empieza a llorar). Yo vengo por ayuda y usted me sale con eso.*

CO: *(utiliza el silencio) Que siente ahorita?*

CL-G: *Sola. Me siento tan sola. Extraño a mi país y a mi familia. Siento que mi esposo no me ayuda y ahora siento que esto no me va a ayudar.*

CO: *Doña Gabriela entiendo que se siente así. Sin embargo, mi preocupación es ayudarla. Entiendo que usted quiere que su hijo se comporte y podemos trabajar en eso, pero me preocupa que el método que utiliza puede crear más problemas en los Estados Unidos. Como informante por mandato es mi obligación por ley informar a las autoridades si considero que un menor está siendo abusado. Me preocupa que usted castigue a su hijo y le deje marcas.*

CL-G: *¡Usted no entiende porque está bien joven! No tiene niños. Me imagino que sus papás igual le enseñaron a respetar a los mayores. Ya esto me está poniendo muy nerviosa.* [Isabel stops the recording]

SUP-V: *¿Qué pasó después de eso?*

CO: *Casi no hablo. Se cerró y no me contestaba mucho. Al final se terminó yendo unos minutos temprano.*

SUP-V: *You asked the right questions and said the right things. It is your responsibility to assess for child abuse.*

CO: *I'm still not sure that it is though.*

SUP-V: *We as counselors are responsible for reporting any suspicion. It is the police's job to investigate if it is or isn't. We need to report this because she has left bruises, which is the law's distinction between spanking and physical abuse.*

Reflection Questions

1. Do you believe that Isabel handled the conversation with Gabriela well? If so, what do you think she did well? If not, how would you have handled it differently?

2. Are there any cultural considerations that influence Isabel's decision to report?

3. Do you believe Victoria is right in stating that this is a reportable case? If so, why? If not, what would you have liked for the supervisor to recommend?

Third Supervision Session

SUP-V: *Hello Isabel. How is everything going?*

CO: *I'm doing ok. Just struggling overall with what happened with Doña Gabriela. She did not return after our last session. I have tried reaching out and I haven't heard anything back. I am concerned about reporting her and not knowing what happened. I know I had to do it by law, but I felt that it caused more pain than helped. It's not fair that she could get in trouble for spanking her child when she is just trying to do her best. Like my mother did that same thing and she was not a bad mother. I'm honestly very angry.*

SUP-V: *Do you feel angry with me?*

CO: *Honestly, I do. I understand why we had to report her, but I felt pushed into doing it. I wish there was something else we could do. I think Latinos get a bad reputation and these are just cultural differences. If we were working in her country, we would be wrong, and she would be right. It's the law but it is based on cultural norms of the U.S. Getting Latinos to come to counseling is already hard and now because they are afraid that they will get in trouble for their cultural differences they are less inclined to come. No wonder there is less use of counseling services! I would too!*

SUP-V: *How would you like to handle it differently?*

CO: *That's the part, I know regardless we would have had to come to the same point. She was leaving bruises. [takes a deep breath]. Maybe I could have taught her about other discipline techniques and have her try them out. Maybe one or two would have worked and she could have seen that she doesn't need to spank him that hard. Then, have a conversation with her that she needs to use these techniques to avoid getting into trouble. Maybe it was too soon. I don't think we gave her a chance to change.*

SUP-V: *It seems to me like you tried bringing up that conversation, but she was closed off to it.*

CO: *I did, yeah. I wonder if the fact that I am young, white-skinned, and educated had something to do with it. I have some privilege in that sense and here I was telling her how to parent her child. I should have talked about that, instead of pretending it didn't matter.*

SUP-V: *Do those differences matter with us?*

CO: *Yeah, they do! Not only are you my supervisor but you are older. I felt like I had no say. I know what it's like to be an immigrant and have your cultural norms be questioned simply because it's not normal here. I don't face losing my children for them and they still feel awful! I should have said something and advocated for her.*

Reflection Questions

1. What are your thoughts and feelings regarding Isabel's position?
2. What do you like and dislike about the supervisor's responses?
3. What supervisor-supervisee considerations are playing in this relationship?

4. What resolution to this case study do you believe benefits the client the most while remaining ethically responsible as a counselor?

Implications for Clinical Practice, Bilingual Training, and Research

The increasing number of bilingual counselors presents challenges for the counseling field, particularly as it relates to bilingual counseling training and supervision. Training programs could consider expanding their definition of bilingual supervision to emphasize both the cultural and linguistic dimensions. Supervision in Spanish is an integral need for bilingual counselors, which is currently deficient (Gallardo et al., 2014; Trepal et al., 2019; Interiano-Shiverdecker et al., 2021). Bilingual counselors require a supervisor who understands the therapeutic complexities and contextual issues concerning their experiences and the populations serviced. By training counselors in bilingual counseling concurrently with their standard counseling curriculum, counselor education programs can help minimize challenges and feelings of incompetence (Castaño et al., 2007; Ivers & Villalba, 2015; Trepal et al., 2019; Verdinelli & Biever, 2009b). Although it may not be feasible for all counseling programs to offer specialized training in bilingual counseling, training programs could strive to provide the appropriate support and resources to bilingual counselors. Some recommendations include recruiting bilingual counselor educators that may help address the unique supervision needs of bilingual counselors; establishing a language/cultural immersion program or offering elective courses on Latine mental health or Spanish counseling skills; inviting guest speakers who have experience conducting counseling in Spanish; and establishing a working partnership with internship sites to ensure that bilingual counselors are getting the training and support they need. Furthermore, if a bilingual supervisor is not accessible, the monolingual supervisor should be educated on the demands of those who provide counseling in a language other than English (Castaño et al., 2007). In addition, programs should consider the nuances in training between tracks such as Clinical Mental Health, Marriage and Family Counseling, and School Counseling. Although all the tracks may involve work with children, school counselors are in a special situation in that they have direct contact with large groups of Latine youth experiencing linguistic challenges, cultural choques, immigration and safety issues, and socioeconomic hurdles.

Similarly, training programs could offer support to any clinical faculty who engage in bilingual clinical supervision. This support may include financial support to attend specialized training, providing opportunities to establish support networks outside of the department, and potential redistribution of their allocation of effort to account for the additional time invested in engaging in bilingual supervision (i.e., looking up resources, translations, risk-assessments).

Establishing connections and/or partnerships with other counseling programs that are currently offering specialized training in this area could be an invaluable resource to bilingual supervisors.

Other recommendations include developing partnerships and collaborations with other departments on campus such as linguistics and social work departments; conducting formalized and systematic research studies examining best practices in bilingual counseling and bilingual supervision; and consulting with other professionals who are bilingual counselors and supervisors.

Conclusion

With the call to infuse multicultural, social justice-oriented frameworks into counseling pedagogy, there appears to be a specific need for bilingual counseling training and supervision. We hope that this chapter can offer supplemental information for supervisees and supervisors to effectively provide bilingual supervision.

Points to Remember

- Bilingual counselors who do not receive adequate training may struggle with their perceptions of self-efficacy.
- Benefits of training and supervision include pride in serving their community, enhanced resourcefulness, and advocacy skills.
- At an individual level, bilingual counselors may have to advocate for not only services in Spanish but also make sure that all documentation is offered in both languages.
- Providing services in Spanish is a way to advocate for quality and access to services, however, it is important to assess your level of comfortability and proficiency in Spanish.
- Acquiring and communicating clinical terminology in Spanish is not only one of the biggest challenges for bilingual counselors but also one

of the main reasons they may experience low self-efficacy when providing services in Spanish.

- Regardless of bilingual counselors' limitations, providing services in Spanish is a form of advocacy.
- Within bilingual supervision, it is important to consider and assess differences in identity development between the client, supervisee, and supervisor.
- Resources such as case conceptualization, tapescripts, and treatment plans in Spanish are critical resources for bilingual counselors.

Resources

- Avila, E. (2000). *Woman Who Glows in the Dark: A Curandera Reveals Traditional Aztec Secrets of Physical and Spiritual Health.* TarcherPerigee.
- Chabram-Dernersesian, A., & de la Torre, A. (2008). *Speaking from the body: Latinas on health and culture.* University of Arizona Press.
- Morrison (2015). *Desarrollo de habilidades clínicas.* Manual Moderno.
- Morrison (2014). *La entrevista psicológica.* Manual moderno.
- Morrison (2014). *DSM-5: Guía para el diagnóstico clínico.* Manual moderno.
- Zavaleta, A. N. (2020). *Curandero Hispanic Ethno-Psychotherapy & Curanderismo: Treating Hispanic Mental Health in the 21st Century.* Authorhouse

References

Alvarado, M., Lerma, E., & Vela, J. C. (2019). Experiences of Spanish speaking counseling students: Implications for the profession. *The Journal of Counselor Preparation and Supervision, 12*(4). https://repository.wcsu.edu/jcps/vol12/iss4/1

American Counseling Association. (2014). *ACA Code of Ethics.* Author. http://www.counseling.org/resources/aca-code-of-ethics.pdf.

American Psychiatric Association. (2013). *Diagnostic and statistical manual of mental disorders: DSM-5* (5th ed.). Author.

Arthur, G. L., & Gfoerer, K. P. (2002). Training and supervision through the written word: A description and intern feedback. *The Family Journal, 10*(2), 213–219. https://doi.org/10.1177/1066480702102014

Bernard, J., & Goodyear, R. (2018). *Fundamental of clinical supervision* (6th ed.). Pearson.

Biever, J. L., Castaño, M. T., de las Fuentes, C., González, C., Servín-Lopez, S., Sprowls, C., & Tripp, C. G. (2002). The role of language in training psychologists to work with Hispanic clients. *Professional Psychology: Research and Practice, 33*(3), 330–336. http://dx.doi. org/10.1037/0735-7028.33.3.330

Biever, J. L., Gómez, J. P., González, C. G., & Patrizio, N. (2011). Psychological services to Spanish-speaking populations: A model curriculum for training competent professionals. *Training and Education in Professional Psychology, 5*(2), 81–87. https://doi.org/10.1037/a0023535

Castaño, M. T., Biever, J. L., González, C. G., & Anderson, K. B. (2007). Challenges of providing mental health services in Spanish. *Professional Psychology: Research and Practice, 38*(6), 667–673. https://doi.org/10.1037/0735-7028.38.6.667

Delgado-Romero, E., De Los Santos, J., Raman, V., Merrifield, J., Vazquez, M., Monroig, M., … Durán, M. (2018). Caught in the middle: Spanish-speaking bilingual mental health counselors as language brokers. *Journal of Mental Health Counseling, 40*(4), 341–352. https://doi.org/10.17744/mehc.40.4.06

Eells, T. D. (Ed.). (2022). *Handbook of psychotherapy case formulation.* Guilford Publications.

Ferdman, B. M., & Gallegos, P. I. (2001). Latinos and racial identity development. In C. L. Wijeyesinghe & B. W. Jackson III (Eds.), *New perspectives on racial identity development: A theoretical and practical anthology* (pp. 32–66). University Press

Fuertes, J. N. (2004). Supervision in bilingual counseling: Service delivery, training, and research considerations. *Journal of Multicultural Counseling and Development, 32*(2), 84–94. https://doi.org/10.1002/j.2161-1912.2004.tb00363.x

Gallardo-Cooper, M., Arredondo, P., Delgado-Romero, E. A., & Zapata, A. L. (2014). *Culturally responsive counseling with Latinas/os.* John Wiley & Sons.

González, L. M., Ivers, N. N., Noyola, M. C., Murillo-Herrera, A., & Davis, K. M. (2015). Supervision in Spanish: Reflections from supervisor-trainee dyads. *The Clinical Supervisor, 34*(2), 184–203. https://doi.org/10.1080/07325223.2015.1058208

Goodman, L. A., Liang, B., Helms, J. E., Latta, R. E., Sparks, E., & Weintraub, S. (2004). Training counseling psychologists as social justice agents: Feminist and multicultural perspectives. *Counseling Psychologist, 32,* 793–837. https://doi.org/10.1177%2F0011000004268802

Ibrahim, F. A., & Heuer, J. R. (2016). *Cultural and social justice counseling: Client-specific interventions.* Springer International Publishing.

Ingram, B. L. (2006). *Clinical case formulations: Matching the integrative treatment plan to the client.* John Wiley & Sons Inc.

Interiano-Shiverdecker, C. G., Robertson, D., Santillan, S., & Stumpf, M. (2023). Exploring language and cultural competence among bilingual counselors who participated in a study abroad program. *Teaching and Supervision in Counseling, 5*(7), https://doi.org/10.7290/tsc05mxpl

Interiano-Shiverdecker, C. G., Robertson, D. L., Zambrano, E., Contreras, J. & Morgan, A. (2021). Development and implementation of a bilingual counseling curriculum. *Teaching and Supervision in Counseling, 3*(3), Article 3. https://doi.org/10.7290/tsc030303

Ivers, N. N., & Villalba, J. A. (2015). The effect of bilingualism on self-perceived multicultural counseling competence. *The Professional Counselor, 5*(3), 419–430, https://doi.org/10.15241/nni.5.3.419

Johal, J. (2017). 'No one ever speaks about it': A qualitative investigation exploring the experiences of multilingual counsellors in practice. *Counselling and Psychotherapy Research, 17*(4), 291–300. https://doi.org/10.1002/capr.12134

Kendjelic, E. M., & Eells, T. D. (2007). Generic psychotherapy case formulation training improves formulation quality. *Psychotherapy: Theory, Research, Practice, Training, 44*(1), 66–77. https://doi.org/10.1037/0033-3204.44.1.66

Killian, K. D. (2001). Differences making a difference: Cross-cultural interactions in supervisory relationships. *Journal of Feminist Family Therapy, 12*(2–3), 61–103. https://doi.org/10.1300/J086v12n02_03

Kozina, K., Grabovari, N., Stefano, J. D., & Drapeau, M. (2010). Measuring changes in counselor self-efficacy: Further validation and implications for training and supervision. *The Clinical Supervisor, 29*(2), 117–127. https://doi.org/10.1080/07325223.2010.517483

Larson, L. M., Suzuki, L. A., Gillespie, K. N., Potenza, M. T., Bechtel, M. A., & Toulouse, A. (1992). Development and validation of the counseling self-estimate inventory. *Journal of Counseling Psychology, 39*(1), 105–120. https://doi.org/10.1037/0022-0167.39.1.105

Lopez, A., & Torres-Fernandez, I. (2019). Exploring the experiences of supervisors and supervisees who engaged in bilingual supervision. *The Journal of Counselor Preparation and Supervision, 12*(1), 10. https://digitalcommons.sacredheart.edu/jcps/vol12/iss1/10

Martinez-Smith, C. (2018). *Bilingual counselors-in-training self-efficacy with counseling in Spanish: A narrative study.* Published dissertation.

McCaffrey, A., & Moody, S. J. (2015). Providing equitable services: Implementing bilingual counseling certification in counselor education programs. *VISTAS online, 33,* 1–11. https://www.counseling.org/docs/default-source/vistas/article_33625c21f16116603abcacff0000bee5e7.pdf?sfvrsn=fc4a412c_8

Perry, V. M. (2016). *A phenomenological investigation of Spanish English bilingual supervisees' experiences in clinical supervision.* Published dissertation.

Persons, J. B. (2008). *The case formulation approach to cognitive-behavior therapy.* Guilford Press.

Ramos-Sánchez, L., Esnil, E., Goodwin, A., Riggs, S., Touster, L. O., Wright, L. K., Ratanasiripong, P., & Rodolfa, E. (2002). Negative supervisory events: Effects on supervision and supervisory alliance. *Professional Psychology: Research and Practice, 33*(2), 197–202. https://doi.org/10.1037/0735-7028.33.2.197

Santiago-Rivera, A. L., Altarriba, J., Poll, N., Gonzalez-Miller, N., & Cragun, C. (2009). Therapists' views on working with bilingual Spanish–English speaking clients: A qualitative investigation. *Professional Psychology: Research and Practice, 40*(5), 436–443. https://doi.org/10.1037/a0015933

Schwartz, A., Rodriguez, M. M. D., Santiago-Rivera, A. L., Arredondo, P., & Field, L. D. (2010). Cultural and linguistic competence: Welcome challenges from successful diversification. *Professional Psychology: Research and Practice, 41*(3), 210–220. https://doi.org/10.1037/a0019447

Seligman, M. E. P. (1993). *What you can change and what you can't: The complete guide to successful self-improvement.* Knopf

Seto, A., & Forth, N. L. (2020). What is known about bilingual counseling? A systematic review of the literature. *Professional Counselor, 10*(3), 393–405. https://doi.org/10.15241/as.10.3.393

Sheperis, D., & Sheperis, C. (2015). *Clinical mental health counseling: Fundamentals of applied practice.* Pearson

Stilen, P., Carise, D., Roget, N., & Wendler, A. (2007). *Treatment planning M.A.T.R.S. utilizing the Addiction Severity Index (ASI) to make required data collection useful.* Mid-America Addiction Technology Transfer Center in residence at the University of Missouri-Kansas City.

Sue, D. W., Sue, D., Neville, H. A., & Smith, L. (2019). *Counseling the culturally diverse: Theory and Practice* (8th ed.). Wiley.

Trepal, H., Ivers, N., & Lopez, A. (2014). Students' experiences with bilingual counseling. The *Journal for Counselor Preparation and Supervision, 6*(2), 21–34. http://dx.doi.org/10.7729/52.1096

Trepal, H., Tello, A., Haiyasoso, M., Castellon, N., Garcia, J., & Martinez-Smith, C. (2019). *Supervision strategies used to support Spanish-speaking bilingual counselors. Teaching and Supervision in Counseling, 1*(1), 19–31. https://doi.org/10.7290/tsc010103.

Verdinelli, S., & Biever, J. L. (2009a). Experiences of Spanish/English bilingual supervisees. *Psychotherapy: Theory, Research, Practice, Training, 46*(2), 158–17. https://doi.org/10.1037/a0016024

Verdinelli, S., & Biever, J. L. (2009b). Spanish–English bilingual psychotherapists: Personal and professional language development and use. *Cultural Diversity and Ethnic Minority Psychology, 15*(3), 230–242. https://doi.org/10.1037/a0015111

· 5 ·

BILINGUAL CASOS: BECOMING
CULTURALLY EFFICACIOUS

In this chapter, we provide case studies to assist you in becoming culturally efficacious bilingual counselors with the knowledge, skills, competence, and confidence to support clients. Each case study specifically deals with common issues that we as bilingual counselors have encountered. We introduce each case study with an abbreviated review of the literature; this is followed by three to four sessions in Spanish and English, and for each session, there are reflective questions. At the end of each case, we provide resources.

Social Justice Framework

As previously mentioned, throughout this book we have situated our theory and practice within a social justice framework. We have suggested that a culturally efficacious bilingual counselor addresses the needs of the client by considering the language preferences of the client as well as the cultural considerations that align with the client's ways of being and thinking. By providing case studies in both English and Spanish, we ensure that linguistic justice centers in our practices and that we attend to our clients' needs. In the case studies, we have also utilized the term *consejere* as a gender-inclusive term for a counselor.

Caso I. Yolanda's Case Study
Dudas de matrimonio

Marriage Counseling

Typical problems that couples bring to the session can include intimacy and communication issues, financial stress, domestic violence, substance use, family-raising concerns, and even partner emotional issues such as anxiety or depression. Latine families may face unique marital challenges, including the loss of familiar environment and support due to migratory experiences, loss of one's culture, unemployment or employment instability, poverty, and internal conflict resulting from acculturation (Hancock & Siu, 2009; Pérez et al., 2013). As a result, marital stress impacts the quality of life and relationships for couples facing financial crises and emotional turmoil. In addition, Latine values integral to the family dynamic are often compromised. For example, *familismo*, or the focus on and value of children and extended family as a strength, may be negatively influenced by marital conflict. Couples might worry that their fighting and conflict will negatively affect their children's well-being and familial relationships (see Chapter 3).

Another challenge faced by this population is the potential for diversity issues within bilingual or multilingual family units. Couples raised in contrasting cultural environments may differ in the language spoken, including code-switching with each other and extended family (see Chapter 2). This may also impact the couple's decision to speak their native language with their children. Often parents decide to speak English because of the pressure to assimilate and to avoid racism and discrimination, which they believe will further the success of their children (Softas-Nall et al., 2015).

Counselors will do well to consider the heterogeneity and individual differences of Latine families, including factors such as national origin, immigration status, social class, acculturation level, and length of residence in the United States (Snyder et al., 2010; see Chapter 3). Understanding the perceived customs of couple behavior and how cultural identity influences relational expectations may help to individualize treatment for Latine couples. Previous research has incorporated marital education programs for Latine populations rather than counseling (Lindahl & Wigderson, 2017). However, these programs do little to focus on cultural diversity and strengths within couples (Hawkins & Fackrell, 2010; Pérez et al., 2013).

Case Presentation

Yolanda's case study focuses on matrimonial issues regarding the betrayal of marriage vows. Additionally, alcohol is used as a coping mechanism. Over the course of three sessions, the counselor works with the couple.

Presentación del Caso

El estudio de caso de Yolanda se centra en cuestiones matrimoniales relacionadas con una traición de los votos matrimoniales. Además, el alcohol se utiliza como un mecanismo de afrontamiento. En el transcurso de tres sesiones, el consejero trabaja con la pareja.

First session:

Yolanda and Lauro have made an appointment to begin their first couples counseling session after being married for 15 years. Lauro recently ended an affair and Yolanda seemed very depressed. The couple has two children in middle school and wanted to keep their family together. Yolanda suffered from episodes of rage and resentment towards Lauro, which resulted in heated arguments in front of their children. Lauro started drinking heavily to cope with his wife's detachment and anger. He reports that their low intimacy motivated his affair and that he would like to reconcile with his wife. The following shows an excerpt of their beliefs around counseling:

LAURO (CL-L): *We didn't grow up believing that counseling was something we needed to do to help ourselves, you just fixed it yourself. You didn't talk to anyone about it, you just tried to stop feeling things on your own.*

COUNSELOR (CO): *I imagine you felt isolated holding all those things in, without being able to go to someone for support.*

CL-L: *I guess so. I just drink so that I don't have to worry, but then it ends up hurting my family, hurting my wife.*

YOLANDA (CL-Y): *Yes, but also, my family worked hard to change that mentality. They now see the benefit in counseling, and I want support for my husband and my marriage because it's not doing us any good the way we are now.*

CO: *You both grew up with different perspectives about how to deal with mental health, but ultimately want the best for each other and this relationship. Tell me about the goals you have for counseling, including your hopes and fears.*

Reflective Questions:

1. What questions may you ask in this first session to gain further understanding of the client's problem?
2. What are some skills you might utilize to make sure the client knows you are listening and have empathy for the problem?
3. What precautions may you want to investigate to ensure your client's safety?

Primera sesión:

Yolanda y Lauro han hecho su primera cita para empezar consejería de parejas después de estar casados por quince años. Lauro recientemente terminó una relación extramarital y Yolanda parece estar muy deprimida. La pareja tiene dos hijos en primaria y quieren mantener a su familia junta. Yolanda sufre de episodios de coraje y resentimiento contra Lauro, y ha resultado en discusiones fuertes enfrente de sus hijos. Lauro ha empezado a tomar mucho para aguantar el distanciamiento y coraje de su esposa. Él reporta que la falta de intimidad con su esposa comenzó su relación extramarital y él quisiera reconciliarse con su esposa. A continuación, se muestra un extracto de sus creencias en torno a la consejería:

LAURO (CL-L): *No crecimos creyendo que la consejería era algo que necesitábamos hacer para ayudarnos, simplemente lo hacías solo. No hablabas con nadie y tratabas de dejar de sentir las cosas solo.*

CONSEJERO/A/E (CO): *Me imagino que te sentiste aislado sosteniendo todas esas cosas, porque no pudiste hablar con alguien para recibir apoyo.*

CL-L: *Supongo que sí. Solo bebo para no tener que preocuparme, pero luego termina lastimando a mi familia, lastimando a mi esposa.*

YOLANDA (CL-Y): *Sí, pero también, mi familia trabajó duro para cambiar esa mentalidad. Ahora vemos el beneficio en la consejería y quiero el apoyo para mi esposo y mi matrimonio porque no nos está haciendo ningún bien de la manera en que estamos ahora.*

CO: *Ambos crecieron con diferentes perspectivas sobre cómo lidiar con la salud mental, pero los dos quieren lo mejor para el otro y esta relación. Cuénteme acerca de las metas que tiene para la consejería, incluyendo sus esperanzas y cosas que podrían temer.*

Preguntas de Reflexión:

1. ¿Qué preguntas puedes hacer en la primera sesión para comprender mejor el problema de la pareja?
2. ¿Cuáles son unas técnicas que pudieras utilizar para que los clientes entiendan que estas escuchando y que empatizas con ambos?
3. ¿Qué precauciones puedes investigar para asegurar el bienestar físico y mental de tu cliente?

Second session:

Yolanda has come to the session with feelings of anger and rage. This past week she found out that Lauro was receiving text messages from the woman from his previous affair. She felt betrayed and hurt. She reported that she was violent with Lauro in the car ride to their session and broke down crying. Lauro sat quietly while Yolanda expressed her fears of never trusting him again and her indecision about leaving him. The following is an example from their session:

CO: *Yolanda, what are some feelings that you have about this situation?*
CL-Y: *I feel sad and frustrated that he keeps betraying me and my trust. I don't think that I can ever really trust that he is being honest with me.*
CO: *It must be hard for you to have all of those hurt feelings. Lauro, what are you hearing Yolanda say?*
CL-L: *That she cannot trust me. But I did not do anything wrong this time. I did not respond and I quickly told her about it and blocked the woman's number. I want to move past this and fix our marriage, but she always exaggerates the situation and it brings us back to step one.*
CO: *Okay so I'm hearing that you were honest with Yolanda in telling her about the text message and are wanting to help in working on building that trust with her again. Yolanda, do you feel that you can also work with Lauro to build your trust?*
CL-Y: *I don't know. I want to. But I just don't know right now.*
CO: *And that's okay if you don't know yet. You are here with Lauro right now and that is the beginning of finding out.*

Reflective Questions:

1. What skills does a counselor utilize within this segment?
2. What else could the counselor have said or asked the couple?

Segunda Sesión:

Yolanda ha venido a la sesión con sentimientos de enojo y furia. La semana pasada se dio cuenta que Lauro estaba recibiendo mensajes de texto de su amante. Ella se sintió muy dolida y traicionada. Ella reportó que fue muy violenta con Lauro en el camino a la sesión y rompió en llanto. Lauro se quedó en silencio mientras Yolanda expresaba sus miedos de no confiar en él otra vez y su indecisión de dejarlo. Lo siguiente es un ejemplo de su sesión:

CO: *Yolanda, ¿qué estás sintiendo en este momento?*

CL-Y: *Siento tristeza y coraje de que me siga engañando. Pienso que no puedo confiar en que él va a ser honesto conmigo.*

CO: *Debe ser difícil sentirse de esa manera. Lauro, ¿Qué escuchas de lo que expresó Yolanda?*

CL-L: *Que no me puede tener confianza. Pero esta vez no hice nada. No le contesté y pronto bloqueé el número y le dije a ella sobre el mensaje. Quiero sobrepasar esto y componer nuestro matrimonio, pero ella siempre está exagerando la situación y regresa al principio— nos lleva a lo mismo.*

CO: *Ok, estoy escuchando que tú estás siendo honesto con Yolanda, diciéndole a ella sobre los mensajes de texto y estás trabajando en que ella vuelva a tenerte confianza. Yolanda, ¿Tú sientes que puedes trabajar con Lauro para que vuelvas a tenerle confianza?*

CL-Y: *No lo sé. Quiero. Pero ahorita no lo sé.*

CO: *Y está bien si no lo sabes todavía. Estás aquí con Lauro y ese es el inicio para comenzar a saber.*

Preguntas de reflexión:

1. ¿Cuáles técnicas utiliza la consejera/o en este segmento?
2. ¿Qué otra cosa podría haber hecho o preguntado la consejera/o a la pareja?

Third session:

The couple has attended two sessions and for this third session, they are ready to start discussing Lauro's alcohol use. While completing the paperwork, Lauro disclosed that his father was an alcoholic, and was worried that he was starting to have the same tendencies of drinking heavily with angry outbursts. He mentioned that his drinking was increasing, and it was starting to affect his daily life. Yolanda also agreed that she was fearful he would drive home drunk after work and injure himself or others.

CO: *Tell me about your alcohol use.*

CL-L: *It just helps. I am so tired at the end of work, and it helps me relax. The problem is that when Yolanda starts getting angry with me, I get very angry. I try not to but it is hard to control it. I have to admit that I do not like how angry I get. She does not help though. I tell her to please not start when I am trying to relax, and she does it anyway.*

CL-Y: *It is never a good time. When I am supposed to talk to you. You work all day and when you get home you just want to sit in front of the TV and drink.*

CO: *It sounds that although it helps you relax, drinking has also made it difficult for you to talk with Yolanda.*

CL-Y: *I am scared of him when he drinks.*

CO: *How so?*

CL-Y: *Well, he just raises his voice.*

CL-L: *I am sorry about that. I try not to.*

CO: *It sounds as if you feel guilty about raising your voice.*

CL-L: *I do.*

CO: *What are some of your reasons for wanting to quit or reduce the amount of alcohol you drink per day? How might you go about it?*

Reflective Questions:

1. How might you help Lauro with this issue?
2. What are some legal and ethical dilemmas associated with this problem?

Tercera Sesión:

La pareja ha asistido a dos sesiones y para la tercera sesión están listos para comenzar a conversar sobre el uso del alcohol de Lauro. Al completar el papeleo, Lauro reveló que su padre era una persona con alcoholismo y está preocupado porque él está empezando a tener las mismas tendencias de beber en exceso con arrebatos de enojo como lo hacía su padre. El mencionó que está bebiendo más y que está afectando su vida diaria. Yolanda también se preocupa que Lauro maneja borracho después del trabajo y podría herirse a sí mismo u otros.

CO: *Cuéntame sobre tu consumo de alcohol.*

CL-L: *Simplemente ayuda. Estoy tan cansado al final del trabajo y me ayuda a relajarme. El problema es que cuando Yolanda empieza a enfadarse conmigo, yo me enfado mucho. Intento no hacerlo, pero es difícil controlarlo. Tengo que admitir que no me gusta lo enojado que me pongo. Sin embargo, ella no ayuda. Le digo que por favor no comience cuando estoy tratando de relajarme y ella lo hace de todos modos.*

CL-Y: *Nunca es un buen momento. Cuando se supone que debo hablar contigo. Trabajas todo el día y cuando llegas a casa solo quieres sentarte frente al televisor y beber.*

CO: *Parece que, aunque te ayuda a relajarte, beber también te ha creado dificultades al hablar con Yolanda.*

CL-Y: *Le tengo miedo cuando bebe.*

CO: *¿Cómo así?*

CL-Y: *Bueno, solo levanta la voz.*

CL-L: *Lo siento. Intento no hacerlo.*

CO: *Suena como que te sientes culpable por levantar la voz.*

CL-L: *Así es.*

CO: *¿Cuáles son algunas de tus razones para querer dejar de fumar o reducir la cantidad de alcohol que bebes por día? ¿Cómo podrías hacerlo?*

Preguntas de Reflexión:

1. ¿Cómo ayudarías a Lauro con esta situación?
2. ¿Cuáles son los dilemas legales y éticos asociados con este problema?

Resources

- Falicov, J.C. (2015). *Latino Families in Therapy* (2nd ed.) Guilford Press.
- The Gottman Institute https://www.gottman.com/couples/
- Johnson, S. M. (2019). *The practice of emotionally focused couple therapy: Creating connection* (3rd ed.). Routledge/Taylor & Francis Group.

Caso II. El caso de Rita
Atendiendo Problemas de Enojo y Agresión

When working with court-mandated clients, counselors may encounter resistance from the client. For counseling to be effective, the client must be motivated to receive counseling services. However, court-mandated clients, or involuntary clients, do not intrinsically feel motivated to be in therapy. Counseling is a mental health profession that uses talk therapy as the primary tool to contribute to the well-being of society (Espín, 2018). As Guilman (2015) stated, "therapy is completely relational, and language is a crucial part of all human relationships" (p. 27). Honoring a client's language preference is important when considering treatment outcomes and a positive therapeutic alliance (see Chapter 2).

Case Presentation

Rita is a 38-year-old woman. She came to the session because of a judge's order. Rita presents with anger and aggression. Such aggression consists of issues with controlling her anger as well as verbal and physical aggression. She repeats this conduct in personal and professional situations. This conduct is present at any time of the day but is evident predominantly at work. After consulting legal representatives, Rita must complete a minimum of five sessions focused on anger management. This is the first time Rita has attended counseling services.

Presentación del Caso

Rita es una señora de 38 años. Rita vino a consulta bajo órdenes de un juez legal. Rita presenta problemas de enojo y agresión. Dicha agresión consiste en que Rita tiene problemas controlando su enojo y agresión verbal y física. Repite esta conducta en situaciones profesionales y personales. Esta conducta se da en cualquier momento del día, y predominantemente en el trabajo. Luego de consultar con los representantes legales, Rita requiere un mínimo de cinco sesiones enfocadas en control de ira. Esta es la primera vez que Rita usa servicios de consejería.

First Session:

The goal of this session is to understand Rita's situation from her point of view and begin to establish a client-counselor relationship. Since the sessions have been ordered, one of the intentions is to give autonomy to the client.

COUNSELOR (CO):	*Hello Rita, glad to meet you. How can I help you?*
CLIENT (CL):	*The judge ordered me to come. If it were up to me, I would not come. I do not want to be here.*
CO:	*Have you been to a counselor before?*
CL:	*No, this is the first time. Maybe I will learn something now that I am here.*
CO:	*You are correct, you can use this time for your benefit and learn new things about yourself. Is there anything that you would like to work on?*

CL: I would like to work on my anger. I do not think I have a problem as the judge claims. I can control my anger, but at that moment I could not. I had been containing my anger for a long time and that day I could not hold it in anymore.

Reflection Questions:

1. Do you have enough information to decide the therapeutic approach with which to understand, conceptualize, and treat Rita's problem?
2. What information do you believe is necessary to obtain to understand Rita's identified problem?

Primera Sesión:

La meta de esta sesión es entender la situación de Rita desde su punto de vista y empezar a formar una relación entre consejera y cliente. Ya que las sesiones son mandadas, una de las intenciones es darle autonomía al cliente.

CONSEJERA (CO):   Hola Rita, mucho gusto en conocerla. ¿En qué le puedo ayudar?
CLIENTE (CL):   El juez me dijo que viniera. Si por mi fuera no vengo. No quiero estar aquí.
CO: ¿Alguna vez ha venido a consejería?
CL: No, esta es la primera vez. A lo mejor aprendo algo ya que estoy aquí.
CO: Tienes razón. Puedes usar este tiempo para tu beneficio y aprender nuevas cosas de ti. ¿Hay algo en lo que te gustaría trabajar?
CL: Me gustaría trabajar en mi enojo. No creo que tenga un problema como dice el juez. Sí puedo controlar mi enojo, pero esa vez no pude. Tenía mucho tiempo guardándome el enojo y ese día ya no aguante.

Preguntas para Reflexión:

1. ¿Tienes suficiente información para decidir la dirección terapéutica para entender, conceptualizar y tratar el problema de Rita?
2. ¿Qué información crees que es necesario obtener para entender a Rita en relación a su problema identificado?

Second Session:

CO: How did you feel after our first session last week?

CL: *I felt fine. Even if I do not want to come, I must come, so I am going to try to use this time to work on the things that I need to improve. One of them is my anger. I know that I have a strong temper, but I do not consider myself a violent person.*

CO: *Definitely, we can focus on the things you want to improve. Can you expand more on what you mean by working on your anger?*

CL: *Not to get angry so much. There are some days in which I can control my anger but there are days in which I cannot. It depends on how much work I have. The days when I have a lot of work, I get home in a bad mood and I feel it is affecting my family and obviously, it affects me at work.*

CO: *I think this is a good place to start. You are realizing how your anger affects you, and as a consequence, the people around you. What do you think if during the week you try to pay attention to when your mood changes? Pay attention if it changes when you are with certain people or in certain places. Next time we can talk about what you noticed.*

Reflection Questions:

1. What approaches could you take in session with the information that Rita has given to you?
2. What external factors must you consider to understand Rita's behavior?
3. What are other activities that you could offer Rita for the coming week?

Segunda Sesión:

CONSEJERA (CO): *¿Cómo te sentiste después de nuestra primera sesión de la semana pasada?*

CLIENTE (CL): *Me sentí bien. Tengo que venir, aunque no quiera entonces voy a tratar de usar este tiempo para trabajar en cosas que necesito mejorar, y una de ellas es mi enojo. Yo sé que tengo carácter fuerte pero no me considero una persona violenta.*

CO: *Definitivamente nos podemos enfocar en las cosas que quieres mejorar. ¿Cuáles son algunas de estas cosas?*

CL: *No enojarme tanto. Hay días en los que puedo controlar mi enojo, pero hay días en los que no. Depende de qué tanto trabajo tenga. Los días que tengo mucho trabajo llegó a la casa de muy mal humor y siento que le está afectando a mi familia y pues obviamente me está afectando en el trabajo.*

CO: *Me parece un buen lugar para empezar. Te estás dando cuenta como tu enojo te afecta a ti y en consecuencia a la gente que te rodea. ¿Qué te parece si durante la semana tratas de poner atención si tu humor cambia cuando estás con ciertas personas o en ciertos lugares? Y la próxima sesión hablaremos de esto.*

Preguntas de Reflexión:

1. ¿Qué direcciones puedes tomar, en sesión, con la información que acaba de proporcionar Rita?
2. ¿Qué factores externos se necesitan considerar para entender el comportamiento de Rita?
3. ¿Qué otras actividades para la semana le ofrecerías a Rita?

Third Session:

COUNSELOR (CO):   *What did you think about the activity that I asked you to do during our past session?*

CLIENT (CL):   *Yes, I liked it. I am not going to say that I did not get mad during the week, but I paid more attention at all the times that I felt angry. I realized that there is a waitress at work who always wants to make me mad but this time I did not let her.*

CO: *You are proud that you were able to control your anger in that situation, Rita. I imagine that you had to make a big effort on your part.*

CL: *Yes, but to tell you the truth, I am tired of the shouting and of people thinking that they can make me angry for every little thing.*

CO: *Tell me, Rita, what did you do this time to not get angry at the waitress?*

CL: *At the beginning I ignored her, but since I saw that she kept talking and accusing me of stealing her tips I went to talk to her. I told her that I had not stolen anything from her and that the next time she should pay attention to her clients the same way we all do and then I went back to work.*

CO: *Then, to have control over your anger, first you had to realize that you were angry because of what the waitress was accusing you of, and then you decided to go talk to her to try to clarify the misunderstanding.*

Reflection Questions:

1. Identify the theoretical techniques implemented in the session.
2. With what other approach could you have processed the activity with Rita at the beginning of the session?

Tercera Sesión:

CONSEJERA (CO):   *¿Qué te pareció la actividad que te pedí que hicieras durante la semana en nuestra sesión pasada?*

CLIENTE (CL):   *Si me gusto, fíjate. No te voy a decir que no me enojé durante la semana, pero puse más atención a las veces que me sentía enojada. Me di cuenta de que en el trabajo hay una mesera que siempre me quiere hacer enojar, pero esta vez no la deje.*

CO: *Puedo ver que te sientes orgullosa porque pudiste controlar tu enojo en esa situación, Rita. Me imagino que tuviste que haber puesto mucho esfuerzo de tu parte.*

CL: *Sí, pero la verdad ya estoy cansada de los gritos y de que piensen que me pueden hacer enojar por cualquier cosa.*

CO: *Platícame Rita, ¿tú qué hiciste esta vez para no enojarte con la mesera?*

CL: *Al principio la ignoré, pero como vi que no se callaba y me estaba acusando de haberle robado las propinas entonces fui a hablar con ella. Le dije que no le había robado nada y que la próxima debe de estar al pendiente de sus clientes como todas aquí lo hacemos y luego regresé a trabajar.*

CO: *Entonces para lograr controlar tu enojo primero te diste cuenta que estabas enojada por lo que la mesera te estaba diciendo y después decidiste tener una conversación con ella para tratar de aclarar el malentendido.*

Preguntas de Reflexión:

1. Identifica las técnicas teóricas implementadas en esta sesión.
2. ¿De qué otra forma hubieras procesado con Rita la actividad al principio de la sesión?

Fourth Session:

CO: *I am glad you feel motivated to do something to feel in control of your anger.*

CL: *Yes, I do too. I realized that my stress is also affecting my relationship with my partner and my son. Sometimes when I get home my son does not want to spend time with me, and I get angry at him because of it. After my anger goes away, I realize that I overreacted and got way too angry.*

CO: *It seems like you feel guilty because you were not able to control your anger and because of that your son did not want to be with you.*

CL: *Yes, I do, but I am not going to ask for forgiveness because then my son is not going to take me seriously. I do not want that to happen.*

CO: *Rita, based on what you are saying it seems like getting angry at your son is not working out for you, but you keep getting angry because you think that is what you have to do for your son to take you seriously.*

Reflection Questions:

1. Identify the reflection techniques utilized in this session.
2. What do you think of Rita's response after the counselor's use of reflection?

3. Practice some alternative responses that would be appropriate to use with Rita.

Cuarta Sesión:

CONSEJERO/A/E (CO): *Me da gusto que te sientas motivada en hacer algo para sentirte en control de tu enojo.*

CLIENTE (CL): *Si yo también. Me di cuenta de que mi estrés también está afectando mi relación con mi pareja y mi hijo. A veces siento que cuando llegó a casa mi hijo no quiere convivir conmigo y siempre me enojo con él por eso. Pero luego cuando se me pasa el enojo, me doy cuenta de que se me pasó la mano porque me enoje demasiado.*

CO: *Parece ser que te sientes culpable cuando esto pasa.*

CL: *Si, mucho. Pero no voy a ir a pedirle perdón porque luego mi hijo no me va a tomar en serio y no quiero que eso pase.*

CO: *Rita, por lo que me dices, parece que enojarte con tu hijo no te está funcionando, pero te sigues enojado porque crees que eso es lo que tienes que hacer para que tu hijo te tome en serio.*

Preguntas de Reflexión:

1. Identifica las técnicas de reflexión utilizadas en esta sesión.
2. ¿Qué opinas de las respuestas de Rita después del uso de reflexión del consejero/a/e?
3. Práctica otras respuestas alternativas que serían apropiadas para usar con Rita.

Resources

- Ribas, R. H. (n.d.) *Entrevista Motivacional.* https://openaccess.uoc. edu/bitstream/10609/142546/10/Habilidades%20de%20comunic aci%c3%b3n%20profesional_M%c3%b3dulo%20did%c3%a1ctico%201 _Entrevista%20motivacional.pdf
- Castrillon Gómez, A., Martin Rocha, E. E., Monsalve, P., & Angarita, D. (2017). *Entrevista motivacional (EM): Herramienta de cambio para consultantes con adicciones durante el estadio de precontemplación a contemplación.* https://repository.ucc.edu.co/server/api/core/bitstreams/52195 23f-4381-4c08-aaec-917a26ea705c/content

Caso III. Caso de Abigail y su sobrino Trauma Inmigrando a los EE. UU

Compared to their U.S.-born counterparts, Latine families are much more likely to have their psychological well-being impacted by trauma (Cleary et al., 2017). Cleary and colleagues (2017) found that Latine children who migrate experience trauma before, during, and after coming to the United States. They found that to address said trauma, "culturally and linguistically appropriate educational material about potential mental health outcomes due to trauma experienced" is critical (p. 1057). Kataoka (2003) investigated the efficacy of using a cognitive behavioral group treatment program for immigrant children in elementary through high school. Their results indicated moderate benefits in reducing PTSD symptoms in their participants. Interestingly, within-group differences showed treatment progress varied by gender and country of origin. These differences underline the importance of clinicians avoiding conceptualizing Latine individuals as comprising a monolithic population (see Chapter 3).

Case Presentation

Alan, 15, reunited with his maternal aunt, Abigail, after immigration detained him five months ago. As a requisite of the immigration program, Abigail must take Alan to a counselor because there were reports of trauma during the trip. Up until now, Abigail has followed all the requisites ordered by immigration. Alan is still angry and quiet with his aunt. Alan keeps telling her that he does not need counseling and needs school even less. Alan says he must work to help his mother who is sick in her country. Even though Abigail loves her nephew and wants to help him, she does not know how to teach Alan to trust her, and she does not know how to talk to him about what happened during the trip. Abigail has asked to talk to a counselor to get support in this case.

Presentación del Caso

Alan, 15, tiene cinco meses de ser reunificado con su tía materna, Abigail, después de haber estado detenido por inmigración. Por requisitos del programa de inmigración que detenía a Alan, Abigail tiene que llevar a Alan a una consejera porque hubo reportes de trauma durante el viaje. Hasta este momento Abigail ha seguido todos los requisitos que inmigración le ha pedido, pero Alan sigue enojado y muy callado con ella. Alan le sigue diciendo a Abigail que él no necesita consejería y mucho menos ir a la escuela porque él tiene que trabajar para poder ayudar a su madre que dejó enferma en su país. Aunque Abigail ama a su sobrino y lo quiere ayudar, ella no sabe cómo enseñarle a Alan que tenga confianza con ella y no sabe cómo platicar con él sobre lo que le pasó en el viaje. Abigail ha pedido hablar con una consejera para recibir apoyo en este caso.

First Session:

Today is Abigail's first session and she has filled up documents about services consent including confidentiality and limitations. Abigail's facial expression changes and she looks confused during the time the counselor reviews the counseling rules.

COUNSELOR (CO):   *I see you have questions. I want you to know this is a safe space for you to ask any questions that come to mind.*

ABIGAIL (CL):   *Yes, yes, I have several questions and even more regarding what you said about confidentiality. I came here with you because my nephew Alan has come to live with me after being detained by immigration. They told me that he had ugly experiences and asked me to bring him here. I have never gone to counseling and I do not understand this very well, but I see that my nephew needs help. He is very stubborn and does not want to go to school. I do not understand him. My sister is very worried, and I do not know what to do.*

CO: *Abigail, I would like for you to talk to me on a first-name basis. I am here to find a solution with you, and I hope you can trust me.*

CL: *Oh, yes, of course.*

CO: *All right, going back to what you were telling me about your nephew, I heard a lot of worry on your part. Help me understand where that feeling of worry is coming from. Tell me a little more about your nephew.*

Reflection Questions:

1. What do you think about this initial session with Abigail?
2. The counselor asked the client to talk to her on a first-name basis. How does this affect the relationship between counselor and client?
3. What would be an alternative open question that the counselor could have used in her last response?

Primera sesión:

Hoy es la primera sesión de Abigail y ha llenado documentos sobre el consentimiento de servicios que incluye confidencialidad y limitaciones. En el momento que la consejera revisa estas reglas de consejería, Abigail se presenta confundida por la manera que cambió la expresión de su cara.

CONSEJERO/A/E (CO): *Noto que tienes preguntas. Quiero que sepas que este es un espacio seguro y que puedas hacer preguntas cuando vengan a tu mente.*

ABIGAIL (CL): *Si, si tengo muchas preguntas y más con lo que comenta sobre la confidencialidad conmigo. Vengo aquí con usted porque mi sobrino, Alan, ha llegado conmigo desde que fue detenido por inmigración. Ellos me contaron que pasó por cosas muy feas y me pidieron que lo trajera aquí. Yo nunca he ido a consejería y no lo entiendo muy bien, pero si miro que mi sobrino necesita ayuda porque es muy necio y no quiere venir ni ir a la escuela. No lo entiendo y mi hermana está muy preocupada y yo no sé qué hacer.*

CO: *Abigail, me gustaría que me hables de "tu", yo estoy aquí para encontrar una solución contigo y espero que puedas confiar en mí.*

ABIGAIL: *O, si claro.*

CONSEJERA: *Bueno, en lo que me contabas sobre tu sobrino escuché mucha preocupación de tu parte. Ayúdame a entender de dónde viene esta preocupación tuya. Cuéntame un poco más sobre tu sobrino.*

Preguntas de Reflexión:

1. ¿Qué opinas sobre esta sesión inicial con Abigail?
2. La consejera le pidió a la cliente que utilizará "tu" y no "Usted". ¿Cómo afecta esto a la relación entre consejera y cliente?
3. ¿Cuál sería una pregunta abierta alternativa que la consejera pudiera usar en su última respuesta?

Second Session:

Abigail has returned to counseling a week after her initial session. Abigail enters the room and reports feeling strange returning because her husband calls her crazy for coming to counseling. Abigail also mentions that lately Alan has been disrespectful and is not doing his homework.

CO: *Correct me if I am wrong. You feel as if you are divided between returning to counseling and not wanting others, like your husband, to look at you differently.*

CL: Well, yes and no. I know that I have to do my chores at home and for my family, but I do not feel that my family helps me or asks how I am doing, much less now that Alan is at home. I feel that I run and run, and I never sit down. When I come here, I feel like I am being selfish for wanting to be here instead of cooking at home or doing something else.

CO: What a heavy emotion it is to feel selfish. Abigail, if you could do anything in the world for one day without any worry, what would you do?

CL: Oh God! I do not know. (Silence) No, I do not know.

CO: Let us try together. Close your eyes ... breathe deeply ... and imagine a day of silence and peace at your favorite place. Where are you?

Reflection Questions:

1. Abigail came to the session with a lot in mind. Why do you think the counselor decided to talk about the way Abigail was feeling instead of counseling about Alan?
2. In this session the counselor begins to use the application of theory. Can you name which theory is she using and how effective was the application in this session?
3. What's your opinion on one area of the counselor's growth?

Segunda Sesión:

Abigail ha regresado a consejería una semana después de su sesión inicial. Abigail entra al cuarto y reporta sintiéndose rara regresando porque su esposo la llama loca por haber entrado a sesiones de consejería. Abigail también menciona que Alan últimamente le falta el respeto y no hace su tarea de escuela.

CONSEJERO/A/E (CO):   Corrígeme si entiendo bien. Te sientes como si estuvieras dividida entre venir a terapia y no querer que otros, como tu esposo, te miren diferente.

ABIGAIL (CL):   Bueno, sí y no. Yo sé que tengo que hacer mis deberes en la casa y para mi familia, pero también no siento que mi familia me ayuda o pregunta como estoy – mucho menos ahora que está Alan en la casa. Siento que corro y corro y nunca me siento. Cuando llegué aquí, siento que soy egoísta por querer estar aquí cuando muy bien pudiera estar cocinando y haciendo algo más.

CO: Que emoción tan pesada la de sentirse egoísta. Abigail, si pudieras hacer cualquier cosa en el mundo sin ninguna preocupación por un día, ¿qué harías?

CL: ¡Hay Dios! No lo sé. [Silencio]. No, no lo sé.

CO: Vamos a intentarlo juntas. Cierra los ojos ... respira profundamente ... e imagínate un día de silencio y paz en tu lugar favorito. ¿Dónde estás?

Preguntas de Reflexión:

1. Abigail entró a la sesión con mucho en mente, ¿Por qué crees que la consejera decidió platicar sobre cómo se sentía Abigail en parte de atender consejería y no sobre Alan? ¿Crees que esta fue una buena decisión de parte de la consejera y por qué?
2. En esta sesión, la consejera comienza a utilizar la aplicación de teoría. ¿Puedes nombrar que teoría utiliza y que tan efectiva era la aplicación en esta sesión?
3. ¿Qué opinas que es un área de crecimiento para la consejera en esta sesión?

Third Session:

After being absent on the last appointment, Abigail returned to counseling. She apologized for her absence and started to talk about Alan. In this session, the counselor focuses on the relationship between Abigail and Alan.

CL: *I know I am not his mother and I understand that he is worried about his mother. I am worried as well. She is my sister and I love her. I know that he came here to be able to help her, but he must understand that he cannot be working because he is a minor. I know that because the caseworker at the shelter where he was detained explained it to me and he also knows that. But he keeps getting angry with me.*

CO: *I can hear that you feel torn, but this time you want to help your sister and can't because of the laws of this country. To understand Alan's situation, could you tell me how you decided for Alan to come to the United States?*

CL: *Well, he decided. My sister has been sick for a year after they found out she has breast cancer. My poor sister is a single mother, and she cannot pay for the treatment that she needs. I have helped her as much as I can, but the money that I make cleaning houses, some months it's not enough even for food. She hasn't been able to work for a few months after she got sick. Alan, being the little man of the house, stopped going to school and began to work to help his mother. One day I received a call from my sister. She was very worried because Alan had disappeared, and she was thinking that the "Mara" had killed him. A few weeks later immigration called telling me that they had detained Alan at the border, and I almost died when they told me.*

CO: *So, you have been responsible for him since then.*

CL: *Yes, he is my nephew, and I love him a lot in good times and bad times. Now that my sister is sick and he is here, I have more responsibility to take care of him, for her.*

CO: *In other words, you feel like an extension of your sister, and now you are like a mother for Alan.*

Reflection Questions:

1. How can the counselor manage Abigail's desire to focus on Alan versus the counselor's goals for Ana?
2. Knowing what you know about familismo and acculturation, what is important for the counselor to consider when working with Ana?

Tercera Sesión:

Después de haber faltado a su cita la última sesión, Abigail regresó a consejería. Ella se disculpa por haber faltado y comienza a platicar sobre Alan. En esta sesión la consejera se enfoca en la relación entre Abigail y Alan.

ABIGAIL (CL): *Yo sé que no soy su madre y entiendo que él está preocupado por su mamá. Yo también estoy preocupada por ella. Ella es mi hermana y la amo. Yo sé que él vino aquí para poder ayudarla, pero él tiene que entender que no puede estar trabajando porque todavía es menor de edad. Eso lo sé porque su trabajadora del caso en el albergue donde estuvo detenido me lo explicó y sé que él lo sabe también. Pero aún sigue enojado conmigo.*

CONSEJERO/A/E (CO): *Escucho que otra vez te encuentras entre los dos sentimientos, pero esta vez es querer ayudar a tu sobrino y hermana, y no poder ayudar por las leyes de este país. ¿Me pudieras contar cómo decidieron que Alan llegará a los Estados Unidos para poder entender la situación de Alan?*

CL: *Bueno, él lo decidió. Mi hermana ha estado enferma por un año después de que le encontraron cáncer en los senos. Mi pobre hermana es madre soltera y no puede pagar por los tratamientos que necesita. Yo le he ayudado lo tanto que yo pueda, pero el dinero que hago limpiando casas no me ajusta unos meses ni para la comida. Después de unos meses de que le dijeron, se puso muy grave y no ha podido trabajar desde entonces. Alan, siendo el hombrecito de la casa, dejó de ir a la escuela y comenzó a trabajar para poder ayudar a su mamá. Un día recibí una llamada de mi hermana que estaba preocupada porque Alan había desaparecido y pensaba que la Mara lo había matado. A las semanas, inmigración me llamó diciéndome que habían detenido a Alan en la frontera y yo casi me muero cuando me dijeron.*

CO: *Así que tú te hiciste responsable de él desde entonces.*

CL: *Pues sí, es mi sobrino y lo quiero mucho en las buenas y las malas. Ahora que mi hermana está enferma y él está aquí, tengo más responsabilidad de cuidarlo para ella.*

CO: *En otras palabras, te sientes como una extensión de tu hermana y ahora eres como una madre para Alan.*

Preguntas de Reflexión:

1. ¿Cómo puede el consejero/a/e manejar el deseo de Abigail de enfocarse en Alan versus las metas del consejero/a/e para Ana?
2. Sabiendo lo que sabes sobre el familismo y la aculturación, ¿qué es importante que el consejero/a/e considere cuando trabaja con Ana?

Resources

- Coalition for Immigrant Mental Health. CIMH *Mental Health Resources*, https://ourcimh.org/mh-resources
- Gsafe (2017). *Stress related to immigration status in students: A brief guide for school.* https://gsafewi.org/stress-related-to-immigration-status-in-students-a-brief-guide-for-schools/
- Inclusive Therapists. *Migrants/ Immigrants/ Refugees—Find Inclusive Therapists, Counselors and Mental Health Care Near You. https://www. inclusivetherapists.com/immigration-diaspora-refugee*

Caso IV. El Caso de Ximena
Ansiedad Social como Estudiante de Primera Generación

Social anxiety disorder (SAD) consists of an individual's fear and avoidance of social situations due to the chance of being judged negatively (American Psychiatric Association, 2013). At least 13% of the global population has presented SAD symptoms once in their lifetime (Baxter et al., 2013; Spence & Rapee, 2016). Additionally, SAD has a prevalence rate of 7% and rates higher for females than males (American Psychiatric Association, 2013). However, among the Latine population living in the United States, no gender differences were found (Polo et al., 2011).

Social withdrawal is a main consequence of SAD because individuals develop a perception that others view them negatively and assume that they are being ridiculed and evaluated (Campbell et al., 2016; Rapee & Heimberg,

1997). Post-event rumination is also a common experience of those with social anxiety, commonly cited as a factor that aids the persistence of the disorder (Campbell et al., 2016). Post-event rumination is the re-experience and focus on the past social event where they perceived failure and caused them great anxiety (Kocovski et al., 2009).

Nordstrom et al. (2014) observed that students with high social anxiety reported a variety of adaptive concerns, such as (1) lower academic and social self-esteem, (2) college adjustment problems, and (3) higher levels of mental health symptoms including obsessive-compulsive behavior, depression, and phobia. Social anxiety decreased in their participants from the beginning of the semester to the end if they did not avoid the repeated exposure to social situations that college provides, similar to exposure therapy. However, this does not apply to those who do avoid exposure due to social situations. Those who avoid social environments will suffer academically, further adding to the difficulty of adjusting to college and increasing the chances of dropping out (Nordstrom et al., 2014). Similarly, Russell and Topham (2012) indicated that students who experience social anxiety isolate themselves and become distressed. This often leads to academic problems.

Case Presentation

Ximena is 19 years old, and she is in her first year as a university student in a university out of town. She is the first in her family to attend a university. Ximena decides to go to the counselor's office and wants to talk to a counselor.

Presentación del Caso

Ximena tiene 19 años y está en su primer año como estudiante universitaria en una universidad fuera de la ciudad. Ella es la primera en su familia en asistir a la universidad. Ximena decide ir a la oficina del consejero y quiere hablar con un consejero.

First Session:

COUNSELOR (CO):   *I am glad you are here. Tell me how and why did you decide to come here today?*
XIMENA (CL):   *I decided to come because I do not have many friends in school. My family does not live here, and I feel sad.*
CO: *You feel lonely and miss your friends?*

CL: *Yes. It is hard for me to make friends. I do not trust people. They always disappoint me.*

CO: *Mhmm. Tell me more about that.*

CL: *I lack trust to empathize with people under new circumstances. I have always been shy ever since I was little. My childhood friends made me feel ashamed by making comments about my body and calling me fat. I feel ugly . . . Well, I know that I am.*

Reflection Questions:

1. In which direction could the counselor continue this dialogue?
2. What is the relationship between Ximena and her worries?
3. How can you prepare for the second session?

Primera Sesión:

CONSEJERO/A/E (CO):   *Me alegra mucho que estés aquí. ¿Cuéntame cómo y porqué decidiste venir hoy?*

XIMENA (CL):   *Decidí venir porque no tengo muchos amigos en la escuela. Y mi familia no vive en esta ciudad. Me siento triste*

CO: *¿Te sientes sola y extrañas a tus amistades?*

CL: *Si. Se me hace difícil hacer amigos. No confió en la gente. Siempre me decepcionan*

CO: *hmm. Cuéntame más de eso*

CL: *Me falta confianza para empatizar con las personas en nuevas circunstancias. Siempre he sido tímida desde que era pequeña. Mis amigos de la infancia me hicieron sentir avergonzada al hacer comentarios sobre mi cuerpo y me llamaban gorda. Me siento fea . . . bueno, sé que lo soy.*

Preguntas de Reflexión:

1. ¿En qué dirección puede el consejero/a/e seguir este diálogo?
2. ¿Cuál puede ser la relación entre el pasado de Ximena y sus preocupaciones?
3. ¿Cómo puedes prepararte para la segunda sesión?

Second Session:

The counselor and the client discuss the summary of the first session and continue to discuss Ximena's trust issues with new people.

co: *When can you trust other people?*

cl: *The only friends I can trust are my family. They understand me and support me.*

co: *You feel safe with them. I imagine that it is hard to be far away from them in difficult times.*

cl: *Yes, I always spent time with them before I came here. I especially miss my sister. We did everything together. Now we almost barely talk because she is working a lot, and I have a lot of homework.*

co: *It is hard to maintain relationships when you are a student and living far away from them.*

cl: *Yes, sometimes I think of going back. I am so lonely here. I know that is not possible. My family expects me to be a successful doctor who makes a lot of money. I do not want to study this. I want to be in the designing business. I told that to my mom once and she scolded me. She told me that it was better for me to sleep on the street, to get used to it because there is no money in that business.*

co: *You feel pressured to please your parents.*

cl: *Yes, I am the only one who has reached a university level. I feel the responsibility to improve their economic situation. As if I have the responsibility to make sure that my family does not have a life of poverty. That makes things more difficult. I hate school, what I am studying. That, besides the fact that I do not have friends, makes me depressed.*

Reflection Questions:

1. What cultural aspects are important to be noticed?
2. How can you prepare for the next session?

Segunda Sesión:

El consejero/a/e y el cliente discuten el resumen de la primera sesión y continúan discutiendo los problemas de confianza de Ximena con personas nuevas.

CONSEJERO/A/E (CO): *¿En qué circunstancias puedes confiar en otros?*

XIMENA (CL): *Los únicos amigos en quien puedo confiar son mis familiares. Ellos me entienden y me apoyan.*

co: *Te sientes segura con ellos. Me imagino que es muy difícil estar lejos de ellos en momentos difíciles.*

cl: *Si, yo siempre pasaba el tiempo con ellos antes de venir aquí. Extraño especialmente a mi hermana. Hacíamos todo juntas. Ahora casi no hablamos porque está trabajando mucho y yo tengo mucha tarea.*

co: *Es difícil mantener relaciones cuando eres una estudiante viviendo lejos de ellos.*

cl: *Si. A veces pienso regresar. Estoy tan sola aquí. Pero yo sé que eso no se puede. Mi familia espera que llegue a ser una doctora exitosa y que gane mucho dinero. Yo no quiero estudiar eso. Yo quiero estar en el negocio de diseño de moda. Le dije esto a mi mamá una vez y me regañó. Me dijo que es mejor que ya duerma en la calle para acostumbrarme porque no hay dinero en ese negocio.*

CO: *Sientes la presión de complacer a tus padres.*

CL: *Si. Soy la única que ha llegado a un grado universitario. Siento la carga y responsabilidad de mejorar su situación económica. Como si fuera mi responsabilidad asegurarme que mi familia no esté viviendo en la pobreza. Esto hace las cosas más difíciles. Yo odio ir a la escuela, mis estudios. Eso, aparte de que no tengo amigos, me causa estar deprimida.*

Preguntas de Reflexión:

1. ¿Qué aspectos culturales son importantes de notar?
2. ¿Cómo puedes prepararte para la próxima sesión?

Third Session:

Ximena canceled three appointments, and this is the first time that she has come back after three weeks. In this session, the counselor continues to talk about Ximena's shyness when talking to new people.

CO: *Hello Ximena! I did not hear from you these last three weeks. How have you been?*

CL: *Yes . . . I know. Forgive me. I missed the first appointment because I had a panic attack. I was walking downtown, and suddenly I felt that everybody was looking at me, judging me. I got nervous, and I wanted to cry and hide.*

CO: *You must have felt a lot of fear. Why do you think it was a panic attack?*

CL: *My heart was beating very fast. I began to sweat. I felt like fainting. I was very afraid.*

CO: *Mhmm. Yes, it sounds like a panic attack.*

CL: *Yes, I felt that everybody was looking at me and talking about me telling me ugly things. Since then, I did not want to get out of my dorm.*

CO: *Wow! Even when your body and mind told you not to get out, here you are. You are very courageous.*

CL: *Mhmm . . . I suppose. I had not thought about it. It's just that I do not want to be suspended from school. I do not want to do that to my family.*

CO: *Are you afraid to disappoint them?*

CL: *(Begins to cry). They have fought a lot so I can have this opportunity (silence). I do not have someone to talk with. My mother is my best friend. They are my only support system. I do not want to tell them because they will not understand. For them, my life is easy because I did not grow up like they did. I know they are going to be frustrated with me.*

Reflection Questions:

1. What is the counselor's responsibility for checking the client's well-being when she did not show up?
2. How do you suggest the counselor should continue future sessions?
3. What techniques and interventions could be helpful to address Ximena's panic attacks and overall anxiety?

Tercera Sesión:

Ximena canceló tres citas y esta es la primera vez que regresa después de tres semanas. El consejero/a/e continúa hablando de la timidez que tiene Ximena al hablar con gente nueva en esta sesión.

CONSEJERO/A/E (CO):   *¡Hola Ximena! No supe de ti estas últimas semanas. ¿Cómo has estado?*

XIMENA (CL):   *Si . . . yo sé. Perdóname. La primera cita que falté fue porque tuve un ataque de pánico. Estaba caminando por el centro y de repente sentí que todos me estaban mirando y que me juzgaban. Me puse muy nerviosa y quería llorar y esconderme.*

CO: *Debes de haber sentido mucho miedo. ¿Qué te hace pensar que fue un ataque de pánico?*

CL: *Pues, mi corazón latía rápido. Empecé a sudar. Sentí que me iba a desmayar. Tenía mucho miedo.*

CO: *hmm..Si eso suena como un ataque de pánico.*

CL: *Si. Sentía que todos me miraban y que estaban hablando de mí, diciéndome cosas feas. Desde entonces no he querido salir de mi dormitorio.*

CO: *¡Guau! Aun cuando tu cuerpo y tu mente te dijeron que no debes salir, aquí estás. Eres muy valiente.*

CL: *hmm . . . supongo que sí. No lo había pensado. Es que no quiero que me suspendieran de la escuela. No quiero hacerle eso a mi familia.*

CO: *¿Tienes miedo de decepcionarlos?*

CL: *(empieza a llorar) Ellos han luchado tanto para que yo tenga esta oportunidad (Silencio). Y no tengo con quien hablar. Mi mamá es mi mejor amiga. Ellos son mi único sistema de apoyo. Y no les quiero decir esto porque sé que no lo entenderían. Para ellos, mi vida es tan fácil porque no crecí como ellos. Sé que solo se van a frustrar conmigo.*

Preguntas de Reflexión:

1. ¿Cuál es la responsabilidad del consejero cuando un cliente no viene a su sesión?

2. ¿Cómo sugieres que el consejero continúe esta conversación en la próxima sesión?
3. ¿Qué técnicas e intervenciones podrían ser útiles para abordar los ataques de pánico y la ansiedad general de Ximena?

Session Four:

The counselor and Ximena pick up from the last session and further discuss her anxiety. Ximena reports that her anxiety is now starting to affect her ability to attend class.

COUNSELOR (CO): Hello Ximena, last week we talked about the panic attack that you had. We also talked about your fears and doubts you have about talking to your family. How have you been since last week?

XIMENA (CL): I have missed many classes. I cannot walk if there are a lot of people going to class. My grades are very low. I only go out to buy food and take it to my room to eat and to be alone. I have spent a lot of time in my room.

CO: Your voice tells me that this situation worries you.

CL: Yes, I want to go to my classes. I want to be with my classmates. Every time I try to talk to other students and make new friends I begin to feel as if I am getting another attack. I start thinking about all the ugly things they might be saying about me.

CO: You feel that everything is focused on you. I also hear that before you get to know your friends you have decided that they are thinking bad things about you.

CL: I could think logically, and I know that they are probably not talking bad about me. I know, but at that moment I cannot control my anxiety.

CO: When was the last time you had a panic attack?

CL: Since the last visit that I missed.

CO: I know you have spent a lot of time alone, but you also told me that you also go out to eat and get out to come here. What techniques have you used in those occasions to overcome the panic?

Reflection Questions:

1. What solution technique is the counselor using in the last line?
2. Which would be another question or comment that the counselor could add to direct the treatment in the line?
3. How can you prepare for the next session?

Cuarta Sesión:

La consejera y Ximena retoman la última sesión y discuten más a fondo su ansiedad. Ximena informa que su ansiedad ahora está empezando a afectar su capacidad para asistir a clases.

CONSEJERO/A/E (CO):   *Hola Ximena, la semana pasada hablamos del ataque de pánico que tuviste. También hablamos de tus miedos y dudas de hablar con tu familia. ¿Cómo has estado desde la semana pasada?*

XIMENA (CL):   *He perdido muchas clases. No puedo caminar por donde hay mucha gente para llegar a la clase. Mis notas ya están muy bajas. Solo salgo para comprar comida y me lo llevo de regreso al cuarto para comer y estar sola. Estoy pasando mucho tiempo encerrada.*

CO: *Tu voz me dice que eso te preocupa mucho*

CL: *Si. Yo quiero ir a mis clases. Quiero estar con mis compañeros. Pero cada vez que trato de hablar con otros y hacer nuevos amigos, empiezo a sentir que me va a dar otro ataque. Empiezo a pensar en todas las cosas feas que a lo mejor están diciendo de mí.*

CO: *Sientes que todo el enfoque está en ti. También estoy escuchando que antes de conocer a amistades, ya has decidido que ellos piensan mal de ti.*

CL: *Yo puedo pensar lógicamente y sé que probablemente no están hablando mal de mí. Lo sé. Pero en el momento, no puedo controlar la ansiedad.*

CO: *¿Cuándo fue la última vez que te dio un ataque de pánico?*

CL: *Desde la primera visita que perdí.*

CO: *Yo sé que has pasado mucho tiempo sola. Pero también me contaste que has salido para comer y también sales para venir aquí. ¿En esas ocasiones, qué técnicas has usado para sobrepasarlo?*

Preguntas de Reflexión:

1. ¿Qué técnica de terapia centrada en soluciones está usando el consejero/a/e en la última línea?
2. ¿Cuál sería otra pregunta o comentario que podría añadir el consejero/a/e para dirigir el tratamiento en la línea?
3. ¿Cómo puedes prepararte para la próxima sesión?

Resources

- National Institute of Mental Health. ¡ESTOY TAN ESTRESADO! https://www.nimh.nih.gov/sites/default/files/health/publications/espanol/ estoy-tan-estresado/estoy-tan-estresado-hoja-informativa.pdf
- National Institute of Mental Health (2022). *Trastorno de ansiedad generalizada: Cuando no se puede controlar la preocupación.* https://www.nimh.nih.gov/sites/default/files/documents/health/publi cations/espanol/trastorno-de-ansiedad-generalizada-cuando-no-se-pue den-controlar-las-preocupaciones-new/trastorno_de_ansiedad_generaliz ada.pdf
- National Society Anxiety Center. https://nationalsocialanxietycenter. com/resources/
- McKleroy, A. (2020). *Essential strategies for social anxiety: practical techniques to face your fears, overcome self-doubt, and thrive.* Rockridge Press.
- Hendriksen, E. (2019). *How to be yourself: Quiet your inner critic and rise above social anxiety.* St. Martin's Griffin.
- Bell, A. (2021). *The highly sensitive person: building social relationships and emotional intelligence as a HSP: How to overcome anxiety and worry and stop emotional overload with eq strategies.* Independently published.

Caso V: Caso de Alexa
Ser AfroLatina y LGBTQ+

When working with culturally diverse individuals, counselors must be aware of how their worldview may impact how they negatively view their client, including awareness of their privilege, marginalization, and potential biases (see Chapter 3). Counselors must provide their clients with a safe platform to unpack their thoughts on issues such as gender, gender expression, sexuality, race, language, or experiences of oppression. Latine individuals often navigate multiple marginalized identities and counselors must be prepared to address these issues as they illuminate themselves in session.

Gender Considerations

Latine families often pass on consejos (advice) to shape their child's behavior and learning. Cultural programming such as gender roles, norms, expectations, and values are implemented through storytelling and testimonios (testimonies). Over time, children grow into adults and eventually solidify their beliefs. Clients may experience cognitive dissonance when individuals challenge or reject their beliefs as they come to new realizations and opinions. In addition, traditional views and bias may be reflected in how they view others and themselves. Domenech Rodriguez (2018) described feeling stumped by the following riddle:

> A father and son were driving when they got in a terrible accident. The father died. The son was rushed to the hospital and wheeled into the operating room. The surgeon rushed in to perform an operation, stopped, and said "I can't operate on him. He's my son." Who is the doctor? (p. 71)

The author discussed feeling "smug" for giving a progressive answer that the son most likely had "two fathers", completely ignoring the possibility that the surgeon was his mother, a female. Latine traditional roles may consider women to be homemakers while considering men to attain career skills and success. They may also consider a woman's sexuality as pure and sacred, tied often to religious values. Having clients explore their understanding of gender roles, including gender identity and expression, will help them to gain insight into how they perpetuate stereotypes or how they are placed in boxed views.

LGBTQ+ Considerations

Cultural values are an integral part of Latine ethnic identity. LGBTQI+ Latine persons often must navigate complicated familial processes including religious and gender ideologies/rhetoric (Schmitz et al., 2020). Religious institution affiliation, specifically Catholicism for many Latine individuals, may shape a client's decision to not share their sexual orientation with others for fear that others can reject and attack them. As a result, rejection and LGBTQ+ discrimination can lead to poor mental health outcomes, including the increase of suicidal behaviors (Sutter & Perrin, 2016). Counselors may do well to support, advocate, and guide clients to develop an awareness of how their mental health is impacted by experiences of discrimination and rejection.

Afro-Latine Identity

Latine individuals make up a group of diverse experiences based on ethnicity, migration patterns, language, generational status, and citizenship (Torres, 2004; see Chapter 3). Despite their ever-growing status in the United States, there is still a tendency to treat Latine individuals as a monolithic group. Disacknowledgement of within-group differences can lead to underrepresentation of unique identities such as Afro-Latine clients, Latine people of African descent. It is important to consider the racialized perspectives of Afro-Latine clients and the historical context from which Latine preference for Whiteness dates to Spanish colonialism (Haywood, 2017). Racism, specifically colorism, can impact Afro-Latine clients which may result in microaggressions and a negative view of self. Additionally, Afro-Latine individuals are influenced by familial racial socialization to either accept or reject their dual identities of color (Haywood, 2017). Counselors may formulate treatment plans surrounding client issues with navigating their biracial identities and recognizing cultural strengths.

Case Presentation

Alexa is a 24-year-old undergraduate student who identifies as Afro-Latina and bisexual. She shared that their preferred pronouns are they/their/them. Their relationships with other women have been kept secret as their family is not accepting of non-traditional relationships. Now that they are living on campus, they are seeking a safe space to discuss these relationships and learn how to adjust to new freedoms.

Presentación del Caso

Alexa es un estudiante universitario de 24 años que se identifica como afrolatine y bisexual. Elle compartió que su pronombre preferido es elle. Sus relaciones con otras mujeres se han mantenido en secreto ya que su familia no acepta relaciones no tradicionales. Ahora que vive en el campus, está buscando un espacio seguro para discutir estas relaciones y aprender a adaptarse a las nuevas libertades.

First session:

Alexa explained that this was their first experience with counseling and was looking forward to having a safe space to discuss their relationships and college experience as a first-generation student.

COUNSELOR (CO): *Hello Alexa, tell me what brings you here today.*

ALEXA (CL): *Well, I am really struggling with my first semester at school. Trying to balance family, school, and relationships. But more than anything it is my relationships that I want to talk about.*

CO: *Ok. Say more about your relationships.*

CL: *Well. (silence). I'm bisexual. My family does not know about that. I grew up in a family environment that was not very accepting of the LGBTQ+ community. So even though I've known for a while that I am bi, most of my relationships with women were kept secret. This always ended up messing up the relationship and we broke up a lot of times because of that.*

CO: *You really didn't feel safe opening up to your family and that affected your relationships.*

CL: *They did and now that I am living on campus, I feel free to be myself and have relationships but I am honestly anxious about it. I have never been able to just be myself and explore my sexuality. I am excited but also scared.*

CO: *That can be something we explore in session if you'd like.*

Reflection Questions:

1. Take a moment and reflect on some of the cultural identities presented in this case. What are some personal beliefs, attitudes, or misconceptions you have that might interfere with counseling this client? How might you overcome them?
2. Describe some of Alexa's self-identities. How might these identities be used in counseling as strengths and resiliency qualities? How might these identities also clash with one another?

Primera Sesión:

Alexa explicó que esta fue su primera experiencia con la consejería y esperaba tener un espacio seguro para discutir sus relaciones y experiencia universitaria como estudiante de primera generación.

COUNSELOR (CO): *¿Hola Alexa, dime qué te trae aquí hoy?*

ALEXA (CL):   *Bueno, realmente estoy luchando con mi primer semestre en la escuela. Tratando de equilibrar la familia, la escuela y las relaciones. Pero más que nada es de mis relaciones que quiero hablar.*

CO: *Ok. Di más sobre tus relaciones.*

CL: *Pues. (silencio). Soy bisexual. Mi familia no sabe nada de eso. Crecí dentro de un ambiente familiar que no aceptaba mucho a la comunidad LGBTQ+. Así que a pesar de que he sabido por un tiempo que soy bi, la mayoría de mis relaciones con las mujeres se mantuvieron en secreto. Esto siempre terminaba arruinando la relación y rompimos muchas veces por eso.*

CO: *Realmente no te sentías segure abriéndote con tu familia y eso afectó tus relaciones.*

CL: *La verdad que sí y ahora que estoy viviendo en el campus, me siento libre de ser yo misme y tener relaciones, pero honestamente estoy ansiose por eso. Nunca he sido capaz de ser yo misme y explorar mi sexualidad. Estoy emocionade, pero también asustade.*

CO: *Eso puede ser algo que exploremos en la sesión si lo deseas.*

Preguntas de Reflexión:

1. Toma un momento y piensa en las identidades culturales presentadas en este caso. ¿Cuáles son algunas de las creencias personales, actitudes o conceptos erróneos que tienes y que tal vez interfieran al aconsejar a este cliente? ¿Cómo podrías superarlos?
2. Describe alguna de las auto-identidades de Alexa. ¿Cómo se pueden usar en consejería para re-enforzar y como cualidades de resiliencia? ¿Cómo podrían estas chocar entre ellas?

Second Session:

Alexa disclosed that they were very moved by the previous session and felt so much relief in opening up to someone. They shared more about their personal life and completed the biopsychosocial. Alexa discussed more in depth about their background and their family's religious identity. They shared that they grew up Catholic and often felt guilty for their sexual identity because it was not accepted in their religion. They felt that their faith was always strong growing up but over time they isolated themselves from their community of faith which created strains in their relationships with family and friends from church. The following are words exchanged between counselor and client:

COUNSELOR (CO):   *It must have been very difficult to lose a piece of yourself and your community due to feeling isolated and ignored.*

ALEXA (CL):   *Yeah, it felt even worse than that. Like a leper, I was rejected. And by the people I loved and cared about, even worse.*

CO: *You felt shunned and cast away. Although, your faith was also an important part of your world. How was that for you?*

CL: *It was so hard. No lo aguante. It became harder to keep my faith in a God who did not accept me for who I am.*

Reflective Questions:

1. The topic of religion is a central issue for this session. How do you feel the counselor could respond to Alexa's internal struggle with their faith?
2. What are some counseling theories you may use moving forward with Alexa? What might be the best fit for the client?

Segunda Sesión:

Alexa reveló que estaba muy conmovide por la sesión anterior y sintió mucho alivio al abrirse con alguien. Compartió más sobre su vida personal y completó el biopsicosocial. Alexa discutió más en profundidad sobre sus antecedentes y la identidad religiosa de su familia. Compartió que creció en la religión católica y a menudo se sentía culpable por su identidad sexual porque no era aceptade en su religión. Sentía que su fe siempre era fuerte mientras crecía, pero con el tiempo se había aislado de su comunidad de fe, lo que creó tensiones en sus relaciones con familiares y amigos de la iglesia. Las siguientes son palabras intercambiadas entre el consejero y el cliente:

CONSEJERO (CO):   *Ha de haber sido muy difícil perder una parte de vos misme y tu comunidad debido a que te ignoraban y sentías aislamiento.*

ALEXA (CL):   *Sí se sintió peor que eso. Como un leproso, era rechazade y todo esto por las personas que me importaban y a quienes quería, era peor.*

CO: *Te sentías desechade y rechazade. A pesar de esto, tu fe era también parte de tu mundo. ¿Cómo te fue con eso?*

ALEXA: *Fue muy difícil. ¡No lo aguante! Me fue más difícil mantener mi fe en Dios quién no me acepta por quién yo soy.*

Preguntas de Reflexión:

1. El tema de religión es un tema central para esta sesión. ¿Cómo piensas que el consejero podría responder a la lucha interna de Alexa con su fe?
2. ¿Cuáles son las teorías de consejería que puedes utilizar para avanzar con Alexa? ¿Cuál sería lo más adecuado para este cliente?

Third session:

Although Alexa has only attended two sessions, they shared a traumatic experience from this past weekend involving them being arrested for a domestic violence charge. Alexa appeared in extreme distress and mentioned that they were experiencing symptoms such as hypervigilance, flashbacks, mistrust, and nightmares. They recalled the memory of being arrested at their home and feeling helpless while they were locked away overnight. They were slowly able to talk through the moments leading to the trauma, including being choked by their girlfriend and having to use physical force to defend themselves. Alexa also mentioned some important implications such as being the only one arrested, despite their girlfriend also being involved in the altercation. She discussed the arrested officers, a Latino male and a White male, and her girlfriend was a White female.

COUNSELOR (CO):	*You mentioned that the officers' race stood out to you, tell me more about that.*
ALEXA (CL):	*Pues eran blanquitos and I'm not, that was obvious. They didn't have to tell me they were discriminatory; it was all over their faces. I opened my mouth and they heard me speaking Spanish and the first comment the Latino cop made was "You don't speak Spanish, don't try me." I'm like being Black and being Latina is not mutually exclusive. You can't just take away my identity because I don't fit your stereotype of what Latino people look like. It's because I'm also Caribbean so I'm dark and my hair doesn't look like yours. I'm not light like you.*
CO:	*You were pissed off that they could dismiss you in that way. Even more than that, this experience was enraging because it highlighted anti-blackness within the Latine community.*
	silence
CL:	*Exactamente. We don't talk about it but Latinos can be racist too. How can I identify with "Latinidad" if it doesn't identify with me?*

Reflective Questions:

1. What are some important things to consider as you move forward with counseling Alexa?
2. How might you broach the topic of race brought up in Alexa's experience?
3. What are some tools that you could provide for psychoeducation on domestic violence and posttraumatic stress disorder?

Tercera Sesión:

A pesar de que Alexa solamente asistió a dos sesiones, elle compartió una experiencia traumática el fin de semana pasado en la cual fue arrestade con cargos de violencia doméstica. Alexa se veía extremadamente angustiade y mencionó que estaba experimentando síntomas de hipervigilancia, reviviendo el momento, desconfianza y pesadillas. Elle recordó ser arrestade en su casa y se sintió indefense mientras era arrestade por una noche. Lentamente pudo hablar de los momentos que provocaron el trauma, incluyendo cuando su novia trataba de ahorcarle y elle tuvo que usar la fuerza para defenderse. Alexa también mencionó unas implicaciones importantes, como el hecho de ser la única persona que fue arrestade a pesar de que su novia también participó en el altercado. Elle mencionó que los oficiales que le arrestaron eran un Latino, un Caucásico, y su novia era una mujer Caucásica.

COUNSELOR (CO): *Mencionaste que la raza de los oficiales se destacó para ti, cuéntame más sobre eso.*

ALEXA (CL): *Pues eran blanquitos y no lo soy, eso era obvio. No tenían que decirme que eran discriminatorios; estaba en todas sus caras. Abrí la boca y me oyeron hablar español y el primer comentario que hizo el policía latino fue: "No hablas español, no juegues conmigo". Como si ser negre y ser latine es mutuamente excluyente. No puedes simplemente quitarme mi identidad porque no encajo en tu estereotipo de cómo se ven los latinos. Es porque también soy caribeñe, así que soy de piel oscura y mi cabello no se parece al tuyo. No soy de tez blanca como tú.*

CO: *Sentías enojo de que pudieran desechar tu identidad de esa manera. Aún más que eso, esta experiencia fue enfurecida porque destacó la anti-negritud dentro de la comunidad latina.*
silencio

CL: *Exactamente. No hablamos de eso, pero los latinos también pueden ser racistas. ¿Cómo podemos identificarnos con "latinidad" si no se identifica con nosotros?*

Preguntas de Reflexión:

1. ¿Cuáles son algunas cosas importantes a considerar para continuar dando consejería a Alexa?
2. ¿Cómo podrías abordar el tema de "raza" mencionado en la experiencia de Alexa?
3. ¿Cuáles son algunas de las herramientas que podrías proveer para psicoeducación en el área de violencia doméstica y desorden de estrés postraumático?

Fourth Session:

Alexa reports this session that they are still having intrusive thoughts and memories of the trauma. Towards the end of the session, Alexa admitted that their girlfriend attempted to contact them and was not sure what to do. The following is an example from their session:

COUNSELOR (CO): *I am sorry to hear that you are still having a difficult time, Alexa. Your reaction is natural given what you experienced. This trauma has had a major impact on your mind and body.*

(CL): *Yeah, I know. I just wish I didn't feel so scared all the time. I keep thinking about how stupid I am for not leaving the apartment sooner when she started to get aggressive with me. I didn't think she would hurt me again.*

CO: *You are pretty upset at the reaction you had under a stressful situation. What was the worst part of it?*

CL: *Feeling trapped and alone. There was a moment that I thought I was going to die, and I just thought, "This is it. I'm never going to see my family again. But I deserve this."*

CO: *That sounds terrifying. You felt you deserved to die. Would you mind telling me about that?*

Reflective Questions:

1. What early messages might have they received about violence in general? Domestic violence?
2. What cultural experiences may have impacted their worldview? Have they been impacted by systematic oppression?
3. Are they a target for racism or heterosexism in addition to their experience of domestic violence?

Cuarta Sesión:

Alexa reporta que, en esta sesión, todavía tienen pensamientos que le perturban y recuerdos del trauma. Hacia el fin de la sesión Alexa admite que su novia trató de ponerse en contacto con ellos y que no estaban seguros de que debían de hacer. Lo siguiente es un ejemplo de la sesión:

CONSEJERO/A/E (CO): *Siento escuchar que todavía tienes dificultades Alexa. Tú reacción es natural debido a lo que has experimentado. Este trauma ha tenido un gran impacto en tu mente y en tu cuerpo.*

ALEXA (CL): *Si, yo sé. Yo sole deseo no sentirme tan asustade todo el tiempo. Sige pensando que fui tan estúpide al no dejar el apartamento pronto cuando ella comenzó a ponerse agresiva conmigo. No pensé que me haría daño otra vez.*

CO: *Tú estás muy molesta con la reacción que tuviste en una situación muy estresante. ¿Cuál fue la peor parte de esto?*

CL: *Sentirme atrapade y sole. Hubo un momento en que pensé que iba a morir y solo pensé, "hasta aquí llegué. Nunca más voy a ver a mi familia otra vez. Pero me lo merezco".*

CO: *Eso suena terrible. Tú sentiste que tu merecías morir. ¿Te gustaría procesar eso más a fondo?*

Preguntas de Reflexión:

1. ¿Qué mensajes previos pudo haber recibido Alexa acerca de la violencia en general? ¿Violencia Doméstica?
2. ¿Qué experiencias culturales pudo haber impactado en su forma de ver el mundo? ¿Ha sido impactade por opresión sistemática?
3. ¿Es vulnerables al racismo o heterosexismo además de su experiencia con violencia doméstica?

Resources

- Blactina. *Amplifying and Empowering Afrolatinx/Afro-Caribbean narratives through digital media, TV, Film & Art.* https://www.blactinamedia.com/
- The Trevor Project. *For Young LGBTQ Lives.* https://www.thetrevorproject.org
- It Gets Better Project. https://itgetsbetter.org

- Centers for Disease Control and Prevention. *LGBTQ Youth Resources.* https://www.cdc.gov/lgbthealth/youth-resources.htm
- Acevedo, E. (2018). *The Poet X.* Quill Tree Books
- Coster, N. (2018). *Halsey Street.* Brilliance Audio;
- Herrera, A. (2019). *American Dreamer: An LGBTQ romance.* Carina Press
- Lee De La Cruz, S. (2021). *I'm a wild seed.* Street Noise Books
- Rice-Gonzalez, C. (2011). *Chulito: A Novel.* Magnus Books

Caso VI: El Caso de Beatriz
Trastornos Alimenticios y la Imagen Corporal en la Población Latine

Eating disorders have a dual impact on mental and physical health and can be life-threatening (Granillo et al., 2005). Although this mental health diagnosis often carries the stigma of being a rich white woman issue, eating disorders impact people of color at alarming rates (Marques et al., 2011). When compared to white non-Hispanic Americans, the Latine population is diagnosed with anorexia nervosa and bulimia nervosa at comparable rates, while the leading diagnosis is binge eating disorder (Pérez et al., 2016). However, it is important to highlight that eating disorders for Latine people are less likely recognized, making diagnosis rates less than accurate (Gordon et al., 2006). There are various reasons for the underdiagnosis. One reason is there is a bias and assumption by medical professionals that Latine do not suffer from eating disorders, which creates a barrier for treatment (Reyes-Rodriguez, 2013). In addition, lack of bilingual counselors and treatment in Spanish also decreases the likelihood of receiving a diagnosis and treatment plan (see Chapter 2).

Acculturative stress also plays a role in body dissatisfaction and disordered eating patterns (Velez et al., 2015; see Chapter 3). This is especially true of Latinas who embody both racial/ethnic discrimination and sexism (Menon & Harter, 2012). Velez et al. (2015) conducted a study exploring the relationships between discrimination and body satisfaction, eating disorder behaviors, and depression. Findings concluded that racist discrimination was positively correlated with body shame, eating disorder symptomatology, and depressive symptomatology. Additionally, they concluded that taking a critical race approach to body image and beauty ideals can produce positive effects for Latinas who suffer from poor body image and shame. Thus, when treating Latine clients, counselors could use a lens that includes systemic and institutional factors.

Case Presentation:

Beatriz is a 33-year-old woman who is diagnosed with bulimia nervosa. She has struggled with this diagnosis since she was 12 years old when she began to use laxatives, weight loss pills, excessive exercise, restriction, and binging behaviors as a way to cope with her home life. Beatriz has stepped down to outpatient services after being in a partial hospitalization program for eight weeks. Her established treatment team is a counselor, registered dietician, and primary care doctor. She is currently medically stable and is not engaging in purging behaviors; however, she continues to battle with urges to restrict food and negative body image.

Presentación del Caso

Beatriz es una mujer de 33 años diagnosticada de bulimia nerviosa. Ella ha luchado con este diagnóstico desde que tenía 12 años cuando comenzó a usar laxantes, pastillas para bajar de peso, ejercicio excesivo, restricción y comportamientos de atracones como una forma de hacer frente a su vida hogareña. Beatriz renunció a los servicios ambulatorios después de estar en un programa de hospitalización parcial durante ocho semanas. Su equipo de tratamiento establecido es un consejero, un dietista registrado y un médico de atención primaria. Actualmente se encuentra médicamente estable y no tiene conductas de purga; sin embargo, continúa batallando con la necesidad de restringir los alimentos y la imagen corporal negativa.

First session:

Beatriz discussed her past medical and psychological history in her recovery process. She shared ways her past trauma in adolescence led to the eating disorder and caused her to spiral into negative self-talk. Beatriz informed the counselor that at an early age, she disliked her body and would often take measures to hide it. Beatriz discussed wearing baggy clothes, avoiding certain fabrics, and avoiding social situations such as swimming or dancing that made others focus on her body. This has led to feelings of isolation, anxiety, and at different points in her life, disordered eating behaviors. The client discussed the bicultural experience of having an eating disorder in her family, where mental health was not recognized. In addition, Beatriz struggled with disconnection from her family since food has always had a cultural significance behind it. Beatriz described specifically how the advice on "taking care of herself" or "tienes que cuidarte" from others has impacted her.

BEATRIZ (CL):   *The ED really disconnected me from my family. We always had get-togethers with all my tias, tios, cousins. Instead of looking forward to them, like everyone else in my family did, I would panic. I was scared that someone would say something about how I looked if I gained weight, or anything that brought attention to my body.*

COUNSELOR (CO):   *You approached these gatherings with the anticipation of being triggered. How did you manage that?*

CL: *Yes! I always feel triggered in social settings. When I could, I would try to get out of going. If I had to go, I was always in my head. What are they thinking about me? Are they judging me? It was especially uncomfortable when we all sat down to eat.*

CO: *I imagine trying to eat while having intrusive thoughts about your body and fearing judgment from others was overwhelming, to say the least.*

CL: *Yeah. Sometimes I would just say I already ate. Other times I would eat but then on the way home, I felt guilty about it.*

Reflective Questions:

1. What questions may you ask this first session to further gain an understanding of the client's problem?
2. What precautions may you want to investigate to ensure your client's safety in the room and navigating triggers?
3. How would you facilitate discussion on the impact of cultural norms such as *respeto* and *familismo* (see Chapter 3) on her experience?
4. What questions or concerns would you want to discuss with the treatment team?

Primera Sesión:

Beatriz habló sobre su historial médico y psicológico pasado en su proceso de recuperación. Ella compartió formas en que su trauma pasado en la adolescencia la llevó al trastorno alimentario y la hizo entrar en una espiral de diálogo interno negativo. Beatriz le informó al consejero que, a una edad temprana, no le gustaba su cuerpo y que a menudo tomaba medidas para ocultarlo. Beatriz habló sobre usar ropa holgada, evitar ciertas telas y evitar situaciones sociales como nadar o bailar que hacían que otros se enfocarán en su cuerpo. Esto ha conllevado a sentimientos de aislamiento, ansiedad y, en diferentes momentos de su vida, comportamientos alimenticios desordenados. La clienta discutió la experiencia bicultural de tener un trastorno alimentario en su familia, donde la salud mental no fue reconocida. Además, Beatriz luchó con la desconexión de la familia ya que la comida siempre ha tenido un significado cultural detrás de ella. Beatriz describió específicamente cómo los consejos de "cuidarse" o "tienes que cuidarte" de otros la han impactado.

BEATRIZ (CL):   *El TA realmente me desconectó de mi familia. Siempre teníamos reuniones con todas mis tías, tíos, primos. En lugar de esperarlos con ansias, como todos los demás en mi familia, entraba en pánico. Tenía miedo de que alguien dijera algo sobre cómo me veía, si aumentaba de peso o cualquier cosa que llamara la atención sobre mi cuerpo.*

COUNSELOR (CO):   *Te acercaste a estas reuniones con la anticipación de que algo desencadenara tus síntomas. ¿Cómo lo lograste?*

CL: *¡Sí! Siempre sentía que mis síntomas se desencadenaban en entornos sociales. Cuando podía, intentaba no ir. Si tenía que ir, siempre estaba en mi cabeza. ¿Qué están pensando de mí? ¿Me están juzgando? Es especialmente incómodo cuando todos nos sentamos a comer.*

CO: *Me imagino que tratar de comer mientras tienes pensamientos intrusivos sobre tu cuerpo y temes el juicio de los demás fue abrumador, por decir lo menos.*

CL: *Sí. A veces solo decía que ya había comido. Otras veces comía, pero luego, cuando iba de camino a casa, me sentía culpable por ello.*

Preguntas de Reflexión

1. ¿Qué preguntas puede hacer en esta primera sesión para comprender mejor el problema del cliente?

2. ¿Qué precauciones puedes investigar para garantizar la seguridad de tu cliente en la habitación y los desencadenantes de navegación?

3. ¿Cómo facilitarías la discusión sobre el impacto de normas culturales como el respeto y el familismo (véase el capítulo 3) en su experiencia?
4. ¿Qué preguntas o inquietudes le gustaría discutir con el equipo de tratamiento?

Second Session:

During the second session, Beatriz felt more comfortable with the counselor and was able to talk more about how her identity and culture impacted the diagnosis. Beatriz highlighted both similarities and differences in how women relate to their bodies in the United States vs. in her culture. She discussed ways she perceives pressure to fit the "thin ideal" while also being curvy. This caused her to become hyper-aware of her body and often compare herself to others.

COUNSELOR (CO):   *What factors have impacted how you see and relate to your body?*
BEATRIZ (CL):   *I would say the way I saw my mom relate to her body in part. She was always going on these weird diets and constantly commented on her body. And also, being exposed to social media and pop culture. It's easy to see how you wish you would look.*
CO: *It is especially easy to internalize messages if you have been exposed to them all your life. What messages have infiltrated your view of self?*
CL: *Well if I don't take part in things to try to be smaller then something is wrong with me. Everyone thinks a Latina should look like JLo or Sofia Vergara. I remember seeing America Ferrera in the movie Real Women Have Curves and wow, I felt understood in so many ways.*

Reflective Questions:

1. In what way would you facilitate dialogue to connect pop culture with internalized negative body image?
2. How could you use Beatriz's family history to highlight its impact?

Segunda Sesión:

Durante la segunda sesión, Beatriz se sintió más cómoda con la consejera y pudo hablar más sobre cómo su identidad y cultura impactan el diagnóstico. Beatriz destacó tanto las similitudes como las diferencias en cómo las mujeres se relacionan con sus cuerpos en los Estados Unidos y su cultura. Ella discutió las formas en que percibe la presión para adaptarse al "cuerpo delgado ideal" y al mismo tiempo tener curvas. Esto hizo que se volviera hiperconsciente de su cuerpo y, a menudo, se comparara con los demás.

COUNSELOR (CO): *¿Qué factores han afectado la forma en que ves y te relacionas con tu cuerpo?*
BEATRIZ (CL): *Diría que la forma en que vi a mi madre relacionarse con su cuerpo en parte. Ella siempre estaba siguiendo estas dietas extrañas y constantemente comentaba sobre su cuerpo. Y también, estar expuesto a las redes sociales y la cultura pop. Es fácil ver cómo te gustaría verte.*
CO: *Es especialmente fácil interiorizar mensajes si has estado expuesto a ellos toda tu vida. ¿Qué mensajes se han infiltrado en tu visión de ti misma?*
CL: *Bueno, que si no participo en cosas para tratar de ser más delgada entonces algo estaba mal conmigo. Todo el mundo piensa que una latina debería parecerse a JLo o Sofía Vergara. Recuerdo haber visto a América Ferrera en la película Real Women Have Curves y wow, me sentí comprendida de muchas maneras.*

Preguntas de Reflexión:

1. ¿De qué manera facilitarías el diálogo para conectar la cultura pop con la imagen corporal negativa internalizada?
2. ¿Cómo podrías usar la historia familiar de Beatriz para resaltar su impacto?

Third Session:

In the third session, the counselor and client reviewed body distortions. Discussions included analyzing how and why she developed body distortions. This has caused her to say "no" to social activities and has fostered feelings of isolation and disappointment. The counselor and client reviewed Beatriz's urge to hide her body and her struggle with distorted thinking patterns.

COUNSELOR (CO): *Looking at the list of body distortions, which ones resonated with your experience?*
BEATRIZ (CL): *For sure, the "beauty bound". This one is definitely me because I always say, I can't wear that because of my body type. Or I shouldn't go dancing or shouldn't go to a party because I don't look the way I want yet.*
CO: *You limit yourself based on what you think you've earned or deserved.*
CL: *Yeah. I can see how I will make up an excuse not to go out, or I will try on a million outfits until I find something that makes me feel less seen. Even when I do go out, I'm always second-guessing myself which takes the fun out of it.*

Reflective Questions:

1. As the counselor, where would you go next with the client?
2. This particular session is cognitive therapy focused. If utilizing a different theory, what would be different in session? Where would the focus turn to?

Tercera Sesión:

En la tercera sesión, el consejero y el cliente revisaron las distorsiones corporales. Las discusiones incluyeron analizar cómo y por qué desarrolló distorsiones corporales. Esto ha hecho que diga "no" a las actividades sociales y ha fomentado sentimientos de aislamiento y decepción. El consejero y el cliente revisaron el impulso de Beatriz de ocultar su cuerpo y su lucha con patrones de pensamiento distorsionados.

COUNSELOR (CO): *Mirando la lista de distorsiones corporales, ¿cuáles resonaron con tu experiencia?*

BEATRIZ (CL): *Por supuesto, la "belleza atada". Este es definitivamente yo porque siempre digo, no puedo usar eso debido a mi tipo de cuerpo. O no debería ir a bailar o no debería ir a una fiesta porque todavía no me veo como quiero.*

CO: *Te limitas en función de lo que crees que has ganado o merecido.*

CL: *Sí. Puedo ver cómo inventaré una excusa para no salir, o me probaré un millón de atuendos hasta encontrar algo que me haga sentir menos vista. Incluso cuando salgo, siempre me cuestiono a mí misma, lo que le quita la diversión.*

Resources

- The Body Positive. https://thebodypositive.org
- National Eating Disorders Association. https://www.nationaleatingdisorders.org
- The Eating Recovery Center. https://www.eatingrecoverycenter.com
- Eating Disorders Anonymous. https://eatingdisordersanonymous.org
- Gaudiani, J. L. (2018). *Sick enough: A guide to the medical complications of eating disorders*. Routledge.
- Schaefer, J., & Rutledge, T. (2003). *Life Without Ed: How One Woman Declared Independence from Her Eating Disorder and How You Can Too*. McGraw Hill

References

American Psychiatric Association. (2013). *Diagnostic and statistical manual of mental disorders* (5th ed.). Author

Baxter, A. J., Scott, K. M., Vos, T., & Whiteford, H. A. (2013). Global prevalence of anxiety disorders: A systematic review and meta-regression. *Psychological Medicine, 43*(5), 897–910. https://doi.org/10.1017/S003329171200147X

Campbell, C. G., Bierman, K. L., & Molenaar, P. C. (2016). Individual day-to-day process of social anxiety in vulnerable college students. *Applied Developmental Science, 20*(1), 1–15. https://doi.org/10.1080/10888691.2015.1026594

Cleary, S. D., Snead, R., Dietz-Chavez, D., Rivera, I., & Edberg, M. C. (2017). Immigrant trauma and mental health outcomes among Latino youth. *Journal of Immigrant and Minority Health, 20*(5), 1053–1059. https://doi.org/10.1007/s10903-017-0673-6

Domenech Rodríguez, M. M. (2018). Staying woke at the intersections. In L. Comas-Díaz & C. I. Vazquez (Eds.), *Latina Psychologists: Thriving in the cultural borderlands* (pp. 71–89). Routledge.

Espín, O. (2018). *Latina Realities: Essays on Healing, Migration, and Sexuality*. Routledge.

Gordon, K. H., Brattole, M. M., Wingate, L. R., & Joiner Jr, T. E. (2006). The impact of client race on clinician detection of eating disorders. *Behavior Therapy, 37*(4), 319–325. https://doi.org/10.1016/j.beth.2005.12.002

Granillo, T., Jones-Rodriguez, G., & Carvajal, S. C. (2005). Prevalence of eating disorders in Latina adolescents: Associations with substance use and other correlates. *Journal of Adolescent Health, 36*(3), 214–220. https://doi.org/10.1016/j.jadohealth.2004.01.015

Guilman, S. R. (2015). Beyond interpretation: The need for English-Spanish bilingual psychotherapists in counseling centers. *James Madison Undergraduate Research Journal, 2*(1), 26–30. http://commons.lib.jmu.edu/jmurj/vol2/iss1/5

Hancock, T. U., & Siu, K. (2009). A culturally sensitive intervention with domestically violent Latino immigrant men. *Journal of Family Violence, 24*, 123–132. https://doi.org/10.1007/s10896-008-9217-0

Hawkins, A. J., & Fackrell, T. A. (2010). Does relationship and marriage education for lower-income couples work? A meta-analytic study of emerging research. *Journal of Couple & Relationship Therapy, 9*(2), 181–191. https://doi.org/10.1080/15332691003694927

Haywood, J. (2017). Latino spaces have always been the most violent: Afro-Latino collegians' perceptions of colorism and Latino intragroup marginalization. *International Journal of Qualitative Studies in Education, 30*(8), 759–782. https://doi.org/10.1080/09518 398.2017.1350298

Kataoka, S. H., Stein, B. D., Jaycox, L. H., Wong, M., Escudero, P., Tu, W., & Fink, A. (2003). A school-based mental health program for traumatized Latino immigrant children. *Journal of the American Academy of Child & Adolescent Psychiatry, 42*(3), 311–318. https://doi. org/10.1097/00004583-200303000-00011

Kocovski, N. L., Segal, Z. V., & Battista, S. R. (2009). Mindfulness and psychopathology: Problem formulation. In *Clinical Handbook of Mindfulness* (pp. 85–98). Springer.

Lindahl, K., & Wigderson, S. (2017) Tools for working with Spanish-Speaking Latino couples. In: L. Benuto (Eds.), *Toolkit for counseling Spanish-Speaking clients*. Springer.

Marques, L., Alegria, M., Becker, A. E., Chen, C. N., Fang, A., Chosak, A., & Diniz, J. B. (2011). Comparative prevalence, correlates of impairment, and service utilization for eating disorders across US ethnic groups: Implications for reducing ethnic disparities in health care access for eating disorders. *International Journal of Eating Disorders, 44*(5), 412–420. https://doi.org/10.1002/eat.20787

Menon, C. V., & Harter, S. L. (2012). Examining the impact of acculturative stress on body image disturbance among Hispanic college students. *Cultural Diversity and Ethnic Minority Psychology, 18*(3), 239–246. https://doi.org/10.1037/a0028638

Nordstrom, A. H., Goguen, L. M. S., & Hiester, M. (2014). The effect of social anxiety and self-esteem on college adjustment, academics, and retention. *Journal of College Counseling, 17*(1), 48–63. https://doi.org/10.1002/j.2161-1882.2014.00047.x

Pérez, C., Brown, M., Whiting, J., & Harris, S. (2013). Experiences of Latino couples in relationship education: A critical analysis. *The Family Journal, 21*(4), 377–385. https://doi.org/10.1177/1066480713488525

Pérez, M., Ohrt, T. K., & Hoek, H. W. (2016). Prevalence and treatment of eating disorders among Hispanics/Latino Americans in the United States. *Current Opinion in Psychiatry, 29*(6), 378–382. https://doi.org/10.1097/YCO.0000000000000277

Polo, A. J., Alegría, M., Chen, C. N., & Blanco, C. (2011). The prevalence and comorbidity of social anxiety disorder among United States Latinos: a retrospective analysis of data from 2 national surveys. *The Journal of Clinical Psychiatry, 72*(8), 15381.

Rapee, R. M., & Heimberg, R. G. (1997). A cognitive-behavioral model of anxiety in social phobia. *Behaviour Research and Therapy, 35*(8), 741–756. https://doi.org/10.1016/S0005-7967(97)00022-3

Reyes-Rodríguez, M. L., Ramírez, J., Davis, K., Patrice, K., & Bulik, C. M. (2013). Exploring barriers and facilitators in eating disorders treatment among Latinas in the United States. *Journal of Latina/o Psychology, 1*(2), 112. https://doi.org/10.1037/a0032318

Russell, G., & Topham, P. (2012). The impact of social anxiety on student learning and well-being in higher education. *Journal of Mental Health, 21*(4), 375–385. https://doi.org/10.3109/09638237.2012.694505

Schmitz, R. M., Robinson, B. A., & Sanchez, J. (2020). Intersectional family systems approach: LGBTQ+ Latino/a youth, family dynamics, and stressors. *Family Relations, 69*(4), 832–848. https://doi.org/10.1111/fare.12448

Snyder, I., Duncan, S., & Larson, J. (2010). Assessing perceived marriage education needs and interests among Latinos in a select western community. *Journal of Comparative Family Studies, 41*(3), 347–367.

Softas-Nall, L., Cardona, B., & Barritt, J. (2015). Challenges and diversity issues working with multilingual and bilingual couples and families: Implications for counseling. *The Family Journal: Counseling and Therapy for Couples and Families, 23*(1), 13–17. https://doi.org/10.1177/1066480714548402

Spence, S. H., & Rapee, R. M. (2016). The etiology of social anxiety disorder: An evidence-based model. *Behaviour Research and Therapy, 86*, 50–67. https://doi.org/10.1016/j.brat.2016.06.007

Sutter, M., & Perrin, P. B. (2016). Discrimination, mental health, and suicidal ideation among LGBTQ people of color. *Journal of Counseling Psychology*, 63(1), 98–105. http://dx.doi.org.libweb.lib.utsa.edu/10.1037/cou0000126

Torres, V. (2004). The Diversity among us: Puerto Ricans, Cuban Americans, Caribbean Americans, and Central and South Americans. *New Directions for Student Services*, 2004(105), 5–16. https://doi.org/10.1002/ss.112

Velez, B. L., Campos, I. D., & Moradi, B. (2015). Relations of sexual objectification and racist discrimination with Latina women's body image and mental health. *The Counseling Psychologist*, 43(6), 906–935. https://doi.org/10.1177/0011000015591287

REFLEXIÓN FINAL

Preparing Culturally Efficacious Bilingual Counselors through Theory and Case Studies followed established recommendations by the ACA *Code of Ethics* (2014), in which professional counselors are called to promote quality of life for clients while removing barriers to services. One of these barriers is the lack of trained bilingual counselors. This book sought to increase professional language acquisition in Spanish through reflection and case studies. We believe in the power of language. We believe that providing a space where clients can comfortably express themselves in their preferred language can help decrease the drop-out rate and increase satisfaction with counseling services in the Latine community. However, as reiterated throughout this book, speaking Spanish is not enough. We hope that this book allowed you to gain clinical terminology in Spanish that increased your competency as a bilingual counselor. Moreover, we believe that bilingual counselors must prepare to address cultural and social justice issues that may negatively impact clients' well-being or impede access to mental health services. One of our main goals was to also integrate bilingual supervision, a currently deficient but critical need for bilingual counselors. Bilingual counselors require a supervisor who understands the therapeutic complexities and contextual issues concerning their experiences and the populations served.

We aspire for this book to join the collection of resources that can facilitate bilingual counselor training and supervision in the United States and worldwide. We hope that this book can also fuel efforts for the profession to develop counselor education standards for bilingual training and supervision. This area lacks recognition as a specialty, despite the growing number of Spanish speakers in the United States. We acknowledged Anzaldúa's influence on our work at the beginning of this book and seek to finish by highlighting her teachings. Throughout "How to Tame a Wild Tongue," Anzaldúa emphasizes the relationship between identity and language. She suggests that language is not only a matter of communication but one of personal identity. We align with Anzaldúa by arguing that bilingual training and supervision is of equal importance to established curricula in English, rather than merely a derivation of it. We hope that throughout this book we have documented the relationship between language and identity and what this means for bilingual counselors and those they seek to serve. Anzaldúa declares "I am my language," emphasizing that the loss of one's language is equivalent to a loss of one's self. We hope that this book can raise our collective voices for clients, ourselves, and the future of bilingual counselor training and supervision.

INDEX

180   INDEX

Critical Studies of Latinxs in the Americas is a provocative interdisciplinary series that offers a critical space for reflection and questioning what it means to be Latinxs living in the Americas in twenty-first century social, cultural, economic, and political arenas. The series looks forward to extending the dialogue to include the North and South Western hemispheric relations that are prevalent in the field of global studies.

Topics that explore and advance research and scholarship on contemporary topics and issues related with processes of racialization, economic exploitation, health, education, transnationalism, immigration, gendered and sexual identities, and disabilities that are not commonly highlighted in the current Latinx Studies literature as well as the multitude of socio, cultural, economic, and political progress among the Latinxs in the Americas are welcome.

To receive more information about CSLA, please contact:

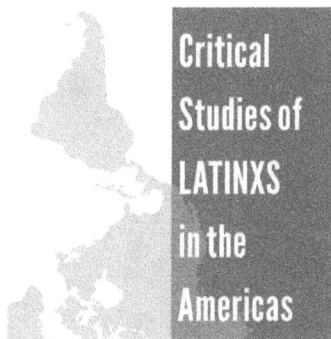

Yolanda Medina (ymedina@bmcc.cuny.edu) &
Margarita Machado-Casas (Margarita.MachadoCasas@utsa.edu)

To order other books in this series, please contact our Customer Service Department at:

peterlang@presswarehouse.com (within the U.S.)
order@peterlang.com (outside the U.S.)

Or browse online by series at:

WWW.PETERLANG.COM